Modern Language Association of America

Approaches to Teaching
World Literature

Joseph Gibaldi, Series Editor

28. Sidney Gottlieb, ed. *Approaches to Teaching the Metaphysical Poets.* 1990.
29. Richard K. Emmerson, ed. *Approaches to Teaching Medieval English Drama.* 1990.
30. Kathleen Blake, ed. *Approaches to Teaching Eliot's* Middlemarch. 1990.
31. María Elena de Valdés and Mario J. Valdés, eds. *Approaches to Teaching García Márquez's* One Hundred Years of Solitude. 1990.
32. Donald D. Kummings, ed. *Approaches to Teaching Whitman's* Leaves of Grass. 1990.
33. Stephen C. Behrendt, ed. *Approaches to Teaching Shelley's* Frankenstein. 1990.
34. June Schlueter and Enoch Brater, eds. *Approaches to Teaching Beckett's* Waiting for Godot. 1991.
35. Walter H. Evert and Jack W. Rhodes, eds. *Approaches to Teaching Keats's Poetry.* 1991.
36. Frederick W. Shilstone, ed. *Approaches to Teaching Byron's Poetry.* 1991.
37. Bernth Lindfors, ed. *Approaches to Teaching Achebe's* Things Fall Apart. 1991.
38. Richard E. Matlak, ed. *Approaches to Teaching Coleridge's Poetry and Prose.* 1991.
39. Shirley Geok-lin Lim, ed. *Approaches to Teaching Kingston's* The Woman Warrior. 1991.
40. Maureen Fries and Jeanie Watson, eds. *Approaches to Teaching the Arthurian Tradition.* 1992.
41. Maurice Hunt, ed. *Approaches to Teaching Shakespeare's* The Tempest *and Other Late Romances.* 1992.
42. Diane Long Hoeveler and Beth Lau, eds. *Approaches to Teaching Brontë's* Jane Eyre. 1993.
43. Jeffrey B. Berlin, ed. *Approaches to Teaching Mann's* Death in Venice *and Other Short Fiction.* 1992.
44. Kathleen McCormick and Erwin R. Steinberg, eds. *Approaches to Teaching Joyce's* Ulysses. 1993.
45. Marcia McClintock Folsom, ed. *Approaches to Teaching Austen's* Pride and Prejudice. 1993.
46. Wallace Jackson and R. Paul Yoder, eds. *Approaches to Teaching Pope's Poetry.* 1993.
47. Edward Kamens, ed. *Approaches to Teaching Murasaki Shikibu's* The Tale of Genji. 1993.
48. Patrick Henry, ed. *Approaches to Teaching Montaigne's* Essays. 1994.
49. David R. Anderson and Gwin J. Kolb, eds. *Approaches to Teaching the Works of Samuel Johnson.* 1993.
50. David Lee Miller and Alexander Dunlop, eds. *Approaches to Teaching Spenser's* Faerie Queene. 1994.

Approaches To Teaching Spenser's *Faerie Queene*

Edited by
David Lee Miller
and
Alexander Dunlop

The Modern Language Association of America
New York   1994

Library of Congress Cataloging-in-Publication Data

Approaches to teaching Spenser's Faerie queene / edited by David Lee
   Miller and Alexander Dunlop.
       p.   cm. — (Approaches to teaching world literature : 50)
   Includes bibliographical references (p.) and index.
   ISBN 0-87352-723-2 — ISBN 0-87352-724-0 (pbk.)
   1. Spenser, Edmund, 1552?–1599. Faerie queene. 2. Spenser,
Edmund, 1552?–1599 — Study and teaching. I. Miller, David Lee,
1951–   . II. Dunlop, Alexander, 1942–   . III. Series.
PR2358.A927   1994
821'.3 — dc20   94-5713

Cover illustration of the paperback edition: *Queen Elizabeth* (the Rainbow
portrait), c. 1600–03. Attributed to Marcus Gheeraerdts the Younger. Photograph
Courtauld Institute of Art.

Published by The Modern Language Association of America
10 Astor Place, New York, New York 10003-6981

Printed on recycled paper

CONTENTS

PREFACE TO THE SERIES

In *The Art of Teaching* Gilbert Highet wrote, "Bad teaching wastes a great deal of effort, and spoils many lives which might have been full of energy and happiness." All too many teachers have failed in their work, Highet argued, simply "because they have not thought about it." We hope that the Approaches to Teaching World Literature series, sponsored by the Modern Language Association's Publications Committee, will not only improve the craft — as well as the art — of teaching but also encourage serious and continuing discussion of the aims and methods of teaching literature.

The principal objective of the series is to collect within each volume different points of view on teaching a specific literary work, a literary tradition, or a writer widely taught at the undergraduate level. The preparation of each volume begins with a wide-ranging survey of instructors, thus enabling us to include in the volume the philosophies and approaches, thoughts and methods of scores of experienced teachers. The result is a sourcebook of material, information, and ideas on teaching the subject of the volume to undergraduates.

The series is intended to serve nonspecialists as well as specialists, inexperienced as well as experienced teachers, graduate students who wish to learn effective ways of teaching as well as senior professors who wish to compare their own approaches with the approaches of colleagues in other schools. Of course, no volume in the series can ever substitute for erudition, intelligence, creativity, and sensitivity in teaching. We hope merely that each book will point readers in useful directions; at most each will offer only a first step in the long journey to successful teaching.

Joseph Gibaldi
Series Editor

PREFACE TO THE VOLUME

Teaching is a labor of love although, like other loves, not without its drudgery. This volume on teaching Spenser is also a labor of love, for the text of *The Faerie Queene* and for those who read or teach it. Many laborers have contributed, beginning with Douglas Macmillan and Hugh Maclean, who initiated the proposal and conducted the survey of teachers. The survey respondents, listed by name at the end of the volume, provided substantial information for the editors, and the contributors in their turn were prompt (without which, nothing) as well as cooperative.

Many colleagues shared their expertise and their judgments with the editors. Some of them retain the anonymity of the review process, but Judith Anderson, Ralph Voss, and Anne Lake Prescott can be thanked by name. Joseph Gibaldi and the book publications staff at MLA headquarters provided strong support for the project. Funds for manuscript preparation and research overhead were provided by the University of Alabama College of Arts and Sciences and by the Hudson Strode Program in Renaissance Studies. The manuscript was prepared with skilled efficiency by Angela Bramlett, and the index by Yeoung Hwa Bae.

David Lee Miller, *University of Kentucky*
Alexander Dunlop, *Auburn University*

Part One

MATERIALS

Introduction

This section is intended for instructors of varying levels of experience as an introduction, update, or review. The editions recommended as classroom texts are relatively inexpensive and generally represent the most recent and authoritative scholarship. The sections headed "Additional Student Readings" and "Aids to Teaching" contain suggestions to help students enrich their readings of *The Faerie Queene* by exploring some of the works in literature and the other arts that formed part of the aesthetic context of *The Faerie Queene*. The "Introductory Bibliography" categorizes and briefly describes for instructors preparing classes or offering guidance to students as many influential and recent scholarly works as space permits.

Classroom Texts

Complete Works

Because of its length *The Faerie Queene* is likely to be taught whole only in courses devoted entirely to Spenser, commonly surveys of his complete works. The only edition of the complete works priced for classroom use is *Spenser: Poetical Works*, edited by J. C. Smith and Ernest de Selincourt. This single-volume edition is relatively inexpensive and of a handy size; it provides reliable texts of all the works, a substantial introduction, and an extensive glossary. These advantages are achieved by the use of very small type closely set in double columns with narrow margins and by the omission of all annotation. The complexity and length of Spenser's work make these drawbacks serious; some may find that they pose an inconvenience for scholarship and a hindrance for teaching.

The Faerie Queene *Complete*

There are two editions of *The Faerie Queene* at classroom price. A. C. Hamilton's edition is a large volume of 753 pages. The text is printed in double columns with adequate margins. Hamilton's copious, thorough, informative notes are printed on the same pages as the text they elucidate, usually in the adjoining column. This arrangement makes the notes immediately available with minimal interruption of the poem but may also confer on the notes the authority of an almost indispensable adjunct to the poem. Clear introductions to the whole poem and to each book summarize and evaluate critical responses to persistent interpretive problems. There are a table of dates, a handy list of characters and their first appearance in the poem, and an extensive bibliography.

The other complete *Faerie Queene*, edited by Thomas P. Roche, Jr., is a thick little paperback with a surprisingly durable binding. The poem is printed with four stanzas on a page and adequate margins. There is a table of dates and a bibliography. The very useful notes are collected in approximately two hundred pages at the back. Whichever edition is selected for classroom use, instructors will want to consult both Roche's and Hamilton's notes. Either edition can be combined with an edition of the shorter poetry to complete the Spenser course.

Selected Works

For courses in which there is less time for Spenser—an early-modern or a Renaissance survey, a course on major Elizabethan poets, or perhaps a quarter-system Spenser course—an edition of selected works recommends itself. The most widely used is the Spenser portion of *The Norton Anthology of English Literature*, fifth edition, edited by Barbara K. Lewalski and Hallett Smith. It includes book 1 and more than half of book 3, *Epithalamion* with eleven sonnets of *Amoretti*, and the "April" and "October" eclogues of *The Shepheardes Calender*. The typographical system is the same for all the books of selections: lexical glosses in the right margin with brief explanatory notes at the bottom. *The Literature of Renaissance England*, edited by John Hollander and Frank Kermode, includes *Epithalamion* with seven sonnets from *Amoretti*, "October," and sixty lines from *Colin Clouts Come Home Againe*, and 150 pages of selections drawn from all books of *The Faerie Queene*. The reedition of Hugh Maclean's *Edmund Spenser's Poetry* by Maclean and Anne Lake Prescott in the Norton Critical Editions series includes *The Faerie Queene* 1, 3, and 7, substantial selections from 2 and 6, the whole *Amoretti* and *Epithalamion*, *Colin Clouts Come Home Againe*, four eclogues of *The Shepheardes Calender*, and a fine revised selection of critical articles. The generous textual and critical selections and full glossing and annotation make this 842-page volume an attractive choice for many undergraduate Spenser courses and for Renaissance poetry courses at every level. Robert Kellogg and Oliver Steele's edition of selections remains popular. It contains *The Faerie Queene* 1, 2, and 7, "November," *Fowre Hymnes*, *Muiopotmos*, and *Epithalamion* with twenty-six sonnets of *Amoretti*; the introductions are excellent. Also available is *Spenser: Selections with Essays by Hazlitt, Coleridge, and Leigh Hunt*, a reprint of a 1923 volume edited by W. L. Renwick. The shortest and least expensive book of selections is A. Kent Hieatt and Constance Hieatt's handy *Spenser: Selected Poetry*, a small paperback including 140 pages of selections from *The Faerie*

Queene 1, 2, 3, 4, and 6, as well as "October" and *Epithalamion* with seven sonnets from *Amoretti*.

Selections from The Faerie Queene

Partial editions of *The Faerie Queene* alone may be useful in courses involving substantial other reading, such as a course on the epic tradition. Currently available are The Faerie Queene: *Books I to III*, edited by Douglas Brooks-Davies; The Faerie Queene *I and II*, edited by P. C. Bayley; and The Faerie Queene *I*, edited by M. C. Jussawala. The Mutability cantos are available separately, edited with an excellent introduction by S. P. Zitner.

Additional Student Readings

Assigned Readings

The possibilities for additional student readings are limited by the nature of the course. In the typical Spenser course, reading *The Faerie Queene* and the major shorter poetry while researching and writing a paper is likely to leave students little time for extensive additional reading. Responses to the survey of Spenser scholars conducted for this volume indicate that instructors normally require some of *The Faerie Queene* and some shorter poetry in both Renaissance and Spenser courses but little non-Spenserian reading in the Spenser course. Because *The Faerie Queene* is so widely and overtly allusive we are unlikely to approach it with New Critical tunnel vision, but possibly we are too much inclined to contextualize it on its own terms—to explain Renaissance theology and politics and literary tradition in the context of the poem rather than the reverse.

One response to this problem is the two-paper system, requiring students to write by mid-semester a paper involving research and analysis of values expressed in a non-Spenserian text, literary or nonliterary, or in a specific aspect of Elizabethan culture that may include the fashions and practices of art, architecture, music, gardening, or clothing, as well as many kinds and levels of political, economic, commercial, religious, or social activities or institutions. The second paper, due toward the end of the semester, requires students to relate the values and structures revealed by a close study of a portion of *The Faerie Queene* to those revealed in the first paper. Such a system requires outside reading according to the interests of the student and promotes awareness of the cultural systems of which *The Faerie Queene* is a part. Time and class size permitting, the sharing of the various perspectives may enrich the reading experience of all the participants.

Recommended Readings

Supplementary or background readings will depend on the focus of the course and the interest and enthusiasm of students; such readings may be useful also as topics for papers. Some ancient works recommended by respondents as background reading include Homer's *Iliad* and *Odyssey*, Vergil's *Aeneid*, Ovid's *Metamorphoses*, and the 1560 *Bible*. Some medieval works recommended as background reading: Augustine's *City of God*, *The Song of Roland*, Wolfram von Eschenbach's *Parzifal*, Dante's *Commedia* and the letter on allegory to Can Grande della Scala, romances of Chrétien de Troyes, Boccaccio's writings on poetry, Chaucer's *The Canterbury Tales*, and Malory's *Morte d'Arthur*. Some Renaissance works recommended as background reading: Ariosto's *Orlando Furioso*, Tasso's *Jerusalem Delivered*, Castiglione's *The Book of the Courtier*, Ficino's *Commentary on Plato's Symposium on Love*, Budé's *De l'institution du prince* (University Microfilms 27287), Camoens's *Lusiads*, Du Bartas's *Divine Weekes and Workes*, More's *History of King Richard III*, Erasmus's *Enchiridion militis christiani*, Sannazaro's *Arcadia*, Sidney's *Arcadia*, Sidney's *An Apology for Poetry*, Elyot's *The Boke Named the Governour*, Hooker's *Laws of Ecclesiastical Polity*, Calvin's *Institutes of the Christian Religion*, the 1559 *Book of Common Prayer*, *The Thirty-Nine Articles of the Church of England*, and shorter writing available in collections such as *The Frame of Order: An Outline of Elizabethan Belief Taken from Treatises of the Late Sixteenth Century*, edited by James Winny; *The Elizabethans*, edited by Allardyce Nicoll; and *The Renaissance Philosophy of Man*, edited by Ernst Cassirer, Paul Oskar Kristeller, and John Herman Randall, Jr.

Introductory Bibliography

Editions

The Faerie Queene 1–3 appeared in London in 1590, 1–6 in 1596, and 1–7 in 1609 and 1611. Subsequent editions include those of John Hughes (London, 1715), John Upton (London, 1758; Upton's copious notes on *The Faerie Queene* have been reprinted in two volumes edited by John G. Radcliffe), Ralph Church (London, 1758), H. J. Todd (London, 1805), F. J. Child (Boston, 1855), J. P. Collier (London, 1862), R. Morris and J. W. Hales (London, 1869), A. B. Grosart (London, 1882), R. E. Neil Dodge (Boston, 1908), and J. C. Smith (Oxford, 1909). The monumental *Works of Edmund Spenser: A Variorum Edition*, in ten volumes, edited by E. Greenlaw, C. G. Osgood, F. M. Padelford, et al. (1932–58), provided the foundation for what has been the most active and the richest half-century of Spenser scholarship, lasting to the present. It remains useful for various kinds of information, especially for sources and analogues.

Reference

Because *The Faerie Queene* is usually thoroughly glossed, students may not feel the need for the *Oxford English Dictionary*, edited by J. A. Simpson and E. S. C. Weiner, but should be encouraged at every point to explore alternative readings. Beyond the editions and the *OED*, the preeminent reference work for *The Faerie Queene* is the massive *Spenser Encyclopedia*, edited by A. C. Hamilton et al. This is the place for both teachers and students to find quick answers to any question about *The Faerie Queene* and its context or to begin a more extensive exploration. Also valuable is Charles Grosvenor Osgood's *Concordance to the Poems of Edmund Spenser*. Naseeb Shaheen's *Biblical References in* The Faerie Queene, Henry Gibbons Lotspeich's *Classical Mythology in the Poetry of Edmund Spenser*, and Charles Huntington Whitman's *A Subject Index to the Poems of Edmund Spenser* may be useful for exploring patterns of theme and allusion. For early Spenser scholarship see Francis R. Johnson's *Critical Bibliography of the Works of Edmund Spenser Printed before 1700*, Jewel Wurtsbaugh's *Two Centuries of Spenser Scholarship*, and Robert M. Cummings's *Spenser: The Critical Heritage*; see also William Wells's "Spenser Allusions in the Sixteenth and Seventeenth Centuries, Part I: 1580–1625," along with Jackson C. Boswell's "Spenser Allusions: Addenda to Wells"; also Richard C. Frushell's "Spenser and the Eighteenth-Century Schools" and Greg Kucich's "The Duality of Romantic Spenserianism." For twentieth-century bibliography see Frederic Ives Carpenter's *A Reference Guide to Edmund Spenser*, Dorothy F. Atkinson Evans's *Edmund Spenser: A Bibliographical Supplement*, Waldo F. McNeir and Foster Provost's *Edmund Spenser: An Annotated Bibliography, 1937–1972*, Bernard J. Vondersmith's "A Bibliography of Criticism of *The Faerie Queene*, 1900–1970," and—indispensable to Spenser scholarship since 1970—the *Spenser Newsletter*, now edited by Jerome S. Dees and available from the Department of English, 122 Denison Hall, Kansas State University, Manhattan 66506-0701. Appearing three times a year, the *Spenser Newsletter* includes reviews of books, summaries of articles, and the annual fall "Spenser Bibliography Update" by John W. Moore, Jr. The only journal devoted principally to publication of articles on Spenser is *Spenser Studies: A Renaissance Poetry Annual*, established in 1980 and edited since by Patrick Cullen and Thomas P. Roche, Jr. The only full biography is Alexander C. Judson's *Life of Edmund Spenser*, which is volume 8 of the Variorum *Works*. Richard Rambuss's enlightening *Spenser's Secret Career* explores the relation between Spenser's lifelong work as secretary to various political and ecclesiastical figures and his poetic career.

Background

The distinction between "background" and "interpretation" is as nebulous as that between "context" and "text." Here we include works that do not undertake to develop a reading of all or part of *The Faerie Queene*. Consequently many works useful for background information, such as James Nohrnberg's *The Analogy of* The Faerie Queene—the work that survey respondents recommend most frequently for background information—or Alastair Fowler's *Spenser and the Numbers of Time*, are listed under "Interpretation." Helena Shire's *A Preface to Spenser* broadly surveys backgrounds of *The Faerie Queene*. Several collections of background documents are available; the choice for editors here is between broader coverage with shorter excerpts and more fully cited documents from a narrower range of topics. Arthur F. Kinney's *Elizabethan Backgrounds: Historical Documents of the Age of Elizabeth I* includes substantial selections relating to government activities. Gerald M. Pinciss and Roger Lockyer's *Shakespeare's World: Background Readings in the English Renaissance* has somewhat shorter selections representing a wide variety of experience. Joel Hurtsfield and Alan G. R. Smith's *Elizabethan People: State and Society* contains very brief excerpts on many topics.

The social and political roles of women in the Renaissance have been much studied in the past decade. Margaret L. King's *Women of the Renaissance* is clear, sensible, and well-documented. Linda Woodbridge's densely learned *Women and the English Renaissance: Literature and the Nature of Womankind, 1540–1620*, Lisa Jardine's provocative *Still Harping on Daughters: Women and Drama in the Age of Shakespeare*, Retha M. Warnicke's *Women of the English Renaissance and Reformation*, with a focus on religious history as a determinant of gender conventions, and Ruth Kelso's classic *Doctrine for the Lady of the Renaissance* are all useful. Louis Adrian Montrose's " 'Shaping Fantasies': Figurations of Gender and Power in Elizabethan Culture" is a provocative analysis focused on the interplay of power around the maiden monarch. Emphasizing particular perspectives are *The Matter of Difference: Materialist Feminist Criticism of Shakespeare*, edited by Valerie Wayne, and Stevie Davies's Jungian study *The Feminine Reclaimed: The Idea of Woman in Spenser, Shakespeare, and Milton*. Camille Paglia's *Sexual Personae*, a peculiar blend of pop philosophy and myth theory, includes a chapter entitled "Spenser and Apollo: *The Faerie Queene*," which some may find useful to provoke classroom discussion. Two excellent collections of essays are *Rewriting the Renaissance: The Discourses of Sexual Difference in Early Modern Europe*, edited by Margaret W. Ferguson, Maureen Quilligan, and Nancy J. Vickers, and *Silent but for the Word: Tudor Women as Patrons, Translators, and Writers of Religious Works*, edited by Margaret P. Hannay.

For background on humanism and education, the revisionist study by Anthony Grafton and Lisa Jardine *From Humanism to the Humanities:*

Education and the Liberal Arts in Fifteenth- and Sixteenth-Century Europe is a good place to start. Valuable earlier studies include Joan Simon's *Education and Society in Tudor England*, Kenneth Charlton's *Education in Renaissance England*, Fritz Caspari's *Humanism and the Social Order in Tudor England*, T. W. Baldwin's *William Skakspere's Small Latine and Lesse Greeke*, and Douglas Bush's *The Renaissance and English Humanism*.

Useful works on sixteenth-century psychology are E. Ruth Harvey's *The Inward Wits: Psychological Theory in the Middle Ages and the Renaissance*, J. M. Bamborough's *The Little World of Man*, and Ruth Leila Anderson's *Elizabethan Psychology and Shakespeare's Plays*.

Social and economic history has been an area of energetic study in recent decades. A representative collection of useful essays on various topics is *Order and Disorder in Early Modern England*, edited by Anthony Fletcher and John Stevenson. Three very helpful one-volume surveys of social and economic structures, conditions, and developments are Joyce Youings's *Sixteenth-Century England*, D. M. Palliser's *The Age of Elizabeth: England under the Later Tudors, 1547–1603*, and Keith Wrightson's *English Society, 1580–1680*. Lawrence Stone's *The Family, Sex, and Marriage in England, 1500–1800* is comprehensive and clear. Louis B. Wright's *Middle-Class Culture in Elizabethan England*, despite his commitment to celebrate what he deems salutary middle-class values, is still useful.

Among works on various aspects of politics and the court, John N. King's "Queen Elizabeth I: Representations of the Virgin Queen" identifies and explains a shift in Elizabethan iconology around 1580 related to sexual and governmental politics; *Spenser and Ireland: An Interdisciplinary Perspective*, edited by Patricia Coughlan, is a small collection of essays on Spenser's Irish politics; Richard C. McCoy's *The Rites of Knighthood: Literature and the Politics of Elizabethan Chivalry* is a thoughtful exploration of the values of the Elizabethan chivalric ethos and the expression of those values in the careers and works of Elizabethan poets, including Spenser; Arthur B. Ferguson's *The Chivalric Tradition in Renaissance England* is less explicitly literary in focus but valuable; John Guy's *Tudor England* is a solid survey of political and religious developments; David Norbrook's *Poetry and Politics in the English Renaissance*, which reviews the politics of modern Renaissance criticism and includes a chapter on *The Faerie Queene*, explores currents of innovative political thought in Renaissance writers; *Patronage in the Renaissance*, edited by Guy Fitch Lytle and Stephen Orgel, is a useful collection of fourteen essays; Frances A. Yates's *Astraea: The Imperial Theme in the Sixteenth Century* explores the expression of the ideal of empire in England and France; Lawrence Stone's *The Crisis of the Aristocracy, 1558–1641* and J. E. Neale's *Elizabeth I and Her Parliaments, 1584–1601* are seminal works.

Useful on science, cosmology, and the occult are *Hermeticism and the Renaissance: Intellectual History and the Occult in Early Modern Europe*, a collection of essays on both general and specific topics edited by Ingrid

Merkel and Allen G. Debus, and *Occult and Scientific Mentalities in the Renaissance*, with writings by Dee, Fludd, Kepler, and others, edited by Brian Vickers. Frances A. Yates's *The Occult Philosophy in the Elizabethan Age* provides a clear introduction to the topic and discusses Spenser and other writers. The studies in this area by S. K. Heninger, Jr., are invaluable: *The Cosmographical Glass: Renaissance Diagrams of the Universe, Touches of Sweet Harmony: Pythagorean Cosmology and Renaissance Poetics*, and *A Handbook of Renaissance Meteorology, with Particular Reference to Elizabethan and Jacobean Literature*, which includes a clear presentation of background information as well as a chapter on Spenser. Wayne Shumaker's *The Occult Sciences in the Renaissance: A Study in Intellectual Patterns* is a thorough and thoughtful survey. Francis R. Johnson's *Astronomical Thought in Renaissance England: A Study of the Scientific Writings from 1500 to 1645* remains useful.

Among works on Renaissance theology and philosophy, A. G. Dickens's standard study, *The English Reformation*, has been revised and updated. *The Cambridge History of Renaissance Philosophy*, edited by Charles B. Schmitt et al., is an excellent collection of essays on many facets of Renaissance natural, moral, and political philosophy and on epistemology, humanism, history, rhetoric, and poetics. In *English Reformation Literature: The Tudor Origins of the Protestant Tradition*, John N. King focuses on the mid-Tudor Protestant literary tradition and its influence on Spenser and others, a subject that has otherwise received little critical attention. Alan Sinfield's excellent brief overview, *Literature in Protestant England, 1560–1660*, has been influential. Patrick Collinson's comprehensive study, *The Elizabethan Puritan Movement*, is standard.

Works on Renaissance aesthetic values, traditions, and ideas are numerous and diverse. Richard Helgerson's *Forms of Nationhood: The Elizabethan Writing of England*, a rich work of cultural and intellectual history intended to broaden the focus of new-historicist scholarship, identifies the senses of national identity of Spenser's generation and the forms in which they are expressed. In *The Poetics of Primitive Accumulation: English Renaissance Culture and the Genealogy of Capital*, Richard Halpern develops a Marxist account of Renaissance poetics. Patricia Fumerton, in *Cultural Aesthetics: Renaissance Literature and the Practice of Social Ornament*, discusses Renaissance aesthetics in terms of the values and interests of the aristocracy. Clark Hulse describes the relation of literature and painting in a changing order of knowledge in *The Rule of Art: Literature and Painting in the Renaissance*; Murray Roston includes a chapter dealing in part with Spenser in his collection of interdisciplinary essays, *Renaissance Perspectives in Literature and the Visual Arts*. Leonard Barkan has written histories of metamorphosis and microcosm, two ideas central to Spenser's art and thought: *The Gods Made Flesh: Metamorphosis and the Pursuit of Paganism* and *Nature's Work of Art: The Human Body as Image of the World*. Suzanne

Woods provides a useful survey of verse theory in *Natural Emphasis: English Versification from Chaucer to Dryden*; other studies of interest on this topic include Leicester Bradner's "Forerunners of the Spenserian Stanza" and Emma Field Pope's "The Critical Background of the Spenserian Stanza." The literature on the allegorical mode is considerable. Jacqueline T. Miller's *Poetic License: Authority and Authorship in Medieval and Renaissance Contexts* includes an insightful discussion of the allegorical nature of *The Faerie Queene*; other useful studies of allegory include Joel Fineman's "The Structure of Allegorical Desire," Michael Murrin's *The Allegorical Epic: Essays in Its Rise and Decline* and *The Veil of Allegory: Some Notes toward a Theory of Allegorical Rhetoric in the English Renaissance*, Maureen Quilligan's *The Language of Allegory: Defining the Genre*, and Angus Fletcher's *Allegory: Theory of a Symbolic Mode*. Other relevant genre studies are Andrew V. Ettin's *Literature and the Pastoral*, which considers book 6 of *The Faerie Queene*, Louis Adrian Montrose's "Of Gentlemen and Shepherds: The Politics of Elizabethan Pastoral Form," Patricia Parker's *Inescapable Romance: Studies in the Poetics of a Mode*, and Thomas Greene's *The Descent from Heaven: A Study in Epic Continuity*. Anne Lake Prescott clarifies the influence of French Renaissance culture in England in *French Poets and the English Renaissance: Studies in Fame and Transformation*. Rosemond Tuve's *Allegorical Imagery: Some Medieval Books and Their Posterity* is an excellent introduction to the Spenserian aesthetic; two influential classic studies of the medieval heritage are Ernst Robert Curtius's *European Literature and the Latin Middle Ages* and C. S. Lewis's *The Allegory of Love: A Study in Medieval Tradition*. On the classical heritage, Don Cameron Allen's *Mysteriously Meant: The Rediscovery of Pagan Symbolism and Allegorical Interpretation in the Renaissance* is useful. Edgar Wind's *Pagan Mysteries in the Renaissance*, Jean Seznec's *The Survival of the Pagan Gods: The Mythological Tradition and Its Place in Renaissance Humanism and Art*, and Douglas Bush's *Mythology and the Renaissance Tradition in English Poetry* are all standard works. On the social and aesthetic aspects of court life, see David Bergeron's *English Civic Pageantry, 1558–1642* and *The Court of Elizabeth the First* by Rachel Percival and Allen Percival, who give special attention to music. On the aesthetics of Renaissance gardens, see Roy Strong's *The Renaissance Garden in England* or Terry Comito's *The Idea of the Garden in the Renaissance*.

Interpretation

Guides, introductions, and handbooks may assist both teachers and students. Russell J. Meyer's The Faerie Queene: *Educating the Reader* is a clear introductory guide for students. Two excellent recent guides are Humphrey Tonkin's *The Faerie Queene* and Elizabeth Heale's The Faerie Queene: *A Reader's Guide*. Simon Shepherd's *Spenser* is appealingly unorthodox but reads texts too reductively to be used without caution. Earlier guides include Douglas Brooks-Davies's *Spenser's* Faerie Queene: *A Critical Commentary on Books I and II*, Mark Rose's *Spenser's Art: A Companion to Book One of* The Faerie Queene, Rosemary Freeman's The Faerie Queene: *A Companion for Readers*, Roger Sale's *Reading Spenser: An Introduction to* The Faerie Queene, Graham Hough's *A Preface to* The Faerie Queene, and H. S. V. Jones's *A Spenser Handbook*.

All the many collections of essays contain valuable work, some appearing originally in the collection and some reprinted. Among the most recent collections, *Unfolded Tales: Essays on Renaissance Romance*, edited by George M. Logan and Gordon Teskey, contains all original essays by distinguished Spenser scholars. *Revisionary Play: Studies in the Spenserian Dynamics* by Harry Berger, Jr., reprints eleven of Berger's extremely influential essays on *The Faerie Queene* from the 1960s. *Studies in* The Faerie Queene, the Spring 1987 issue of *English Literary Renaissance*, edited by Arthur F. Kinney, presents all original essays. Harold Bloom's *Modern Critical Views: Edmund Spenser* includes twelve essays from 1961 to 1985 and a new piece by Donald Cheney. Earlier collections include Peter Bayley's The Faerie Queene: *A Casebook*, with essays from 1715 to 1975; R. C. Frushell and B. J. Vondersmith's *Contemporary Thought on Edmund Spenser* containing all original essays; Judith Kennedy and James A. Reither's *A Theatre for Spenserians*, also with all original essays; A. C. Hamilton's *Essential Articles for the Study of Edmund Spenser*, a rich collection comprising thirty-one articles on *The Faerie Queene* published between 1936 and 1972; Paul J. Alpers's *Edmund Spenser: A Critical Anthology*, which excerpts critical and editorial comment from the Renaissance to the modern era, and *Elizabethan Poetry: Modern Essays in Criticism*, including seven essays on *The Faerie Queene*, several highly influential, two original in this volume; John R. Elliott, Jr.'s *The Prince of Poets: Essays on Edmund Spenser*, with comments on Spenser by other poets, two eighteenth-century pieces on *The Faerie Queene*, and five from 1961 to 1966; Harry Berger, Jr.'s *Spenser: A Collection of Critical Essays*, including six essays on *The Faerie Queene* from 1961 to 1968; and W. R. Mueller's *Spenser's Critics*, a retrospect of work from 1715 to 1949.

The following paragraphs present in various categories a selection of criticism as points of entry into the vast body of writing on *The Faerie Queene* during the last fifty years. The categories are meant to be roughly descriptive but by no means definitive; most of the works could fit in more than one category. Older articles are included sparingly. To achieve a broader bibliographic representation in a limited space, we have not mentioned again separately the essays available in the collections cited above.

Among broadly focused studies of *The Faerie Queene* Gary Waller's "Spenser and *The Faerie Queene*" is useful as a chapter-length introduction to the poem; A. Bartlett Giamatti's *Play of Double Senses: Spenser's* Faerie Queene is a good short overview intended for students; James Nohrnberg's massive *The Analogy of* The Faerie Queene, the most comprehensive study, is invaluable both for its analysis of the relation between the books and for its thorough attention to themes, sources, traditions, and allusions.

Stephen Greenblatt's *Renaissance Self-Fashioning: From More to Shakespeare* initiated a rich tradition of exploration of the importance for our reading of *The Faerie Queene* of Spenser's function and image as poet in his culture. Notable in this tradition are Elizabeth J. Bellamy's "The Vocative and the Vocational: The Unreadability of Elizabeth in *The Faerie Queene*," Louis Adrian Montrose's "The Elizabethan Subject and the Spenserian Text" (which, despite its limited specific engagement with *The Faerie Queene*, may be, because of its brilliant insights and comprehensive focus, the best brief introduction to new-historicist theory and practice), David Lee Miller's "Spenser's Vocation, Spenser's Career," and Richard Helgerson's *Self-Crowned Laureates: Spenser, Jonson, Milton, and the Literary System.*

Among general studies of *The Faerie Queene* focused on narrative, rhetoric, and language, "Narrative as Rhetoric in *The Faerie Queene*" by Harry Berger, Jr., synthesizes much of the best work. A. Leigh DeNeef's insightful *Spenser and the Motives of Metaphor* explores the relation between poet and reader in the indeterminate metaphorical and allegorical process; Paul J. Alpers's "Narration in *The Faerie Queene*" and *The Poetry of* The Faerie Queene, which insists on the consistency of the poem's narrative mode, remain valuable both in their own right and as progenitors of much current scholarship; Jerome S. Dees in "The Narrator of *The Faerie Queene*: Patterns of Resonance" offers an insightful analysis of the narrator's commentaries on the story; John Webster's "Oral Form and Written Craft in Spenser's *Faerie Queene*" is helpful in appreciating aspects of Spenser's narrative practice.

Among general studies of themes, images, and their sources, Judith Anderson's "The Antiquities of Faeryland and Ireland" explores Spenser's idealized view of the past in *The Shepheardes Calendar*, *A View of the Present State of Ireland*, and *The Faerie Queene*. Judith Dundas's *The Spider and the Bee* is valuable for its attention to the visual aspect of the text and its relation to the theory and practice of painting in the Renaissance. Thomas H. Cain's *Praise in* The Faerie Queene thoughtfully considers not only the forms of praise of Elizabeth in *The Faerie Queene* but also those of Spenser's self-representation as encomiast. John Erskine Hankins in *Source and Meaning in Spenser's Allegory* discusses Spenser's allegory, particularly his representation of the moral virtues, in the context of Renaissance writers on allegory. Maurice Evans offers in *Spenser's Anatomy of Heroism: A Commentary on* The Faerie Queene a comprehensive reading stressing the poem's didactic purpose of fashioning gentlemen. C. S. Lewis's *Spenser's Images of Life*, a readable short overview of ideas, images, and methods, written in part by Alastair Fowler from Lewis's notes for his Cambridge lectures, can serve as a companion to a first reading of *The Faerie Queene*. Donald Cheney's *Spenser's Image of Nature: Wild Man and Shepherd in* The Faerie Queene, which focuses on pastoral motifs, may be described as predeconstructive in its view of the text as an infinitely expanding series of paradoxes, contrasts, and opposing forces resistant to doctrinal definition. Kathleen Williams's *Spenser's World of Glass: A Reading of* The Faerie Queene, which stresses the notion of unity beneath the complexity of detail; William Nelson's *The Poetry of Edmund Spenser: A Study*, which surveys the shorter poems as well; and A. C. Hamilton's *The Structure of Allegory in* The Faerie Queene, which clarifies fundamental aesthetic principles of the poem, are still useful standard works.

Psychological studies are of various kinds. David Lee Miller introduces Lacanian concepts in *The Poem's Two Bodies* to demonstrate through a series of specific readings the specular relation of the forms of the 1590 *Faerie Queene* to Spenser's imperial national politics, patriarchal social politics, and Neoplatonizing theology on the one hand and Tudor historical and legal writing and practice on the other. Other studies include *The Sacred Marriage: Psychic Integration in* The Faerie Queene, a Jungian reading by Benjamin G. Lockerd, Jr.; Robert L. Reid's "Man, Woman, Child, or Servant: Family Hierarchy as a Figure of Tripartite Psychology in *The Faerie Queene*," which treats triadic groupings as moral symbols based on Renaissance psychology; and Isabel G. MacCaffrey's *Spenser's Allegory: The Anatomy of Imagination*, a richly subtle discussion of the poem as a model of Spenser's mind and universe.

Among general readings of *The Faerie Queene* in terms of political and military institutions, concepts, and behaviors, Michael West argues in "Spenser's Art of War: Chivalric Allegory, Military Technology, and the Elizabethan Mock-Heroic Sensibility" that the incongruities of Spenser's treatment of war and chivalry are partly "unconscious self-parody," partly "deliberate burlesque" and that they help create an embryonic form of seventeenth-century mock-heroic style. Pamela Joseph Benson in "Rule, Virginia: Protestant Theories of Female Regiment in *The Faerie Queene*" suggests that Spenser's praise of Queen Elizabeth in fact proceeds from a Calvinist belief in the inferiority of women. Michael O'Connell in *Mirror and Veil: The Historical Dimension of Spenser's* Faerie Queene explores the reciprocal relation between the poem's moral allegory and its historical allusiveness.

Among general studies focusing on philosophy, religion, astrology, or numerology, Sean Kane in *Spenser's Moral Allegory* situates his reading of *The Faerie Queene* within his broad reading of Western intellectual history. Recently there has been renewed interest in Spenser's Protestantism. John N. King's *Spenser's Poetry and the Reformation Tradition* offers a thorough and specific discussion of Spenser's works as part of the tradition of Tudor Protestantism. Similarly, Ann E. Imbrie in " 'Playing Legerdemaine with the Scripture': Parodic Sermons in *The Faerie Queene*" explains the biblical language of many of Spenser's villains by reference to English hermeneutic and homiletic theory and practice. Ernest B. Gilman in the third chapter of *Iconoclasm and Poetry in the English Reformation: Down Went Dagon* explores the tensions that inform Spenser's pictorialism in an age radically ambivalent about images. Anthea Hume's *Edmund Spenser: Protestant Poet* emphasizes the primacy of Protestantism in Spenser's intellectual synthesis. Neoplatonism remains a subject of scholarly interest. Robert Cummings's "Spenser's 'Twelve Private Morall Virtues' " suggests that Spenser's concepts of "magnificence" and of "twelve private moral virtues" are clarified by, and may be derived from, the treatment of virtues and vices in the *Corpus hermeticum*. Elizabeth Bieman elaborates the theology of Christian Neoplatonism and its relation to Spenser's works in her *Plato Baptized: Towards the Interpretation of Spenser's Mimetic Fictions*. Kenneth Gross in *Spenserian Poetics: Idolatry, Iconoclasm, and Magic* problematizes our ideas of Spenser's theology and aesthetics. On magic in *The Faerie Queene* see the series of articles by Patrick Cheney: " 'And Doubted Her to Deeme an Earthly Wight': Male Neoplatonic 'Magic' and the Problem of Female Identity in Spenser's Allegory of the Two Florimells," " 'Secret Powre Unseene': Good Magic in Spenser's Legend of Britomart," "Spenser's Completion of the Squire's Tale: Love, Magic, and Heroic Action in the Legend of Cambell and Triamond," and, with P. J. Klemp, "Spenser's Dance of the Graces and the Ptolemaic Universe." Alastair Fowler's *Spenser and the Numbers of Time* is a wonderfully rich source of information on numerology. Robert Ellrodt's classic study, *Neoplatonism in the Poetry of Spenser* is still useful, though his analysis has been the subject of much revision.

Among general interpretations of *The Faerie Queene* involving other poets or literary or artistic traditions, principles, or circumstances, studies of relations between Spenser and Milton are the most numerous. In "Couples, Canons, and the Uncouth: Spenser and Milton in Educational Theory" Annabel Patterson considers the reasons for this scholarly interest. John C. Ulreich, Jr., explores in "Making Dreams Truth, and Fables Histories: Spenser and Milton on the Nature of Fiction" the poets' transformations of the Orpheus myth. In "From Allegory to Dialectic: Imagining Error in Spenser and Milton" Gordon Teskey distinguishes the allegorical mode of Spenserian narrative from the mimetic and historical mode of Miltonic narrative. In "Augustine, Spenser, Milton, and the Christian Epic" Marshall Grossman explores fundamental conceptual differences between Spenser and Milton in relation to an Augustinian paradigm. Other important works on the topic include Maureen Quilligan's *Milton's Spenser: The Politics of Reading*, John Guillory's *Poetic Authority: Spenser, Milton, and Literary History*, Richard Mallette's *Spenser, Milton, and Renaissance Pastoral*, Joseph A. Wittreich's *Visionary Poetics: Milton's Tradition and His Legacy*, Richard Neuse's "Milton and Spenser: The Virgilian Triad Revisited," A. Kent Hieatt's *Chaucer, Spenser, Milton: Mythopoeic Continuities and Transformations*, and Patrick Cullen's *Infernal Triad: The Flesh, the World, and the Devil in Spenser and Milton*.

No doubt the grandest recent comparative Spenser project is *Translations of Power: Narcissism and the Unconscious in Epic History*, in which Elizabeth J. Bellamy undertakes the psychoanalysis of epic history, with focus on the *Aeneid, Orlando furioso, Gerusalemme liberata*, and *The Faerie Queene*. Some other general studies of *The Faerie Queene* in relation to the work of other authors include Anne Higgins's clear and perceptive "Spenser Reading Chaucer: Another Look at the *Faerie Queene* Allusions." S. K. Heninger's *Sidney and Spenser: The Poet as Maker* explores the relation of Sidney and Spenser in the context of Renaissance literary theory. In "The Passing of Arthur in Malory, Spenser, and Shakespeare: The Avoidance of Closure" A. Kent Hieatt suggests possible structural and political implications of Spenser's use of Arthurian legend. Peter DeSa Wiggins in "Spenser's Anxiety" discusses Spenser's relation to Ariosto. Colin Burrow's "Original Fictions: Metamorphoses in *The Faerie Queene*" argues that Spenser uses transformations to develop a vision of fecundity and vitality opposed to Ovid's sense of unregenerative sexual hostility and misdirection. In "Spenser's *Georgics*" William A. Sessions argues the structural and thematic importance for *The Faerie Queene* of Vergil's work. Judith Anderson in *The Growth of a Personal Voice:* Piers Plowman *and* The Faerie Queene demonstrates the fundamental conceptual, structural, and stylistic similarities between the two works.

John D. Bernard's *Ceremonies of Innocence: Pastoralism in the Poetry of Edmund Spenser* is a comprehensive and judicious study of Spenserian pastoralism that both reflects and revises earlier new-historicist work by Montrose and others. Theresa M. Krier's *Gazing on Secret Sights: Spenser, Classical Imitation, and the Decorums of Vision* compares Spenser's handling of visual intrusion into mysteries with that of Vergil and Ovid. Other recent studies of Spenser's pictorialism are Stanley Stewart's "Spenser and the Judgement of Paris" and Mason Tung's "Spenser's 'Emblematic' Imagery: A Study of Emblematics." On music, Robin Headlam Wells in "Spenser and the Politics of Music" argues the ambivalence of Elizabethan attitudes toward, and Spenserian representations of, music. Patricia Fumerton's stimulating and perceptive "Relative Means: Spenser's Style of *Discordia Concors*," though limited in its identification of the defining character of Spenser's style as the abrupt juxtaposition of contraries, is the best recent stylistic study of *The Faerie Queene*. Richard Helgerson examines the stylistic tension between "Gothic" and "Roman" in *The Faerie Queene* in "Barbarous Tongues: The Ideology of Poetic Form in Renaissance England."

Among studies of all or parts of book 1 with focus on allegorical interpretation or intellectual history, John N. Wall's *Transformations of the Word: Spenser, Herbert, Vaughan* supports his view of Spenser as "the quintessential poet of the Church of England" with perceptive analyses of book 1 and of *Amoretti and Epithalamion*. Jeffrey Knapp's "Error as a Means of Empire in *The Faerie Queene* I" is a provocative exploration of the relation between imperialism and pastoralism, with emphasis on books 1 and 6. Richard Mallette's "The Protestant Art of Preaching in Book One of *The Faerie Queene*" places Redcrosse's progress in learning to listen and learn in the context of Reformation homiletics. In two pieces, "The True Saint George" and "What Spenser Meant by Holinesse: Baptism in Book One of *The Faerie Queene*," Harold L. Weatherby argues for the influence on Spenser of Eastern and patristic theology and liturgy. "Holiness as the First of Spenser's Aristotelian Moral Virtues," Gerald Morgan's careful reading of book 1 in relation to Renaissance Aristotelianism deriving from Thomas Aquinas, invites further inquiry into an area that has received relatively little attention, as scholars have busied themselves with the extent of Spenser's Platonism, and offers a new response to the much discussed problem of Spenser's declaration of the allegorical and structural significance of the "twelve private morall vertues, as Aristotle hath devised." Carol V. Kaske's "The Dragon's Spark and Sting and the Structure of Red Cross's Dragon-Fight" is a close examination of the religious allegory in cantos 11 and 12. Mary R. Falls in "Spenser's Kirkrapine and the Elizabethans" argues that Kirkrapine represents not the abuses of the Church by clergy expelled in the dissolution of the monasteries by Henry VIII but, rather, abuses of the Church by Elizabethans. A. S. P. Woodhouse's "Nature and Grace in *The Faerie Queene*," exploring the relation between books 1 and 2, has been controversial and influential.

Studies of book 1 that focus on theme, style, or literary tradition include Anne Lake Prescott's "Spenser's Chivalric Restoration: From Bateman's *Travayled Pylgrime* to the Redcrosse Knight," an enlightening comparison of book 1 with a 1569 chivalric pilgrimage allegory adapted from a fifteenth-century Burgundian work. Shirley Clay Scott's exemplary thematic study, "From Polydorus to Fradubio: The History of a *Topos*," traces through Western literature the Vergilian topos of a bleeding, speaking tree to show Spenser's unique sense of his religious allegory and of his relation to literary tradition. In "'A Gentle Knight Was Pricking on the Plaine': The Chaucerian Connection" Judith Anderson argues that Spenser's diction creates a delicate layering of Chaucerian parody at the beginning of book 1 and at the end of the Mutability cantos. Thomas P. Roche, Jr., in "The Menace of Despair and Arthur's Vision, *Faerie Queene* I.9," examines verbal and conceptual patterns in the "despair canto" to suggest that Spenser conceives of cantos as coherent units.

Among studies of book 1 with psychological focus, Elizabeth Bellamy's "Reading Desire Backwards: Belatedness and Spenser's Arthur" is a brilliant, lucidly written analysis, chiefly Lacanian, of Arthur's dream in canto 9. In "Spenserian Psychology and the Structure of Allegory in Books 1 and 2 of *The Faerie Queene*" Robert L. Reid argues that Spenser's concept of the psyche is a modified Platonic tripartite scheme that informs books 1 and 2 in fundamental ways.

Studies of all or parts of book 2 focused on theme, style, literary tradition, or the other arts include John Rooks's "Art, Audience, and Performance in the Bowre of Bliss," an informative exploration of the representation of music in the Bower of Bliss and its implications for the episode and for the work generally. Theresa M. Krier's "The Mysteries of the Muses: Spenser's *Faerie Queene*, II.3, and the Epic Tradition of the Goddess Observed" analyzes the methods and goals of Spenser's modification of the ancient tradition of describing the numinous woman. Stephen Greenblatt's provocative essay "To Fashion a Gentleman: Spenser and the Destruction of the Bower of Bliss" in his *Renaissance Self-Fashioning* reads canto 12 in the context of the literary and cultural history of sixteenth-century England and has served to redirect the discussion of the relation between art and ideology in *The Faerie Queene*. In "A Numerical Key for Spenser's *Amoretti* and Guyon in the House of Mammon" A. Kent Hieatt suggests that the forty stanzas of Guyon's descent to the house of Mammon (7.26–66) constitute a numerical and thematic link to the forty Lenten sonnets of *Amoretti*. Though the theoretical ground has shifted somewhat beneath *The Allegorical Temper: Vision and Reality in Book II of Spenser's* Faerie Queene by Harry Berger, Jr., it has been the most influential work on book 2 and remains the point of departure for most recent work.

Studies of book 2 in the context of intellectual history are many. Richard Mallette in "The Protestant Ethics of Love in Book Two of *The Faerie Queene*" argues that the separation of books 1 and 2 into realms of grace and nature violates the ethic of love in which Spenser participated. Richard Waswo's situation of the British chronicles of canto 10 in the tradition of the West's myth of the foundation of civilization in his "The History That Literature Makes" may be of interest to those wishing to integrate Spenser into courses in world or Western literature or civilization. Harold L. Weatherby in "Two Images of Mortalitie: Spenser and Original Sin" suggests that Spenser's ideas of the Fall and of Original Sin derive from patristic theology rather than from the Augustinian tradition and shows the implications of this insight for book 2. Philip Rollinson's brief but careful and richly annotated "Arthur, Maleger, and the Interpretation of *The Faerie Queene*" places Spenser's Arthur in the context of Western intellectual history. Lauren Silberman in "*The Faerie Queene*, Book II, and the Limitations of Temperance" reads book 2 as largely ironic, an example of the application of inappropriate methods to the enterprise of making sense of the sensual world. Gerald Morgan's "The Idea of Temperance in the Second Book of *The Faerie Queene*" is an enlightening exploration of Spenser's concept of temperance in terms of both Scholastic and Protestant theology. Sean Kane's "The Paradoxes of Idealism: Book Two of *The Faerie Queene*" explores the ideological implications of Spenser's allegory from medieval and modern viewpoints. Michael Murrin's provocative "The Rhetoric of Faeryland" explores the relation of Spenser's faerie land to Western traditions. In "The Goodly Frame of Temperance: The Metaphor of Cosmos in *The Faerie Queene*, Book II," James Carscallen clarifies Guyon's career as a knight of temperance in relation to the broader concept of the universal temperance of the elements of nature.

Among studies of book 2 with psychological focus James Vink's "Spenser's *Straftraum*: Guyon's Evil Descent" presents a perceptive, generally Freudian reading of Guyon's experience in Mammon's cave. In "Augustinian Psychology in *The Faerie Queene*, Book II" Carol V. Kaske argues that book 2, widely considered the most classical of *The Faerie Queene*, is informed by thought rooted in the Bible and coded by the Church fathers. Robert L. Reid in "Alma's Castle and the Symbolization of Reason in *The Faerie Queene*" shows how the intricacies of Aristotelian and Platonic faculty psychology subserve the moral allegory of book 2. Jerry Leath Mills explores in a series of articles the relation of the historical chronicles in cantos 9 and 10 to Guyon's career and to the virtue of temperance and clarifies related structures of numerology and faculty psychology derived from sources such as Bateman, Bryskett, and Bodin: "Prudence, History, and the Prince in *The Faerie Queene*, Book II," "Spenser and the Numbers of History: A Note on the British and Elfin Chronicles in *The Faerie Queene*," "Spenser, Lodowick Bryskett, and the Mortalist Controversy: *The Faerie Queene* II.ix.22," and "Symbolic Tapestry in *The Faerie Queene* II.ix.33."

After three decades *The Kindly Flame: A Study of the Third and Fourth Books of Spenser's* Faerie Queene by Thomas P. Roche, Jr., remains the best general guide to books 3 and 4 and the place to enter the scholarly discussion of them. Spenser scholars surveyed for this volume recommended *The Kindly Flame* more frequently than any other critical work on *The Faerie Queene* in any category.

A number of more recent studies read book 3 in terms of specifically literary traditions. Two dealing with Ariosto include Lauren Silberman's "Spenser and Ariosto: Funny Peril and Comic Chaos," a comparison of Spenser's humor surrounding Britomart with the more cynical humor of Ariosto, and Elizabeth Bellamy's "Androgyny and the Epic Quest: The Female Warrior in Ariosto and Spenser." On Ovid, Silberman argues in "The Hermaphrodite and the Metamorphosis of Spenserian Allegory" that his allusions function to defer the problem of coping with human sexuality. Silberman's "Singing Unsung Heroines: Androgynous Discourse in Book 3 of *The Faerie Queene*" suggests that Spenser's transformation of topoi from Ariosto and Ovid subverts both the Platonic ontology that links male and female with form and matter and the Petrarchan poetics that pairs male and female with subject and object. Mihoko Suzuki in "'Unfitly Yokt Together in One Teeme': Vergil and Ovid in *Faerie Queene* III.x" finds in the events surrounding Malbecco's banquet an Ovidian subtext qualifying the Vergilian ethos that Spenser may have found too restrictive. "Escaping the Squire's Double Bind in Books III and IV of *The Faerie Queene*" by

Reed Way Dasenbrock, a provocative and insightful study of the roles of squires, argues that Spenser sharply criticizes the Petrarchan tradition as he embraces an ethic of reciprocal love. The fifth chapter of Andrew Fichter's *Poets Historical: Dynastic Epic in the Renaissance* focuses on the careers of Britomart and Artegall to show the shift, traced through Vergil, Augustine, Ariosto, and Tasso, from classical epic to Christian epic, in which love is compatible with and fundamental to empire. Donald Cheney's "Spenser's Hermaphrodite and the 1590 *Faerie Queene*," a discussion of themes and structures in relation to classical artistic and literary traditions, treats ideas to which subsequent commentators have returned repeatedly.

Studies of book 3 in a context of political or intellectual history include Heather Dubrow's "The Arraignment of Paridell: Tudor Historiography in *The Faerie Queene* III.ix," an analysis of the voices and perspectives of the accounts by Paridell and Britomart of their heritages. William A. Oram's "Spenser's Raleghs" explores in terms of the generic demands of allegorical romance and the pastoral the relation between the events of Ralegh's career and Spenser's allusions to Ralegh. Margaret Olofson Thickstun in "Spenser's Brides Errant" offers a perceptive reading of the career of Britomart as female hero in a Pauline-Puritan tradition that ascribes to women individual conscience and potential moral heroism at the same time as it prescribes the subordination of women. Bruce Thomas Boehrer in " 'Careless Modestee': Chastity as Politics in Book 3 of *The Faerie Queene*" argues that the simultaneous exaltation and effacement of the queen serves "to displace the anxiety of royal legitimacy and issue from the person of the queen." James W. Broaddus in "Renaissance Psychology and Britomart's Adventures in *Faerie Queene* III" draws on Renaissance physiology and faculty psychology to clarify Spenser's treatment of love and sexuality. Pamela J. Benson in "Florimell at Sea: The Action of Grace in *Faerie Queene*, Book III" undertakes to clarify the theological allegory of Florimell's story and especially her relationships with the fisherman and Proteus. In his vaguely Jungian "The Mothers in *The Faerie Queene* III" Jonathan Goldberg notes mythic patterns related to the transition from maidenhood to motherhood and argues that maternity in book 3 is a spiritual concept and its chastity a *castitas animae*. Dwight J. Sims argues in "The Syncretic Myth of Venus in Spenser's Legend of Chastity" that the book takes its meaning and structure from the syncretic tradition of Neoplatonic mysteries, especially as expressed in Pico's conception of the three Venuses.

Among studies of language, structure, or theme in book 3, Sayre N. Greenfield's perceptive "Reading Love in the Geography of *The Faerie Queene*, Book Three" provides a succinct overview of some structures and a thoughtful discussion of Spenser's concept of structure. Sheila T. Cavanagh looks at the ambiguities of Arthur's relations with women from a Derridean perspective in " 'Beauties Chace': Arthur and Women in *The Faerie Queene*" in Christopher Baswell and William Sharpe's *The Passing of Arthur*. In the same volume Judith

Anderson's "Arthur, Argante, and the Ideal Vision: An Exercise in Speculation and Parody" suggests that Argante is a parodic antitype of Gloriana;
in her " 'In Liuing Colours and Right Hew': The Queen of Spenser's Central
Books" Anderson identifies an undercurrent of criticism of Queen Elizabeth
in books 3 and 4. Susanne Lindgren Wofford in "Gendering Allegory: Spenser's Bold Reader and the Emergence of Character in *The Faerie Queene*
III" argues that sexual tension works through the characters to create interpretations that subvert the authority of the narrative and force us to read
against as well as with the allegory. Humphrey Tonkin in "Spenser's Garden
of Adonis and Britomart's Quest" looks closely at the metaphor of generation
in the garden of Adonis and its relation to Britomart's story.

Notable among studies of all or parts of book 4 is Jonathan Goldberg's
Endlesse Worke: Spenser and the Structures of Discourse, probably the most
influential Spenser book of the eighties; rather than try to explain away the
disruptions and deferrals of book 4, Goldberg identifies the "freeplay" of
the narrative as its essential quality. Marvin Glasser in "Spenser as Mannerist Poet: The 'Antique Image' in Book IV of *The Faerie Queene*" is interested in placing Spenserian stylistic traits such as those identified by Goldberg
—"fluidity of form," temporal and spatial dislocation, self-reflexivity, disjointed perspective and proportions, antitheses held in stasis—in a context
of European aesthetic history by noting affinities with paintings by Parmi-
gianino, Breughel, and El Greco. Most recent work has in general not followed Goldberg. Mark Heberle's "The Limitations of Friendship" seeks to
explain the indeterminacy of the narrative by clarifying aspects of the moral
allegory. Alan MacColl's "The Temple of Venus, the Wedding of the Thames
and the Medway, and the End of *The Faerie Queene*, Book IV," strongly
critical of poststructuralist readings, especially Goldberg's, reads cantos 10
and 11 as a tableau of mythic symbolism within the Christian tradition.
David O. Frantz in "The Union of Florimell and Marinell: The Triumph
of Hearing" relates canto 12 to the Renaissance debate concerning the hierarchy of the senses and suggests that Spenser's concern with this question
informs *The Faerie Queene* generally. David W. Burchmore argues in "Triamond, Agape, and the Fates: Neoplatonic Cosmology in Spenser's Legend
of Friendship" that Neoplatonic mythology and numerology inform the story
of the "-mond" brothers and book 4 generally. The identification of Timias
as Ralegh and the interpretive problems and opportunities related to
Spenser's topical allusiveness are explored in James P. Bednarz's "Ralegh
in Spenser's Historical Allegory," Donald Cheney's "Spenser's Fortieth Birthday and Related Fictions," and William A. Oram's "Elizabethan Fact and
Spenserian Fiction."

Topical allusiveness is of some concern for most studies of book 5. Clare
Carroll's "The Construction of Gender and the Cultural and Political Other
in *The Faerie Queene* 5 and *A View of the Present State of Ireland*: The
Critics, the Context, and the Case of Radigund" is an incisive, no-nonsense

evaluation of the politics of book 5 and of *View* and the politics of modern criticism of those works. Mark Heberle's "Aristotle and Spenser's Justice" presents evidence for Aristotelian influence. In "Spenser's Malengin, Missionary Priests, and the Means of Justice" Elizabeth Heale argues that Malengin represents the threat to Elizabeth's monarchy and the Protestant commonwealth posed by the covert Roman Catholic priesthood in England. Sheila T. Cavanagh in " 'Such Was Ireland's Countenance': Ireland in Spenser's Prose and Poetry" suggests that Spenser saw the Irish situation as a prototype of the tragedy of the fallen world and defends his analysis of that situation as compassionate. In contrast, Ciaran Brady in "Spenser's Irish Crisis: Humanism and Experience in the 1590's" looks at book 5 in the light of his identification of internal contradictions in *A View of the Present State of Ireland*, which he describes as "a sustained exercise in bad faith." In "Murdering Peasants: Status, Genre, and the Representation of Rebellion," Stephen Greenblatt considers Talus's overthrow of Grantorto as part of a progression in Renaissance attitudes, which he traces from Dürer to Shakespeare, toward the suppression of popular rebellion. Donald V. Stump in "The Two Deaths of Mary Stuart: Historical Allegory in Spenser's Book of Justice" argues persuasively that Britomart's overthrow of Radigund figures not the death of Mary but rather events of Elizabeth's early years, so that book 5 can be read as a chronological allegory of Elizabeth's long struggle with Mary. In "Isis versus Mercilla: The Allegorical Shrines in Spenser's Legend of Justice" Stump suggests that the court of Mercilla represents Spenser's ideal of the justice of a golden age that supercedes the silver-age justice of the temple of Isis. Carol Stillman in "Nobility and Justice in Book Five of *The Faerie Queene*" argues that a concept of personal and institutional nobility is fundamental to Spenser's allegory of justice. Angus Fletcher in *The Prophetic Moment: An Essay on Spenser* takes a typological, mythographic approach. Judith Anderson in " 'Nor Man It Is': The Knight of Justice in Book V of Spenser's *Faerie Queene*" argues persuasively that Artegall's seeming limitations are consistent with his allegorical function and identity. James E. Phillips in "Renaissance Concepts of Justice and the Structure of *The Faerie Queene*, Book V" suggests that Spenser follows the practice of Renaissance legal theorists in treating his topic under the categories of justice absolute, equity, and mercy and that this division is the organizational principle of the book. W. Nicholas Knight's "The Narrative Unity of Book V of *The Faerie Queene*" offers a systematic reading of the imagery and narrative as representing a process of education in justice and equity for Artegall. Jane Aptekar's *Icons of Justice: Iconography and Thematic Imagery in Book V of* The Faerie Queene focuses on the philosophical allegory, with its contradictory elements, in the context of iconographic tradition. T. K. Dunseath's *Spenser's Allegory of Justice in Book Five of* The Faerie Queene focuses on the framework of the moral allegory, the role of the book in resolving earlier themes, and the affinity of Artegall with other titular heroes. René

Graziani in "Elizabeth at Isis Church" argues that Elizabeth's final dealings with Mary, Queen of Scots inform canto 7.

Among studies of all or parts of book 6, Jacqueline T. Miller's innovative "The Courtly Figure: Spenser's Anatomy of Allegory" argues that, through Calidore, Spenser critiques his rhetorical strategies, exposing his complicity in the discourse of power and compromising the good discipline he wishes to impart. Anne Shaver's perceptive "Rereading Mirabella" treats the love resister as "a whipping girl for untouchable royalty," her episode expressing the widely felt threat to social hierarchies posed by Elizabeth's independence from marriage. Elizabeth J. Bellamy in "Colin and Orphic Interpretation: Reading Neoplatonically on Spenser's Acidale" argues for open rather than static reading of the vision on Mount Acidale as a self-reflexive Neoplatonic myth about the origins of poetry. Also involving Neoplatonic concepts is Seth Weiner's complex but illuminating argument in "Minims and Grace Notes: Spenser's Acidalian Vision and Sixteenth-Century Music" that the dance of the graces involves an elaborate symbolism based on musical terms and concepts. Kenneth Borris in " 'Diuelish Ceremonies': Allegorical Satire of Protestant Extremism in *The Faerie Queene* VI.viii.31–51" reads Serena's brush with the cannibals as a satiric allegory on English Puritanism; his "Fortune, Occasion, and the Allegory of the Quest in Book Six of *The Faerie Queene*" is a more general treatment of courtesy as a commitment to virtue whereby humankind may be liberated from fortune. Similarly Michael Tratner in " 'The Thing S. Paule Ment by . . . the Courteousness That He Spake Of': Religious Sources for Book VI of *The Faerie Queene*" reads the book as an allegory based on Elizabethan Protestantism, especially a theology of grace. Focusing instead on literary tradition, Margaret P. Hannay in " 'My Sheep Are Thoughts': Self-Reflexive Pastoral in *The Faerie Queene*, Book VI, and the *New Arcadia*" suggests that situations in which a prince teaches a princess-shepherdess to read his Petrarchan, pastoral, and chivalric posturings constitute also poets' attempts indirectly to instruct their queen to read their fictions. Julia Reinhard Lupton's "Home-Making in Ireland: Virgil's Eclogue I and Book VI of *The Faerie Queene*" offers the novel proposal that, working variations on Vergil's first eclogue, Spenser pastoralizes the Iron Age Ireland of book 5 into the golden world of book 6, integrating the personal with the political. Debra Belt in "Hostile Audiences and the Courteous Reader in *The Faerie Queene*, Book VI" suggests that contemporary prefatory addresses to readers help define courtesy in ways pertinent to Calidore's career and clarify Spenser's strategy toward his readers. Paul J. Alpers in "Spenser's Late Pastorals" argues that Melibee and Colin Clout represent a pastoral alternative to the heroic ideal into neither of which Calidore can be successfully assimilated. David Lee Miller in "Abandoning the Quest" explores the important connection between the courtier and the poet, suggesting that Calidore's progress from political court to contemplative vision entails the abandonment of the quest to realize the workings of the divine in public life and that on another level the poem as vision is limited by its impulse to act as didactic poetry. Humphrey Tonkin's *Spenser's Courteous Pastoral: Book Six of* The Faerie Queene deservedly remains the standard work on the book, offering a systematic reading of the narrative and sensible discussions of relevant themes, concepts, and backgrounds and of the book's relation to the whole. Richard Neuse's "Book VI as Conclusion to *The Faerie Queene*" is a careful analysis of Calidore as an antihero whose courtesy is a shallow civility inhospitable to religion, poetry, and contemplation.

Most of the work on *Two Cantos of Mutabilitie*, the letter to Ralegh, and the dedicatory sonnets is included in more broadly focused works or in anthologies already cited. Among the others is Carol Stillman's discovery, presented in "Politics, Precedence, and the Order of the Dedicatory Sonnets in *The Faerie Queene*," that the dedicatory sonnets are arranged in exact accordance with the heraldic rules for precedence. In " 'Figuring Hierarchy': The Dedicatory Sonnets to *The Faerie Queene*" David Lee Miller discusses the ideological and aesthetic implications of the dedicatory sonnets. About the letter to Ralegh there is much uncertainty. The "Annuall feaste" at Gloriana's court, which Spenser describes in the letter as the occasion of the adventures of *The Faerie Queene*, John N. Wall identifies in "Orion's Flaming Head" as Christmas. Jerry Leath Mills in "Spenser's Letter to Raleigh and the Averroistic *Poetics*" suggests that Spenser thought his overall plan derived theoretically from Aristotle's *Poetics*, which he likely knew in a medieval version. On the *Cantos of Mutabilitie* Sherman Hawkins's "Mutability and the Cycle of the Months" is standard. Spenser's use of Ovid as "a literary source and challenge" for the cantos is discussed in Michael Holahan's "*Iamque opus exegi*: Ovid's Changes and Spenser's Brief Epic of Mutability." Harold L. Weatherby in "The Old Theology: Spenser's Dame Nature and the Transfiguration" claims that Spenser derived central concepts of the cantos from the Greek Church fathers. Russell J. Meyer argues in " 'Fixt in Heauens Hight': Spenser, Astronomy, and the Date of the *Cantos of Mutabilitie*" that Spenser drew on the work of contemporary astronomers and in fact described in the cantos an actual lunar eclipse that occurred after April 1595.

Aids to Teaching

The most widely recommended visual texts are the portraits of Queen Elizabeth, which Roy Strong discusses in *Gloriana: The Portraits of Queen Elizabeth I*, and Alciati's 1581 *Emblemata*. Other works used by instructors include books of hours such as *The Belles Heures of Jean, Duke of Berry*, edited by Millard Meiss; calendars such as the *Kalendar and Compost of*

Shepherds; paintings by Bosch, Breughel, Botticelli, and Dürer; Blake's *Faerie Queene*; and the Spenser murals in the Enoch Pratt Library in Baltimore. Some instructors have shown the films *A Man for All Seasons* and *Anne of the Thousand Days*, both available on videotape. One instructor has found that discussion of *Star Trek* as a heavy-handed modern allegory helps students with little antiquarian interest appreciate the mode of *The Faerie Queene*; *Star Wars* might also work well. Tudor perpendicular architecture provides an interesting analogue to *The Faerie Queene*. Useful slide sets are Frank B. Sear's *Perpendicular and Tudor* and *Elizabethan and Jacobean* in the series *The Architecture of England*. In music the obvious analogue is polyphony; some may prefer to introduce the concept with very simple music, such as that of *English Lute Duets* by John Johnson, John Dowland, and others, available on cassette from the Musical Heritage Society of Ocean, New Jersey.

Illustrations

Visual materials can help the instructor emphasize a number of interesting elements in *The Faerie Queene*. The essays by Clark Hulse and Julia M. Walker in this volume offer contrasting strategies for using the following illustrations in the classroom.

Fig. 1. Attributed to Marcus Gheeraerdts the Younger. *Queen Elizabeth I* (the Ditchley portrait). C. 1592. Oil on canvas. National Portrait Gallery, London. Used with permission.

NON SINE SOLE
IRIS.

Fig. 2. Attributed to Marcus Gheeraerdts the Younger. *Queen Elizabeth I* (the Rainbow portrait). C. 1600–03. Oil on canvas. Marquess of Salisbury, Hatfield House. By courtesy of the Marquess of Salisbury.

Fig. 3. The Monogrammist HE. *Queen Elizabeth and the Three Goddesses.* 1569. Oil on panel. Hampton Court Palace. By gracious permission of Her Majesty the Queen.

Fig. 4. Quentin Massys the Younger. *Queen Elizabeth* (the Sieve portrait). 1583. Oil on canvas. Pinacoteca Nazionale, Siena. Used with permission.

Fig. 5. Attributed to "H." *Sir Walter Ralegh*. 1588. Oil on panel. National Portrait Gallery, London. Used with permission.

Fig. 6. Titian. *The Rape of Europa*. 1562. Oil on canvas. Isabella Stewart Gardner Museum, Boston. Used with permission.

Fig. 7. Detail. Titian. *The Rape of Europa*. 1562. Oil on canvas. Isabella Stewart Gardner Museum, Boston. Used with permission.

Fig. 8. Girolamo Porro. Frontispiece to canto 33. Lodovico Ariosto, *Orlando furioso* (Venice, 1583), 368. Engraving. Courtesy of the John M. Wing Foundation, The Newberry Library, Chicago.

Part Two

APPROACHES

Introduction

David Lee Miller

Introductions tend inevitably to stress continuity and coherence. Yet the essays in this collection, not to mention the dozens that might have been added, testify equally to the inexhaustible variety of *The Faerie Queene*, or what Renaissance criticism would have called its copiousness. Few literary works so unmistakably exceed one's grasp. Although *The Faerie Queene* remains the longest poem in English, its plenitude is principally a function not of sheer mass but of something else—suggestiveness, resonance, endless readability. William Empson, whose remarks on the Spenserian stanza in *Seven Types of Ambiguity* are as perceptive as anything else written on *The Faerie Queene*, describes this elusive quality well: "[W]hen there are ambiguities of idea," he writes,

> it is whole civilisations rather than details of the moment which are their elements; [Spenser] can pour into the even dreamwork of his fairyland Christian, classical, and chivalrous materials with an air, not of ignoring their differences, but of holding all their systems of values floating as if at a distance, so as not to interfere with one another, in the prolonged and diffused energies of his mind.   (34)

If *The Faerie Queene* is hard to teach—and I have found it harder than any other poem in English except Blake's *Jerusalem*—the reason owes something to its most distinctive quality, this abundance that renders all endings and assertions "provisional" (Alpers, "Narration" 27).

Yet this same quality makes the poem infinitely adaptable, a sleeping Proteus that no one course can contain but that will sing for almost any syllabus. My advice on teaching the poem has always been, Do less, and do more with it. Even in graduate seminars, I find it most rewarding to keep on *introducing* the poem; more than twenty years after it started, my own introduction is not yet finished. I imagine this is what C. S. Lewis meant by the remark that he had never met a reader who *used* to like *The Faerie Queene*. If we can just make the right introductions, if we can start the conversation, we will have done what a teacher can.

The "approaches" in this section are intended to start many conversations. Some offer guidance to instructors teaching Spenser for the first time. Others should appeal to nonspecialists seeking selections from *The Faerie Queene* for courses designed around such topics as poetry and the visual arts, gender and eroticism, the discourse of colonialism, or traditions of romance narrative. Many will also have value for specialists who teach the poem repeatedly and at every level of the curriculum but have never quite realized the lesson plan of their dreams.

The essays are divided between introductory strategies and those ranging freely within the zodiac of curricular invention. With two exceptions, the first group all take book 1 as their purview. Judith Anderson lays out a classic strategy for teaching the opening cantos as Spenser's reading lesson. Her essay strikes a keynote for the collection as a whole, urging close attention to the reading process in which the text engages us and wary hesitation in the face of the obvious. A more synoptic approach allows Raymond-Jean Frontain to address the problem beginning teachers often find most daunting: how does one integrate *The Faerie Queene* into a coherently organized historical survey of English literature?

Evelyn Tribble shares Anderson's resistance to "solving" the difficulties of the text, even at the introductory level. Here, as in the essays by Theresa Krier and John Webster, the still pervasive influence of Alpers's *The Poetry of* The Faerie Queene is evident. Tribble grounds this pedagogy historically in Protestant biblical hermeneutics as exemplified by Tyndale. John Timpane extends this concern with the interpretive process in his argument for using the poem to teach composition, and vice versa; he suggests making a virtue of the necessity we are under to teach basic reading and writing skills at the same time as we introduce literary texts.

Krier challenges Coleridge's infamous distinction between the abstractness of allegory and the concreteness of the symbol, arguing that students can best read the allegorical personae of book 1 by attending to details of bodily form and carriage, especially the body's relation to such simple natural forms as light and water. Her emphasis on *virtù* as the physical expression of virtue complements Frontain's use of the hero as a figure around which to organize the standard survey course. The first section closes with an essay on teaching book 2. Webster bases his approach on one of Spenser's favored strategies, the subtle deployment of proverbs in ambiguous contexts, where they function not as summary ethical judgments but as gnomic invitations to further reflection. Like Timpane, Webster links class discussion to writing exercises that encourage interpretive thinking; his aim is to help the poem engage students in "a continual sifting of the culture's wisdom."

The second group of essays begins with approaches to *The Faerie Queene* that use visual media. As Clark Hulse remarks, such comparisons are especially apt because the ethics and dynamics of visual experience are so prominent a theme in the poem. To explore Spenserian allegory in relation to Renaissance painting, then, means to question the poem's mimetic processes and assumptions, encouraging students to "re-create within themselves Spenser's logic of representation." Julia Walker develops a particular thematic focus, reading portraits of Elizabeth against the narrative of Britomart in books 3–5; in both she traces the resonance of a major historical shift in representations of the queen, related to the complex sexual politics of female rule in a patriarchal society.

Anne Shaver extends the concern for sexual politics in a survey of Spenser's female characters. Her essay, like Walker's, focuses on Spenser's qualified resistance to feminine rule, but Shaver extends the implications of this issue to the portrayal of powerful women throughout the poem. On specific points of interpretation Shaver's essay may be contrasted with many that follow, including Dorothy Stephens's, A. Leigh DeNeef's, and Margaret Hannay's; the special value of its overview is to indicate patterns that may not be prominent in local contexts but nevertheless tend to dominate the whole. Shaver's conclusion is that there must be distinct limits to feminist idealization of *The Faerie Queene*, which tends to affirm a hierarchical view of gender.

We close the volume with a series of essays on teaching individual books. Diana E. Henderson finds book 3, with its largely secular allegory of desire, more accessible to students than the spiritual allegory of book 1. The challenge is to cope with the book's multiple interwoven plots, which can easily confuse readers who expect a continuous narrative; Henderson suggests turning this multiplicity to advantage by using it as a topical guide to the richness of Elizabethan literary language. Stephens, meanwhile, makes the thoroughly unconventional option of teaching book 4 sound surprisingly attractive. Like Walker, Shaver, and DeNeef, she grants considerable emphasis to the thematization of gender; the pleasant surprise is that her approach to the Legend of Friendship locates alternative spaces of feminine intimacy within the largely patriarchal order of the poem.

Two essays on teaching the Legend of Justice offer new perspectives on what is traditionally the most problematic book. Sheila Cavanagh uses theoretical readings on the discourse of colonialism together with Elizabethan accounts of Ireland to help students grasp the persistent Irish subtext of book 5; her aim is not to render Spenser's views palatable but to render them significant by establishing a coherent historical and political context for them—and perhaps to make modern readers less complacent by extending that context to include comparable elements in our own historical situation. Edwin D. Craun takes book 5 as an occasion to theorize problems in the relation of law to justice, examining Artegall's and Mercilla's decisions as part of a genuinely cross-disciplinary comparison between philosophical and fictional discourses on the topos of justice.

The emphasis in essays on comparative teaching—whatever the medium or discourse to be juxtaposed with poetry—consistently falls on the importance of reciprocal analysis as opposed to "application." DeNeef makes a similar point: instead of using psychoanalytic concepts to read *The Faerie Queene*, he suggests ways of reading passages from books 2 and 6 so as to rethink our understanding of the gaze, a notion from Lacan that has gained currency among literary critics interested in feminism and psychoanalysis. Hannay offers another context for teaching book 6 in her account of a course on pastoral romance. Sidney's two versions of *Arcadia* form a series with Spenser's Legend of Courtesy and Lady Mary Wroth's *Urania*. The emphasis on generic intertextuality suggests that the process of retrospection and revision begun by Sidney in the *New Arcadia*, and carried forward by Spenser and Wroth, offers a model for the interpretive activity of student readers; issues of gender, class, and politics lend continuity and contemporary interest to the exploration of genre.

For all the variety of their aims and interests, the fifteen essays gathered here cannot pretend to encompass the possibilities for teaching Spenser's *Faerie Queene*. Their collective value then is not to round out a conspectus of classroom approaches but to reassert the importance simply of reading and teaching this extraordinary text. Spenser has never had the readership other major authors enjoy; even my own institution, which offers a traditional English major centered on canonical British writers, lists undergraduate courses in Chaucer, Shakespeare, and Milton, but not Spenser. *The Faerie Queene* may be the most undervalued classic in the canon of English poetry. Much could be said about the venerable tradition of condescending to Spenser that begins with Jonson and Milton—both writers for whom Spenser's prestige cast a longer shadow than did Shakespeare's. But at the present moment of intellectual and institutional crisis, characterized by expanding canons and contracting budgets, there is no guarantee that Spenser's poetry will even be condescended to very widely in the next century. This volume of essays bears witness to the belief that Spenser should be read better and more often—and to the hope that he will be.

"The Hard Begin": Entering the Initial Cantos

Judith H. Anderson

My title comes from Spenser's third book, where Merlin counsels Britomart to persevere in her quest, not fearing "The hard begin, that meets . . . [her] in the dore" (3.21).[1] I intend it to acknowledge the challenge Spenser's allegorical narrative presents to a modern reader and to suggest that Spenser's own beginning in book 1 is the best introduction to his poem. In taking a title from the third book for an essay on teaching the first, I also want occasion to emphasize that book 1, rather than book 3, the likely alternative, is the most effective place to begin a study of Spenser. Although book 3 is appealing as a love quest with a woman at its center and as a romance structure in which allegory is looser and less dominant than in book 1, I have never taught book 3 alone without being frustrated by what students miss—what they simply cannot see or "read" in it—if they do not have book 1 for reference and contrast. In short, while I have taught book 3 by itself for thematic, generic, or historical reasons and will do so again, I find no substitute for the first two cantos of book 1 in introducing the techniques and assumptions that underlie *The Faerie Queene*. It is here that a student learns most effectively to read Spenserian narrative and to recognize the allegorical dimensions that permeate Renaissance literature, including even as poignant a work as *King Lear*.

If students are unlikely to have had prior acquaintance with an overtly allegorical work, I explain at the start that *The Faerie Queene* is a romantic story about a knight, a woman, various temptations, and several monsters but that it is also a narrative embodying explicit and sustained meanings that go beyond the literal level of the knight's adventures: Redcrosse is a knight but he also represents holiness and, as it punningly turns out, wholeness. Even more exactly, although he represents the quest for holiness and wholeness when he is first seen, he does not truly embody them until the end of the story. Similarly, Una is a woman and the beloved of Redcrosse, but she is also Truth, Unity, Oneness; and when Redcrosse fights a serpent woman in the first canto, he fights both a monster and various sorts of error. Just how the combination of romantic story and allegory works in the poem can best—indeed, can only—be understood by closely following their interaction in the opening cantos.

While my aim is to get to Spenser's opening cantos, the path to them lies through his first proem. A desirable strategy when teaching book 1 is to offer enough commentary on this proem to justify its presence, since the most misleading impression a student can form at the outset is the one modern expectations make easy, namely that the proem is merely a flourish and hence that Spenser's style is *simply* ornate (so much verbiage) rather than skillful, functional, and significant. At the same time, however, unless the class is advanced and already acquainted with *The Faerie Queene*, I think it unwise to offer at the beginning the extensive analysis of words or topoi, whether traditional or specifically Spenserian, that is only available to students after they have read at least half the poem. What I do first is simply to comment on the traditional nature of the poet's voice and its reference to his own past ("Lo I the man" who progressed from pastoral to epic, from *The Shepheardes Calender* to *The Faerie Queene*), a voice whose parallel in book 1 will be Redcrosse's movement from pastoral plow field to court (10.65–66). For students who are new to Spenser, I relate this voice to Chaucer's at the beginning of *The Canterbury Tales* or to traditions in Renaissance painting—for example, the combination of a traditional motif with a contemporary patron or with a depiction of the artist on the threshold of the painting's inner space. Traversing the middle stanzas of the proem more quickly, I ask students to pause over the poet's address to the queen in the fourth stanza, noting that she is at once inspiration, subject, and audience of the poet's verse and that his role is conceived as being cooperative with hers; I mention as well that the queen is throughout the poem the measure of the relation of an ideal (or "antique") image to the present age, and therefore of faerie land to history and of fiction to life.[2] On notes such as these, which intrigue students, we proceed to the opening of canto 1.

This is the point at which I most want the students, whatever their level, to participate actively in analyzing the poem. It is significant that Spenser's narrative begins not with an abstraction or a label like "Holiness" but with an image that has to be interpreted and responded to not merely in detail but also in sequential detail. At the very threshold of *The Faerie Queene*, readers are thus asked to recognize as a basic assumption of meaning that Spenserian description characteristically unfolds in a *process* that their perceptions must trace. I prefer to move step-by-step through each of the opening three stanzas, asking of the first what sort of story the students would expect if they met it in isolation, what details in it seem odd, and what might be gained by not naming Redcrosse immediately. In the second stanza, I ask what dimension is added and, again, whether any line or detail seems not to fit; and in the third, what further dimension is added and particularly what line 8, "his new force to learne," might mean. By the time we have finished with the first three stanzas, a process frequently requiring half a class period, students are engaged with the process of the poem itself and aware of their own ability to respond to it, even if they have yet to digest a library of footnotes. They grasp the functional value of Spenserian description and the extent to which its puzzling details, especially if patterned, are at once to be examined closely and held in suspension, since an explanation of them is often tantalizingly incomplete when they first occur (e.g., the simultaneously puzzling and suggestive meaning of the word *pricking* in line 1, the anger of the knight's steed, his own seeming jollyness yet seeming solemn sadness). Questions are to be raised, indeed raised insistently, but not as yet necessarily answered.

At the beginning of the poem, the worst mistake, one virtually guaranteed to lose the students, is to hurry. The other is to assume that they prefer literary pabulum to the complexity (and complication) that makes the poem worth reading. Entering this poem takes time, which, of course, will have to be made up somewhere else. Other parts of the poem will have to be slighted, covered in lecture, or skipped altogether. In my experience, however, there is no substitute for careful, close reading at the outset. Once the students begin to recognize the way Spenser's allegorical narrative works, they are better able on their own to interpret parts of the poem either excluded from later classes or treated more summarily.

Following the description of Redcrosse come the simpler, less extensive descriptions of Una and the Dwarf. Conspicuously, even Una, like Redcrosse, is initially unnamed, a fact that demands our reading the image that *is* at this point her existence. Of particular interest to me has been the contrast between the implicit speed of Una's lowly ass and of Redcrosse's foaming steed and the brief appearance of Una's milk-white lamb, a symbol of her innocence never seen again in the poem. Both the assimilation of the lamb into Una's purity and the discrepancy between Redcrosse's speedy "pricking" (fast riding, galloping) and the necessarily slower movement of her humble mount (especially in view of the lamb on a leash and the heavily laden Dwarf to the rear) afford an opportunity to talk about the purpose of Spenser's conspicuous defiance of the usual standards of realism. I have often found this a good point to discuss as well the purpose of his choice of archaic language, which I take both to allude to the native Chaucerian tradition and to be a means of distancing the faerie world from the workaday one. Of course Spenser's occasionally archaic diction and spellings also afford puns on ambiguous or etymological meanings, as Martha Craig has demonstrated for the early cantos of book 1. In the opening canto of *The Faerie Queene*, my underlying concern is ever with the conditions of meaning that pertain to the poem. Unless these make sense to students and engage their interests, the poem is not going to speak to them.

In the middle of the sixth stanza, once the figuration of Redcrosse and Una has been completed, the forward movement of the narrative begins in earnest as a sudden cloudburst forces them to take cover. Even as the storm begins, however, the narrator's description seems to impede a reader's progress, attracting attention to its own verbal details. The suddenness and hideousness of the storm are ominous, the more so in conjunction with the anger of Jove, whose sexually suggestive violence in pouring rain into "his Lemans lap" hardly seems appropriate to the Christian God. Repetition of the seemingly innocent word *shroud* also resonates oddly. Exactly what these signs mean both invites attention and remains elusive.

The storm "enforces" Redcrosse and Una to seek shelter, and they spy nearby a nameless wood, characterized only as a "couert"—"A shadie groue . . . That promist ayde the tempest to withstand." As readers for whom the forward movement of Redcrosse and Una—the real "action" of the story —has just started, we anticipate its further development: their prompt entry into the wood and an account of what happens to them there. Instead, for a sequence of five lines in which the principal actors and their need to act momentarily seem forgotten, we confront a prolonged description of the wood itself. But why? What does it accomplish? Presumably, Redcrosse and Una are being soaked to the skin while the narrator surveys the landscape.

Intervening between their first seeing the wood and their entering it ("Faire harbour that them seemes; so in they entred arre"), the narrator's leisurely description is conspicuously intrusive in every way. Yet this description presents the situation they confront as, "enforst" by the rainstorm, they seek shelter, and its leisureliness ensures that we confront it as well. Like the initial description of Redcrosse, that of the wood requires close reading: how does it call attention to itself and what information does it convey? Too suspicious a reading (this wood is simply evil) is as misguided as one too trusting (this wood is wholly good). In view of the rainstorm, Redcrosse and Una's decision to enter the wood is sensible and even unavoidable; no alternatives are visible in the text or in life as Spenser here depicts it.

Throughout this first episode, our position as readers roughly parallels that of Redcrosse and Una. When they enter the condition recognized only eventually by Una as "the wandring wood" and "*Errours den*," they appear to join the narrator in praising various trees, both their characteristics and their uses: "The sayling Pine, the Cedar proud and tall, / The vine-prop Elme, the Poplar neuer dry, / The builder Oake, sole king of forrests all." Although this catalog of trees ends with "the Maple seeldom inward sound," the unfortunate maple is immediately preceded by "the Ash for nothing ill" and "The fruitfull Oliue": like Redcrosse and Una, we are engaged in seeing (reading) a wood that suggests human experiences of various sorts (st. 8–9). If alerted by the initial description of this wood ("that heauens light did hide, / Not perceable with power of any starre"), we might notice that concerns within it are limited to the (merely) human order; if familiar with the context of relevant arboreal catalogs in Ovid's *Metamorphoses* (10.90–104) and Chaucer's *Parliament of Fowls* (lines 176–82), two of Spenser's sources, we might further detect the scent of danger, but the only failure of which we can convict Redcrosse and Una as they drift toward Error's den is their relaxation of alertness to such nuances amid the delights of the wood. They are not reading their surroundings closely enough, but until they actually reach Error's den, I doubt many readers would recognize this to be their problem—at once the wandering characters' problem and their own.

When Redcrosse and Una suddenly are lost "in diuerse doubt" in the wood, wandering "too and fro in wayes vnknowne," they take the path "that beaten seemd most bare." This path leads them to the cave of Error, which "plaine none might . . . see, nor she see any plaine" (st. 16). Once Error has been defeated, however, Redcrosse and Una keep not to the path beaten bare but to the one "which beaten was most plaine" (st. 28); now they can see it. The suggestive distinction between a bare path and a plain path and the association of Error with a lack of clear sight underline the extent to which the episode in the Wandering Wood is essentially an exercise in perception.

The epic similes that seemingly interrupt but actually interpret Redcrosse's battle with Error—the comparison of Error's "parbreake" to the fertile swelling of the Nile and of her monstrous spawn to a cloud of gnats in a pastoral landscape—afford other images to be read closely, both as early indicators of the way Spenser adapts this ancient form of comparison to allegorical narrative and for their specific bearing on Redcrosse's subsequent adventures. For example, the murmurings of the gnats are recalled in the sound of swarming bees in the cave of Morpheus and are among the many details that connect this cave of Sleep to the waking experiences of the Redcrosse Knight within the first canto. On a more general level, the epic similes embedded in Redcrosse's struggle with Error make clearer the extent to which the natural world and especially its expression in human nature bear on the Legend of Holiness. In these similes, the potency and weakness, the attraction and corruption in the natural world become explicit. This theme is submerged but present from the beginning of the canto, when Jove violently pours his rain into the lap of his mistress, or "Leman," and Redcrosse and Una first set eyes on the "loftie trees" in the Wandering Wood. While nature is by no means depicted as simply evil in the similes describing Redcrosse's battle with Error, these comparisons connect the natural world to Error's fiercest attacks and Redcrosse's weakness. Looking ahead to a related incident in the second canto, at this point I am likely to ask students what meaning they find in the emblem, or condition, of Fradubio (2.33)—a man in the straitjacket of the natural world and a mirror image of what Redcrosse himself will soon become.

After defeating Error—or seeming to defeat her, since the themes and images of the battle will haunt Redcrosse's quest—the knight next meets Archimago. In an early edition of *The Norton Anthology*, there used to be a footnote at this point identifying Archimago as "Hypocrisy" and explaining his wicked designs on Redcrosse and Una. The footnote was deleted when the editors realized it was the equivalent of a note on page 1 of a murder mystery identifying the murderer and thoroughly thwarting the reader's responses to the unfolding of the fiction. It was Exhibit A in a course on how *not* to read *The Faerie Queene*.

At first, while some verbal nuances are suspect, nothing is definitively evil about Archimago's appearance, and his image, like Redcrosse's and Una's, requires sequential reading. In the case of Archimago, however, the increasing pressure of time and the absence of immediate moral definition usually lead me to employ a more synoptic approach. After glossing his name — arch-magician (from Latin *magus*), arch-image, or, perhaps, even image maker—I ask the students whether they consider him a tempter wholly external to Redcrosse. More particularly, I want to know whether they recall the epithets—virtual tags—that are repeatedly attached to his figure. Before long we usually find ourselves looking at the beginning of the second canto, stanzas 5 and 6 to be exact, where Redcrosse, led by "the old man" (elsewhere the "aged sire"), sees the lewd coupling of a false Una with a false squire and burns with "bitter anguish of his guiltie sight." The insistent epithet "old man," in contrast to the "new man" who wears but needs also to fit "the whole armor of God" (Eph. 6.11–17), suggestively aligns Archimago with the unregenerate flesh—the Old Adam: this old man has an inherent relation to Redcrosse, and Redcrosse's "guiltie sight" is both his own beholding eye and that which he sees, or thinks he sees. When Redcrosse wanders (the word is Spenser's) away from Una, he flies "from his [own] thoughts and gealous feare" (2.12). He runs away not only from her but also from himself.

Having established the relation of Archimago to Redcrosse and the primarily interior significance of his temptation, we return to its earlier stages and specifically to the dreamscape of Morpheus's cave. Here I have found the cinematic analogy of a split screen a useful way of suggesting the resemblance between the dreamscape and the setting and situation in which Redcrosse sleeps: for example, Morpheus "drowned deepe" in his cave of Sleep, with a "trickling streame" and "euer-drizling raine" to lull him, parallels Redcrosse "drownd in deadly sleepe" within the hermitage, whereby "a Christall streame did gently play." The origin of the lustful dream that Archimago's "sprite," or spirit, seeks and finds in the realm of Sleep is clearly not alien to—or really outside—Redcrosse's nature.

When Redcrosse wakens from sleep, his Morpheus-like state, his response confirms his implication in Archimago's seemingly objective temptation. He starts up in a "great passion of vnwonted lust, / Or wonted feare of doing ought amis" (1.49); either he has never had this experience before ("vnwonted"), or he has it all the time ("wonted"). I have never met a group of students who did not recognize the obvious psychological possibilities in his response and their relation to the "too solemne sad" knight first seen in canto 1. Redcrosse clearly has not come to terms with his own nature, and his failure to do so has the potential to destroy him.

The final stanza of the first canto sets the knight's predicament in a clearer, if still more troubled, perspective and also exemplifies a characteristic Spenserian technique that is often employed when the distinction between a seemingly objective reality and a subjective one is blurred. By this point in Redcrosse's temptation by Archimago, the old man's "sprites"—the one that elicits a lustful dream from Sleep and the one that animates a false Una—have affected the knight deeply enough to waken him. Although he is grieved by Una's supposed falseness and muses over its meaning, he lacks sufficient faith in her to see through it:

> At last dull wearinesse of former fight
> Hauing yrockt asleepe his irkesome spright,
> That troublous dreame gan freshly tosse his braine,
> With bowres, and beds, and Ladies deare delight:
> But when he saw his labour all was vaine,
> With that misformed spright he backe returned againe.

To whom does the pronoun "he" in the final couplet refer? Is it really clear that the "irkesome spright" refers to Redcrosse's spirit rather than to one of the sprites that tempts him? Whose labor is "vaine," the knight's or the tempter's? Lines such as these hardly intimate the firmness of Redcrosse's resistance or, as far as Archimago is concerned, the futility of further temptation. The blurring of reference in them suggests the beginning of an active cooperation between the troubling sprite of the tempter and the troubled sprite, or spirit, of Redcrosse. Their ambiguities thus mirror the state of Redcrosse's affairs. Notably, these ambiguous lines occur at the end of a canto, where, at least for some space of time, we are literally left with them, momentarily denied reassurance or clarification. The narrator of *The Faerie Queene* is fond of such timing and tries it again in the final stanza of canto 2, where the identities of Redcrosse and Duessa overlap in a layered series of wavering referents.

The narrator's concluding observations on Archimago's successful temptation of Redcrosse serve, in effect, to outline the basic structure of much of the rest of book 1. When Redcrosse abandons Una, Archimago realizes triumphantly that "his guests" have been "diuided into double parts," a description that refers both to their psychic fragmentation (one from the other and, inseparably, within each) and to their physical separation. From this point on, Redcrosse's and Una's paths run inversely parallel, often alternating in successive cantos: as Redcrosse degenerates, slipping progressively into a merely natural and pagan existence, Una moves up a kind of evolutionary ladder from the Lion, the half-human Satyrs, and Satyrane to Arthur, the best and most Christian of knights.

When Redcrosse and Una (Holiness, or Wholeness, and Oneness, Unity) separate, Archimago decides "the person to put on / Of that good knight"— literally to impersonate Redcrosse. He dons "mighty armes" and "siluer shield" and wears a "bloudy crosse" on his breast, with the result that "Full iolly knight he seemde, and well addrest, / And when he sate vpon his courser free, / *Saint George* himself ye would haue deemed him to be" (2.11). The verbal echoes of the description of Redcrosse in the opening stanza of canto 1 are exact, insistent, and ironic. They bring full circle the opening questions and puzzles concerning the nature of that untried knight in dented armor. Their irony touches on his pretension and more generally on the deception of all appearances. Above all, it reflects on the fallibility of human judgment: probably most readers "deemed" the figure first met in canto 1 a simple representation of Holiness—already what he has yet to endeavor to become. To an extent, the best readers among us might have been suspicious when we first met all that "seeming" in the opening stanzas, but I doubt that most of us questioned the authenticity of the bloody cross or expected the narrator to turn with such irony against us and against the symbolic resources of his own art: "*Saint George* himself ye would haue deemed him to be." That even Spenser's first book is from its outset surprisingly open to such problems and complications of meaning might finally be the single most important point for a student to grasp.

NOTES

[1]I quote from Roche's edition of the entire poem. But even when teaching the whole of Spenser's epic romance, I invite students also to use the edition of books 1 and 3 by Hugh Maclean and Anne Lake Prescott if they want the convenience of lexical glosses and other notes on the same page as the text. Those who are unfamiliar with Renaissance language welcome this convenience. (For book 1, Lewalski and Smith in *The Norton Anthology* also provide notes on the same page as the text.)

[2]On the cooperation of the poet and the queen in producing the poem, see Cain, ch. 2, especially pp. 51–54. Here and in the pages that follow, my argument reflects essays I have previously published, which could be consulted for more extensive discussion: " 'In Liuing Colours and Right Hew': The Queen of Spenser's Central Books" treats the relation of an ideal image to the present age, particularly in the proems; " 'A Gentle Knight Was Pricking on the Plaine': The Chaucerian Connection" concerns Spenser's use of the word *pricking* in book 1. I have analyzed the epic similes in the battle with Error at greater length in *The Growth of a Personal Voice: Piers Plowman and The Faerie Queene* 27–29; pp. 23–36 concern Redcrosse's and Una's entry into the Wandering Wood, and pp. 29–30 examine the cave of Morpheus.

"Add Faith unto Your Force and Be Not Faint": Teaching Book 1 in the Sophomore Survey

Raymond-Jean Frontain

Christian values, Robert Crosman argues, are "intrinsically and irremediably anti-epic":

> To expect a Christian poem is to expect a story that . . . encourages a reader to look favorably upon a system of values that exalts humility, obedience to God, love of one's enemies, passivity, spirituality, and other-worldliness. To expect an epic, on the other hand, is to expect a poem of physical action: wars, battles, and great deeds by active, martial heroes. . . . Worldly triumph is the theme of epic, while the Christian theme is one of worldly defeat as the necessary prelude to spiritual victory. (6)

In attempting to reconcile classical and Christian ideals, Renaissance humanists had to mediate "between one view which sees heroism as something external—triumphing over an opponent—and another view which sees heroism as something internal—a quality of soul which cannot always be manifested in deeds" (Cantor ix).

Spenser's meditation on, and mediation between, these contradictory heroic ideals is the focus of my unit on book 1 in the sophomore survey course (for which my texts are volume 1 of *The Norton Anthology of English Literature*, 5th edition, edited by M. H. Abrams, and the Norton Critical Edition of Shakespeare's *Hamlet*). Through lecture, but particularly through carefully orchestrated discussion, I attempt to establish the Redcrosse Knight's pivotal place in a continuum of heroes that ranges from Beowulf and Sir Gawain to Hamlet, Milton's Samson, and (in the second half of the course the following semester) "the poet's mind" whose growth is the epic action of Wordsworth's *Prelude*. In the Redcrosse Knight, I argue, can best be seen the progressive interiorization of epic action, a process by which we can map the emergence of the modern hero.

In the "October" eclogue of Spenser's *Shepheardes Calender*, when Cuddie questions why he should continue writing poetry, Piers exhorts him to turn from pastoral to epic verse:

> Abandon then the base and viler clowne,
> Lyft up thy selfe out of the lowly dust;
> And sing of bloody Mars, of wars, of giusts.
> Turne thee to those, that weld the awful crowne,

> To doubted Knights, whose woundlesse armour rusts,
> And helmes unbruzed wexen dayly browne.
>
> (Abrams 539)

So Spenser himself must have thought when, plotting his career along the Vergilian trajectory, he put aside his "lowly Shepheards weeds" to "sing of Knights and Ladies gentle deeds" and "blazon broad" the "fierce warres and faithfull loves" that he hoped would "moralize" his song.

But Piers's exhortation aims at celebrating a peculiarly static epic heroism. Referring to armor and helmets that rust through disuse, Piers projects under fair Eliza a state similar to the famous *pax Romana* under Caesar Augustus anticipated by Vergil's *Aeneid*. Having already proven themselves so "doubted" or dreaded in battle that no one will dare challenge them, Eliza's knights guarantee a spiritual state that has been achieved through physical combat. It is precisely this delicate balancing between a physical and a spiritual heroic that distinguishes Redcrosse Knight from Beowulf and Milton's Samson. On the romance level of the poem, Redcrosse is, like Beowulf, a hero of force; on the Christian or allegorical level, however, his force must be informed by faith. For "what man is he," Spenser's narrator asks,

> that boasts of fleshly might,
> And vaine assurance of mortality,
> Which all so soone, as it doth come to fight,
> Against spirituall foes, yeelds by and by,
> Or from the field most cowardly doth fly?
> Ne let the man ascribe it to his skill,
> That thorough grace hath gained victory.
> If any strength we have, it is to ill,
> But all the good is Gods, both power and eke will.
>
> (1.10.1)

Beowulf's heroism depends almost exclusively on his Achillean qualities of courage and brute strength; so long as fallen Samson understands his heroic mandate in purely historical terms, however, he remains in bondage to despair. Spenser delicately balances between these two extremes, and therein lies the peculiar quality of Redcrosse Knight as hero.

In preparing students to read "The Legende of the Knight of the Red Crosse, or of Holinesse," I outline the Christian humanist debate on the nature of the hero as I find it analyzed in Paul Cantor, Frank Kermode, John Steadman, and Michael West ("Renaissance Ideal"). "To imitate the ancient Herculeses, Alexanders, Hannibals, Scipios, Caesars and that ilk is contrary to the profession of the Gospel," Rabelais's Grandgousier advises. "Is it not true that what the Saracens and Barbarians once called prowess, we term wickedness and brigandry?" (qtd. in Cantor 6; trans. Leclerq). Cantor juxtaposes Achilles's boasting of his triumph over Hector (and other examples of the hero's humiliation of his fallen victim) with Jesus's prescriptions of behavior in his Sermon on the Mount:

> Judged by these principles, Achilles is headed straight for hell. Jesus is in every respect the antithesis of the classical hero: he is humble rather than proud, merciful rather than vengeful, passive rather than aggressive, and forgiving of sins rather than unyielding in hatred. In classical terms, one might question whether there is in fact anything heroic at all about Jesus, but the tendency of Christianity is to redefine heroism so that suffering misery becomes a higher or deeper form of heroism than inflicting misery.   (4–5)

The Christian king, as commentators from Augustine's time down to Spenser's emphasize, must rule as much by the Bible (*sapientia*) as by the sword (*fortitudo*; see J. King, *English Reformation* 188–89). The problem for the Renaissance poet was finding "the appropriate moral formula (fortitude, wisdom, magnanimity, etc.)" for the epic hero (see Steadman, *Milton's Epic Characters*, pt. 1).

After introducing these concerns I assign two cantos per meeting for the next six class meetings, directing students to divide a notebook page into three columns. I ask them to jot down in the first two columns specific references to when and how Redcrosse Knight reminds them of Beowulf and of Sir Gawain (the two instances of heroism that we've encountered thus far in the term) and, in the third, references to when he resembles neither but seems to be acting in a comparatively new way. In particular I ask them to consider what qualities each poem celebrates as heroic, what kind of triumph each hero enjoys, what cultural values he fights to sustain or implement, and what kind of crucial challenges he faces. I encourage students to read with their cultural memories in overdrive, as it were, alert to parallels and deviations.

I try to ensure that discussion of cantos 1 and 2 during our next meeting makes at least three points:

1. *Physical versus spiritual heroism.* The most obvious parallel that students notice on first entering into Spenser's poem is that both Redcrosse Knight and Beowulf fight dragons but that the circumstances under which they do so are radically dissimilar. Therein lies the peculiar challenge of Spenser's poem. Beowulf fights not simply to put an end to the dragon's marauding and thus save his beleaguered people but to liberate the treasure that "the worm" is hoarding. As part of the Anglo-Saxon heroic economy, he would distribute the treasure among his thanes, who would then be obligated to follow him into his next battle. The only personal incentive to undertake such dangerous action is the glory that the hero may win, which explains the importance of the poet or scop within this heroic system.

Redcrosse Knight, on the other hand, fights a dragon named Error, who, in her death agony, vomits "books and papers" as well as "loathly frogs and toads which eyes did lack" (st. 20). His battle is as much spiritual and intellectual as it is physical. Indeed, he wins only when Una encourages him to "add faith unto your force, and be not faint," thus showing "what ye bee" (st. 19). Despite the biblical and metaphysical overtones of Beowulf's story, these are not the levels on which Beowulf carries out his heroic enterprise. Spenser's heroism, on the other hand, depends finally on spiritual discernment: Redcrosse Knight must learn to recognize deceit and thus avoid falling victim to Error. Spenser's heroic economy is spiritual, the poet inviting the reader to penetrate the veil of allegory as forcefully as Redcrosse Knight must struggle with Error; "reading" in Spenser becomes heroic activity. (Making this point as early as possible deflects student complaints about how difficult *The Faerie Queene* may at first seem to be. According to the implied Spenserian code, only "weenies" will not persevere with Spenser's allegory. Teaching in the Bible Belt, I find that Spenser's implicit association of critical reading with spiritual redemption is a particularly persuasive encouragement to careful reading.)

2. *Education of the hero.* When Beowulf undertakes to rescue Heorot from Grendel's nightly assaults, he has already proved himself in the sea fight with Breca; and when he bests the dragon in its lair he is old and a proven veteran of many wars. Likewise, as Sir Gawain appears at Arthur's Christmas court, he is neither young nor old; he has shown himself "the father of fine manners" (line 919) and is still capable of doing great actions but has grown soft resting on his laurels. The Green Knight's challenge—with its emphasis on the disparity between Arthur's knights' reputation and their present softness (lines 258–64, 309–15)—teaches Gawain the importance of exercising the virtue he has already proved lest it grow dull. Redcrosse Knight, on the other hand, is woefully inexperienced in warfare and unskilled with horses:

> Yet armes till that time did he never wield:
> His angry steede did chide his foming bitt,
> As much disdayning to the curbe to yield.
> (1.1)

Far more than *Beowulf* or *Sir Gawain and the Green Knight*, book 1 is an education narrative, concentrating more heavily on the process that Redcrosse must go through to be able to fight than on the climactic martial encounter itself.

I emphasize this by asking students to parallel Redcrosse Knight's psychological or spiritual development with Beowulf's and Gawain's. Two-thirds of the way through his song, the Anglo-Saxon scop notes that at one time the Geats "did not reckon . . . [Beowulf] brave, nor would the lord of the

Weather-Geats do him much gift-honor on the mead-bench. They strongly suspected that he was slack, a young man unbold." But "change came to the famous man," the scop continues, "for each of his troubles" (Abrams 63–64). The reader understands only in retrospect that Beowulf's competition with his boyhood friend Breca — in which he tested himself by staying immersed in the cold northern waters fighting sea monsters for five days and nights— was the narrative's indication of Beowulf's psychological transformation or maturation (39–40).

But from the start, Spenser gives every indication that Redcrosse Knight's psychological and spiritual maturation process is at least as important as the deeds that his maturity will allow him to accomplish, if not more so, his end being written typologically in his beginning. The "dominant reference" of Spenser's allegory, as Harry Berger points out, is psychological, every encounter until canto 10 having "the double aspect of progress and risk" (*Revisionary Play* 65–66). Spenser's method, Berger demonstrates, is to unfold Redcrosse Knight's psyche or soul into an environment through allegorical names and "pointers" (68; see also Hough 99). What is more, Spenser presents the process of the hero's psychological development in specifically Protestant terms, thus intensifying the spiritual nature of heroism. As Anthea Hume reads book 1, "Spenser's version of the St. George legend steadily unfolds the facts of man's proneness to sin, his self-imprisonment, his need for rescue by a more-than-human power, the psychological crises he will pass through after grace has begun to work in him, and his untimely victorious struggle with Satan" (74; see also Heale, *Reader's Guide* 25, 33). Whereas *Beowulf* is a diptych, presenting the hero's life in two representative panels, Spenser's book 1 is a moving picture, capturing in extraordinary detail the process by which Redcrosse Knight achieves holiness. Redcrosse is clearly closer to Gawain than to Beowulf in this regard, Gawain's successful resistance to Lady Bercilak's three seduction attempts proving finally more significant than his withstanding the Green Knight's ax blows: his fate is decided by the way he faces moral temptation, not physical challenge. But the *Gawain* poet, like the *Beowulf* poet, is not interested in the process by which his hero becomes capable of withstanding such temptation. Spenser's interest in interiority is a particularly Renaissance, even Protestant, phenomenon.

3. *The romance of the hero.* Mention of Gawain's attempted seduction by Lady Bercilak, and of the pivotal role played by Morgan le Faye (revealed only at the end of the story), allows for an easy segue to discussion of Redcrosse Knight's relations with both Una and Duessa/Fidessa. As one of my students bluntly put it, Redcrosse has a girlfriend and Beowulf does not. Indeed, Beowulf seems curiously sexless, there being little time for romance in the Anglo-Saxon heroic world, where women are allowed little more power than as dispensers of mead and as the diplomatic pawns of their fathers and brothers. Duessa, however, is like Morgan, a witch and a

sower of discord; Fradubio might easily have included himself among the men undone by perfidious women whose litany the Green Knight recites when consoling Sir Gawain (lines 2414–29). If Beowulf couldn't care less about getting the girl, for Gawain and Redcrosse Knight women are both dangerous temptations and the prizes a man wins when he succeeds in his heroic endeavor.

But Spenser and the *Gawain* poet allow their heroes to be romanced with a difference. Redcrosse Knight's refusal or inability to confront his repressed or hitherto unacknowledged sexual feelings for Una when in Archimago's hut makes for a far more subtle psychological experience than do Gawain's courtly parrying of Lady Bercilak's seduction attempts; the parallel scenes of Lord Bercilak at the hunt prevent the bedroom scenes from finally being about love at all, effectively distracting attention from Gawain's interior experience. Likewise, the "fall" of Redcrosse Knight in canto 7 (st. 1–6), when he removes his armor to dally with "Fidessa" in the shade, is too psychologically acute to allow him to be handily stereotyped with Adam, Solomon, Samson, and David. (I am particularly grateful for Richard Levin's recent essay analyzing the love plot of book 1.) Morgan le Faye's machinations, when they are finally revealed at the end, surprise the reader as much as they do Gawain. Not so in Spenser: prodded by the poet to "read" the spiritual reality that lies behind Una's veil and Duessa's disguise, readers find themselves in serious trouble if they persevere in their naïveté for as long as Redcrosse does.

The main point I summarize for students at the end of this initial discussion is that while Redcrosse Knight's adventures take place both externally and internally—on both a martial and a spiritual plane—it is the interior or spiritual dimension of his experience that is finally the more important. And, within the narrow bounds of our survey-course anthology selections, this identifies Redcrosse as a radically different kind of hero. Explaining to Arthur her search for a champion who will defeat the dragon that has enthralled her parents and kingdom for four years, Una sighs:

> Full many knights adventurous and stout
> Have enterprizd that Monster to subdew;
> From every coast that heaven walks about,
> Have thither come the noble Martiall crew,
> That famous hard atchievements still pursew,
> Yet never any could that girlond win,
> But all still shronke, and still he [the dragon] greater grew:
> All they for want of faith, or guilt of sin,
> The pitteous pray of his fierce crueltie have bin.   (7.45)

And, as Arthur himself later comments:

Nothing is sure, that growes on earthly ground:
And who most trustes in arme of fleshly might,
And boasts, in beauties chaine not to be bound,
Doth soonest fall in disaventrous fight,
And yeeldes his caytive neck to victours most despight.

(9.11)

In the larger scheme of things, martial power is but vanity; spiritual power is all that matters. The first ten cantos describe Redcrosse Knight's painful education in the vanity of "fleshly might" and "beautie," the final two cantos his triumph as Una's long-sought-for champion, strong in faith and free from a paralyzing consciousness of his "guilt of sin."

As students continue reading book 1, I ask them to pay particular attention to the ways in which Arthur and Una function as models of Christian heroism from whose examples Redcrosse Knight learns right standards of behavior. The "wonted strength" that Redcrosse needs to master his "mishaps," Arthur tells him after freeing him from Orgoglio's dungeon, is "patient might" (8.45); Arthur's account of his dream of the fairies' queen, as Mark Rose points out (110–11), is a parable of just such faith and patience. Even more significant, my students generally find, is the example that Una offers Redcrosse. Beautiful and rich yet wise and humble, she bears her reverses with patience and generosity (see 7.27, for example). After overcoming her own despair with Arthur's help, she is able to help Redcrosse resist the temptation to suicide. Even her fulfillment in marriage to Redcrosse must be delayed as, like every other Christian saint, she patiently accepts the postponement of her final bliss until she can be fully delivered from the onslaughts of time. In making Una a type of Christian heroism, Spenser not only brilliantly deploys romance conventions surrounding the long-suffering woman but draws on such biblical models as Ruth and Judith, members of the supposedly weaker sex who deliver, and ensure the prosperity of, their people.

As the term continues, we find the further development of Spenser's type of heroism in *Hamlet* and *Samson Agonistes*. The physically heroic action Hamlet must undertake in avenging his father's murder pales in comparison with the psychologically heroic action as he struggles, like Redcrosse Knight, with the problem of interpretation in a world of dangerous appearances, defending the "pales and forts of reason" (1.4.28). The old "problem" of Hamlet's four-act "delay" simply does not come up, I have found, when students come to *Hamlet* after book 1 of *The Faerie Queene*. Likewise, "the paradox of activity in apparent inaction" that John Steadman finds in *Samson Agonistes* takes on an even deeper resonance when students understand how much farther to the other side of the balance Milton has pushed the terms of Spenser's equation:

For the greater part of the drama [Samson's] position appears to be static: he does not initiate any action, and despite his threats of violent destruction against two of his Philistine visitors, his only real activity appears to be that of his understanding and will. Throughout the morning it is his strength of mind, not his physical power, that is being exercised, perfected, and put to the proof.

(*Milton and Paradoxes* 224)

Hamlet and Milton's Samson achieve heroism less through a mixture of faith and force than through the triumph of mind or spirit alone. The climax of Milton's dramatic poem is the "rousing motions" that Samson feels, which "dispose / To something extraordinary [his] thoughts" (lines 1382–83). His physical act of heroism—the destruction of the temple of Dagon with all the Philistine worshipers—appropriately takes place offstage.

In an exploration of "the heroic ordeal of individuation and the mythic patterns that surround it," George deForest Lord distinguishes between tragic narrative patterns, which are "marked by the failure of the hero to develop a personality that is a fully individuated self from one that is constituted by the ego," and comic ones, which relate "both the success of the hero in search of himself and his success in restoring or preserving his culture" (1, 3). The comic hero, Lord notes, "must be capable of humility, courage, and psychological flexibility to respond to his archetypal ordeals successfully and in a way that allows for personal development"; he "achieves physical triumphs whose ultimate validity depends on their being profoundly psychological as well." By way of illustration, Lord contrasts the tragic Achilles with comic heroes Odysseus, Aeneas, Dante the pilgrim, and the Son in Milton's *Paradise Regained*, all of whom "exemplify the paradox of true heroic strength: that it cannot be seized by direct action, only by humility or patience" (3–4).

Lord neither considers Beowulf, Gawain, and Redcrosse Knight nor distinguishes among the immediate social, political, and economic pressures that dictate each poet's conscious selection of narrative event and deployment of language. Yet I find Lord's archetypal approach not only a helpful way of considering heroism but a particularly useful way of concluding discussion of book 1. Spenser's first ten cantos, in Lord's scheme, deal with the archetypal getting of self-knowledge, the final two cantos with the restoration or preservation of his culture. It is important to discuss Redcrosse Knight's self-knowledge in Protestant theological terms (Hume) and to consider how he introduces a peculiarly modern heroism onto the literary stage. But it is just as important for undergraduates to understand how Spenser's hero transcends his creator's most immediate religious and political concerns to become a hero not just for his own but for all ages.

I counter colleagues' protestations that *The Faerie Queene* is simply too difficult to teach in the survey course with the observation that Milton becomes much easier to teach when students come to *Paradise Lost* and *Samson Agonistes* after two weeks on book 1. Not only are students better able to enjoy the comically grotesque aspects of Milton's War in Heaven, but they appreciate more fully his idea of an "inactive" hero and of a "paradise within." What is more, on those few occasions when a student continues with me into the second semester, I notice that prior exploration of Redcrosse's internalized heroism renders all the more available Wordsworth's daring in making "the growth of the poet's mind" into epic action and even explains why and how the action of Eliot's *Waste Land* can take place in blind Tiresias's mind.

The Open Text: A Protestant Poetics of Reading and Teaching Book 1

Evelyn B. Tribble

This volume is dedicated to "approaches" to teaching—the word, suggesting as it does both a movement toward and a certain tentativeness, is appropriate not only for teachers but for all readers of *The Faerie Queene*. The remoteness of the text seems to demand approaches rather than direct assault. This remoteness, the central challenge one faces in teaching *The Faerie Queene*, can be attributed to any number of factors: the deliberately archaic language, the static formal qualities of the verse, which resist the forward movement of the narrative, the range of reference no longer immediately available to modern readers, the characters who resist assimilation to novelistic subjectivity, the narrative voice that recedes as much as it guides.

Given what seem such formidable impediments to the approach, what kind of readers ought we to ask our students to be? I suggest we encourage students to be "erring" readers of book 1, readers who wander around the surface of the narrative, resisting the temptation to read quickly, resisting the desire to retreat to an authoritative voice. The retreat to authority—teacher, *Norton* notes, Cliffs Notes, even the arguments to the cantos—can involve readers in an effort to solve the poem and thus eradicate local difficulties and, implicitly, the process of reading itself. In what follows, I sketch the ways that book 1 itself attempts to produce an errant reader and historicize that reader within a Protestant poetics of reading. I conclude by considering a few of the problematics of such an approach.

To read book 1 of *The Faerie Queene* is to experience "diverse doubte" at a number of levels. The argument to the first canto of *The Faerie Queene* exemplifies this doubt, for it is both simple and duplicitous, one thing and two: "The Patron of True Holinesse, / Foule Errour doth defeate."[1] The subject of this sentence is ambiguous: does Holiness defeat Error or Error Holiness? The unfolding action seemingly clarifies this ambiguity, for Redcrosse Knight defeats "the vgly monster plaine" and is congratulated by Una: "ye haue great glory wonne this day" (1.14, 1.27). But to retrospectively erase this ambiguity is to misread, to impose a single allegorical reading (Holiness defeats Error) that ignores the local ambivalence present in the episode: Una's earlier warning, the "greedy hardiment" of the knight (1.14), the belittling comparison of the warrior to a clown annoyed by gnats. Two stanzas later, Redcrosse Knight meets another form of error, this time disguised as Truth, a polyvalent allegorical figure. Only retrospectively and indirectly do readers learn of the limitations of the initial victory. The reader is reviser here, reading recursively, looping back to resee earlier conclusions about the text.

Even on local levels readers are invited to perform the difficult task of discriminating between seemingly similar phenomena. The narrative often frustrates attempts to construct a scheme or an ordering principle. For example, the word "goodly" is used to describe Duessa and is twice used for Lucifera's castle. Armed with this knowledge, readers might well be suspicious of the "goodly knight" of canto 7 who, like Lucifera, is associated with brightness and carries, of all things, a dragon as his emblem. Yet this knight is of course Arthur, and so the suspicious reading needs revision in the light of what is discovered through forward movement. Or consider the multivalency of lions, associated with Una, with the seven deadly sins, and with Kirkrapine. Or the image of liquefication, linked throughout book 1 with sexual licentiousness but finally applied to the union of Una and the Redcrosse Knight.

How are we to encourage our students to see these as more than random anomalies frustrating their attempts to get a handle on the text? To the extent to which we make reading a goal-oriented task (as, full of fire and greedy hardiment, we seek to cover all the material in the survey), we discourage erring readers and encourage solving the text. I suggest that students should not attempt to master *The Faerie Queene*, to domesticate it and seek to erase local discontinuities. Rather, the external action should be relocated *within* readers; the journey is what matters. Paul Alpers in particular argues persuasively that *The Faerie Queene* is a "rhetorical" text, that Spenser "depends upon the reader to see and make connections that are not made by any phenomena within the poem"; "[h]e trusts the reader to see the relation and coherence of the points made and attitudes expressed by the various parts of the poem" (*Poetry* 113, 119). This formulation is a persuasive way of describing the reader's role in *The Faerie Queene*, but it provides no historical account of why such a reader should be produced. I propose a historically grounded locus for understanding the reader's role in *The Faerie Queene*: early Protestant accounts of reading the Bible, particularly those of William Tyndale. Spenser's text can be seen as participating in a reconfiguration of readers that is Protestant in origin.

Reading is perhaps the central issue of early Protestantism, and Protestant-Catholic polemic tends to center on the question of the capabilities of the individual reader. Thomas More, for instance, argues strenuously that the "common consent of the whole holy church" is needed to guide individual readers; interpretations at odds with the body of the Church are by definition wrong (More 114–15). In contrast, Reformers, arguing that the Scriptures are "plain," often use the tropes of sight and light to figure the experience of reading Scripture. Tyndale argues that the Church has attempted to "amaze" the people by expounding Scripture "in manye senses before the vnlerned laye people (when it hath but one symple literall sense whose light the owles can not abydye)" (*Pentateuch* 3). The truth of the Bible is figured as a blinding light capable of exposing hypocrisy or deceit.

But seeing is not the same thing as reading, and Reformers began to develop theories of reading that took account of its process, its unfolding effect
on the individual believer. Stephen Greenblatt has pointed to Tyndale's keen
awareness of the reading process as temporal (*Renaissance Self-Fashioning*
103). The reader gets to predestination only after experiencing the gospels
and the early chapters of Romans; to skip over the first part is to distort
the meaning of the Bible and to invite despair: "After that, when thou art
come to the eighth chapter and art under the cross and suffering of tribula-
tion, the necessity of predestination will wax sweet, and thou shalt well
feel how precious a thing it is" (Tyndale, *Prologue* 505). This is a radically
internalized view of reading, relying heavily on the manipulation of response
that underlies so many humanist educational programs.

In the preface to his *Pentateuch*, Tyndale gives the following advice to
readers:

> Cleave unto the texte and playne storye and endeavaure thi self to
> serch out the meaning of all that is described therein and the true sense
> of all manner of speakyngyes of the scripture, of proverbs, similitudes,
> and borrowed speech, whereof I entreated in the end of the obedience,
> and beware of sotle allegoryes. And note everything ernestly as things
> partayning vnto thine own herte and soule.   (161)

This passage is one of many in Tyndale that advocate adhering to the "literal"
sense, the "plain" meaning of the Bible apparent to all readers, or rather
all readers who read by referring the Bible inward, to their own hearts and
souls. But the Bible does not merely provide an inert object of contemplation; Tyndale describes an actively engaged reader, one who searches out
meaning, shuttling between self and text. What prevents this inward direction from collapsing into solipsism is the adherence—cleaving—to the literal
sense of the text. The central readerly activity that Tyndale describes is contextualization, a method he consistently opposes to willful allegorization;
the Bible is no mere base from which to extrapolate one's own narratives.
Throughout *The Obedience of a Christian Man*, as well as his prologues
to the books of the New Testament, Tyndale stresses the importance of contextual reading—if one gets lost when reading Scripture, one does not appeal
to some arbitrary frame of reference (an allegorical interpretation, sanc-
tioned by authority, that has little to do with the text). Instead, one goes
back to the text itself, comparing one part with another and carefully considering context to determine local meaning.

This theory of reading has its origins in polemic, most notably a long
attack on the Bishop of Rochester's "Sermon of the Condemnation of Martin
Luther," in which Rochester "proveth by a shadow of the Old Testament"
that the Pope "is Christ's vicar and head of Christ's congregation" (Tyndale,
Obedience 208). Rochester proves this point by arguing that Moses "signifieth

Christ, and Aaron the Pope." Tyndale vigorously attacks Rochester for interpreting "figures" as though they held the same signification throughout
the Old and New Testaments: "Understand, therefore, that one thing in
the scripture representeth divers things. A serpent figureth Christ in one
place, and the devil in another; and a lion doth likewise." Thus Aaron represents different things in different places: when he was Moses's disciple,
he represented "not Peter only or his successor . . . but signifieth every disciple of Christ." When Aaron made the golden calf in Moses's absence, there
he "representeth all false preachers, and namely our most holy father the
pope" (209). Tyndale goes on to attack Rochester for playing "bo-peep" with
the Scriptures—jumping out at any moment and imposing his own allegorical
meaning on the text. He "feareth not to juggle with the holy scripture of
God. . . . But even after this manner-wise pervert they the whole scripture
and all doctors; wresting them unto their own abominable purpose, clean
contrary to the meaning of the text, and to the circumstances that go before
and after" (208).

For both the Tyndalian and the Spenserian reader, figures are multivalent;
they do not possess a predetermined, stable meaning but instead take on
significance contextually. And this meaning must be discovered by the reader
—it is not provided. Readers must make their ways through a text that is
on the one hand easy—its meanings are not arcane and abstruse but profoundly simple—and on the other difficult, in that a correct reading demands
effort, demands faith.

To consider the implications for reading and teaching *The Faerie Queene*,
teachers and students should work against playing "bo-peep," against standing above the text and imposing a fixed meaning on a particular figure or
incident. Just this tendency is exhibited by student editions of the poem as
well as by Cliffs Notes—to stabilize polyvalence by imposing an overly
schematized or reductive allegorical reading. Thus the notes to the fourth
edition of *The Norton Anthology* (those of the fifth are considerably more
nuanced) read *The Faerie Queene* as though it were *Pilgrim's Progress*, arbitrarily identifying the dwarf as "reason," for instance. The Cliffs Notes work
similarly, blandly telling students that Duessa "stands for" Queen Mary,
as though one could simply substitute one for the other in all instances.

It might at first seem strange to juxtapose Spenser and Tyndale in the
context of allegorical reading, since Tyndale constantly warns against "subtle
allegories," while Spenser of course describes his project as "a continued
allegory, or dark conceit." Yet, paradoxically, Tyndale's antiallegorical
thought provides a way of understanding Spenserian allegory. Readers are
to avoid an overly schematized reading, one that prematurely concludes
or elides the reading process; but they are also to see that allegorical readings
cleave to the text—the literal meaning does not merely provide a sort of
springboard for one's own story (the modern equivalent of this is perhaps
"a poem can mean anything a reader wants it to mean"). The Protestant

reader both cleaves and confers, producing provisional meanings by reading with the text (con-text).

Such a poetics is clearly grounded in a certain confidence in the reader's good faith: recall that Alpers sees Spenser as "trusting" and "depending upon" the reader's abilities. Tyndale draws on a similar confidence in his insistence that the literal sense is indeed available to the reader, who can use it to his or her own edification: "There is no story or gest, seem it never so simple or so vile unto the world, but that thou shalt find therein spirit and life and edifying in the literal sense: for it is God's scripture, written for thy learning and comfort" (*Obedience* 301).

Yet there is a contradiction at the heart of any Protestant poetics: the individual reader must interpret, but not individually so. Figures and allegories are slippery things, and readers may misread, wrest, misinterpret, smuggle their own meanings into the text. Tyndale continually inveighs against readers who "misuse" the text, particularly the Old Testament, in this way. In his Pentateuch translation, he comments, "The most parte think [the Old Testament] nothing necessary but to make allegoryes, which they fayne every man after hys awne brayne at all wyle adventure without any certain rule" (293–94). Tyndale fears that allegories are constantly prey to solipsism, to interpretive productions that reflect no truth but the misshapen fantasies of the reader's own brain.

Tyndale goes on to prescribe the "rules" that must be followed in reading or fashioning allegories. First he defines allegories as "examples or similitudes borrowed of strange matters and of another thinge then that thou entreatest of." Their use is "to declare and open a text that it may be the better perceaved and understoode" (*Pentateuch* 294). But allegories, while educative, are fundamentally suspect, for the very qualities that make them good for teaching also render them beguiling:

> Finallye beware of allegoryes, for there is not a more handsome or apte a thing to begile withall than an allegory, not a more sotle and pestilent thinge in the world to persuade a false mater than an allegorye. And contrary wyse there is not a better vehementer or myghtyer thing to make a man understand with all then an allegorye. For allegoryes make a man quick witted and prynte wysdom in hym and maketh it to abyde, where bare wordes go in at the one eare and out at the other.   (*Pentateuch* 295)

This is a fundamentally contradictory view of allegory, here conceived locally as a trope or figure of speech. Allegories can persuade but, like rhetoric itself, that persuasive power can be used for good or ill. Finally the only guarantee of correct reading is the willingness to remain within the parameters of faith: "which allegories I may not make at all the wild adventures: but must keep me within the compass of the faith and ever apply mine allegory to Christ and unto the faith" (*Obedience* 305). Tyndale identifies a potential slippage between the figures of speech in the Bible and about the Bible and the reader's own fantasies; he continually polices the border between liberty and compass to prevent the productive power of the reader from misproducing, from straying into the realm of papistical "juggling."

In the letter to Ralegh, Spenser exhibits a similar ambivalence toward the conjunction of allegory and the reader. "Knowing how doubtfully all Allegories may be construed," he writes, "I haue thought good aswell for auoyding of gealous opinions and misconstructions, as also for your better light in reading thereof . . . to discouer vnto you the general intention & meaning" of the book (Roche, *Edmund Spenser* 15). Like Tyndale, he values allegories for their didactic efficacy: "So much more profitable and gratious is doctrine by ensample, then by rule." Yet "some" will prefer to have "good discipline deliuered plainly in way of precepts, or sermoned at large, as they vse, then thus clowdily enwrapped in Allegoricall deuices." But allegories sit better with the "vse of these dayes seeing all things accounted by their showes, and nothing esteemed of, that is not delightfull and pleasing to commune sence" (16). Plain precepts might be clear, but they will go unread; in contrast, the pleasing surface of allegories allures readers. Yet that very pleasure can distract, lead the eye to wander, to construe doubtfully, jealously, cloudily. The references to malign interpretation that frame the 1596 edition of *The Faerie Queene* indicate that Spenser's initial confidence in the referentiality of language is eroded by the experience of its proliferative potential.

I conclude with misreading as a kind of disclaimer. If we encourage students to become erring readers, we cannot guarantee that they will not stray, indeed become entirely lost. And this possibility raises pedagogical questions similar to the interpretive dilemmas faced by Tyndale. Invitations to wander are inevitably false—or at least the liberty we extend to our students risks being compromised by the compass of the classroom. We want our students to "discover for themselves," yet we also want them to discover the right things; the very word implies retrieving something already there. This dilemma perhaps is lessened if we do not attempt to posit a false freedom—we cannot and should not pretend that our classrooms are unconstrained by the institutional conditions of contemporary academia or that the teacher is not "in charge" in a fundamental sense. But I would suggest that it is possible to view error—even error straying outside what we, versed in the historical and social contexts of Spenser's work, consider the correct "compass" of interpretation—as productive rather than simply recalcitrant.

NOTE

[1]All quotations from *The Faerie Queene* are taken from the Roche edition.

Hymen, Shield, and Journal:
The Task of Interpretation

John Timpane

English 210 at Lafayette College is a semester-long sprint from *Beowulf* to Milton. We have time for only book 1 of *The Faerie Queene* and perhaps the Mutability cantos. One particular class had reached book 1, canto 6, in which Una teaches the "salvage nation" in the forest. Una had just refused the worship of the savages, and "they her Asse would worship fayn" (st. 19).[1] At this point, Ed McDow, an African American student, raised his hand. Annoyed that no one else had noticed the obvious, he said, "This is an allegory for imperialism. And it's racist, too. Una and her ass are both white, and she comes like some god to the poor savages." Another student said, "Where did *that* come from?"

A week or so later, we reached canto 7 and Arthur's shield, "closely covered" and seamless. I asked that all-purpose question, "Now, what does Arthur's shield remind you of?" Before she could take it back, Gretchen Wise called out, "Elizabeth's hymen!" Almost immediately, another student said, "Ex*cuse* me?" Not knowing how to explain or defend her insight, Gretchen seemed embarrassed—not so much because of its intimate connotations as because she had made such an intellectual leap before her classmates had.

Ed's and Gretchen's difficulties remind us that to teach *The Faerie Queene* is to teach interpretation. Few works display such a clear and self-conscious effort to define the audience, occasion, and purpose of writing and to guide (and sometimes prevent) interpretation. That is why I use Kenneth Burke's pentad (xvii) as a way into "A Letter of the Authors"—for here, in Spenser's letter, more clearly than in any other text in English 210, are act (the writing of *The Faerie Queene*—including Spenser's efforts to persuade, move, impress, and please), scene (the time and place of writing, and how these facts impinged on that writing), agency (the tools and instruments—including the stories, characters, metaphors, genres, and narratorial exertions—Spenser employs), agent (Edmund Spenser, a man who lived a certain controversial life that may or may not be reflected in the work), and purpose (why Spenser wrote this poem). As Burke reminds us constantly, to apply this model is already to be interpreting, to be looking for motives.

True, one can teach reading and writing with any literary text—perhaps any text at all. But for the teacher of the English literature survey or of the undergraduate Spenser seminar, *The Faerie Queene* presents an unusually good opportunity. No matter our methods or critical practices, our paper topics inevitably challenge our students to become interpreters (from *interpres*, agent, negotiator, go-between)—to say what they think the poem means, how it achieves that meaning, what values it expresses, what effect it has on the reader, and how it achieves that effect. Spenser teachers should take full advantage of the opportunity—that is, actually teach interpretation with Spenser and Spenser with writing. That opportunity is quickly becoming an obligation.

In our composition textbook, *Writing Worth Reading*, Nancy Huddleston Packer and I sketch out a model of interpretation consisting of three "levels" (a metaphor of convenience—these levels are really elements on a developmental continuum). On the *literal* level the student performs a bare-bones practical reading, confining her- or himself strictly to the text. On the *speculative* level lies informed speculation, careful educated guessing on a scale wider than the text allows but still responsible for an accurate, comprehensive awareness of the text. The *ethical* level comprises speculation about the philosophical, moral, and ethical implications and values arising from the speculative reading. Other levels open up as speculation builds on speculation. Our model is descriptive rather than prescriptive, broached in the hope of helping teachers and students set standards for papers on literature. In the same spirit, I would like to apply this scheme to student writing on Spenser, identifying at each level the operations to be performed, the hazards to be risked, and the special challenges with *The Faerie Queene*. I take my examples from papers by sophomores and juniors in English 210, with thanks to the authors, who had a chance to edit their contributions.

Literal interpretation stays close to the explicit language of *The Faerie Queene*; the interpreter seeks to demonstrate patterns, repetitions, and connections that, beginning and ending in the literal language of the poem, can be more or less quantified. This is what Christopher Lamphier does in his paper comparing the vocabularies of good and evil in book 1:

> Una is first described in 1.1.6 with adjectives such as "lovely," "faire," "pure," "innocent," and "vertuous." Yet the vocabulary of perfection seems more restricted than for evil. When Duessa is disrobed in canto 8, her body is attacked with adjectives such as "bald," "overgrowne," "filthy," "scald," "rotten," "sowre," "wrizzled," "rough," and "scabby" —and that is from stanza 47 only. More are found in stanzas 46 and 48, as well as in stanzas 40 and 41 of canto 2.

Literal interpretation resembles Piaget's "first-order" concrete intellectual operations, the ordering, seriating, arranging, and classifying of immediately given data or *things* (Inhelder and Piaget 249)—the things in this case being the words, phrases, and patterns the student writer finds in the text. This level is not wholly inductive; it involves some limited hypothetical reasoning, "deductions from the actual immediate situation" (Inhelder and Piaget 16). Besides, most literal interpretations serve a thesis. Lamphier's is that "there seem to be more words to describe evil than to describe good, perhaps because there are more dimensions to evil than there are to perfection."

There exists a professional danger of impatience with literal interpretation, as though, being fundamental, it were also elementary. But more and more teachers are incorporating literal interpretation—in the form of journals, freewriting, and exploratory essays—into their classes. In *Teaching with Writing* Toby Fulwiler describes how teachers can use journals to introduce, focus, and summarize class sessions. When my students hit an interpretive crux, I often ask them to take out their journals and write about their expectations going into the readings, the surprises they encounter, the things they find unclear or challenging. At the end of class, I often pose the main question of the day: "Is Redcrosse a truly self-made knight, or does his power ultimately rest with Una and the Faerie Queene? And what difference does it make?" With a text as dense as *The Faerie Queene*, such forms of writing can help the student comprehend the text and prepare to write about it.

As Linda Flower puts it, reading for comprehension has many important virtues, chief among them being that it can produce a "structured, elaborated mental representation of meaning" ("Negotiating" 247). And Janet Emig reminds teachers of writing that "the higher cognitive functions, such as analysis and synthesis, seem to develop most fully only with the support of a system of verbal language—particularly of written language" (123). Make a place, then, for the literal interpretation; honor its role in the development of a student's critical faculty. Good literal interpretation can spur fresh attention to the text. Further, it is essential to become good at literal interpretation, for all scrupulous and careful readers begin here. That is because—and this reveals a well-kept secret, one might even say a professional scandal, about deductive thinking—almost all deduction proceeds from prior intense induction.

Hazards abound, the two most common being banal quantification and plot summary. It is rarely enough to count, and it is never enough to recount. Teachers expect a deductive moment in which the writer makes something of the data. That is why few literal interpretations remain literal. Most mix literal and speculative interpretation, setting particulars in context as they are presented, thus weaving an argument that, although ultimately inductive, incorporates a great deal of simultaneous deduction. Erica Kesselman presents this sort of argument in her essay on the pervasive water imagery of book 1:

> The eyes of Redcrosse are bathed in "sad humour" as he is "drownd in deadly sleepe" (1.1.36). Archimago uses the sensual appeal of water to hypnotize the mind into the lull of slumber—and vulnerability. Morpheus employs the soothing aural aspects of a waterfall and of waves lapping to relax conscious control of the mind and catalyze the release of unconscious jealousy and desire.

Concrete particulars—the quotation, the references to the sounds of waterfall and waves—find a context in Kesselman's deductive generalization at the end of the passage. Her dash from "slumber" to "vulnerability" is also deductive.

In speculative interpretation, writers construct hypotheses to account for their data. Here is where Ed McDow, contrasting the white Una with the dark "salvage nation," found that Spenser uses color as a symbol of racial and cultural superiority. Here is where Gretchen Wise, contemplating her connection between Arthur's seamless shield and Elizabeth's *membrana intacta*, found a family of metaphors about the conservation of absolute power. This is the realm of inferential reasoning, Piaget's "formal" or "second-order operations," or thinking about thought as distinct from thinking about particular things. Readers perceive the form of an artistic or intellectual construct and tackle this form apart from its particulars (Inhelder and Piaget 15–16).

Christine Elliott does just this when she considers Spenser's attack on appearances in book 1:

> Spenser implies that appearance, while important, is always only a small though distinctive aspect of the whole. Spenser thus makes not only an insightful but also a courageous statement about the condition of things in his society. In a time when status meant everything, Spenser is crying out for acknowledgment of the soul.

Had her whole paper remained this general, it probably would not have worked. As Stephen Toulmin and his coauthors note in *An Introduction to Reasoning*, aesthetic arguments oblige the writer to explain with extreme care (as Elliott does elsewhere in her paper) the connections between claim and evidence. Toulmin calls such explanations *warrants*; he notes that in aesthetic arguments warrants very often must be supported with *backing*. Although many people—including me—have championed the Toulmin model as a way to teach argumentation, I find that its greatest usefulness in advanced courses is as a revision tool. Rather than try to insert warrants and backing mechanically (often such elements are implicit), students can use the model to analyze their own arguments in preliminary drafts. Warrants and backing need not be spelled out in many cases; the Toulmin model can help students determine when to spell them out.

Reaching the speculative realm lays bare three huge communication gaps particularly relevant to *The Faerie Queene*: (1) students have never been told that they can, should, and indeed are expected to, speculate; (2) students have no models of or standards for speculation; and (3) students are hesitant to leave conservative literal interpretation for the less conclusive ground of speculation. Teachers can address these gaps by furnishing models and standards. There are clear, incisive professional speculators out there, and analyzing their performances can serve the double purpose of training and encouragement. One good professional reader is Simon Shepherd, who in his book *Spenser* takes pains to write clearly while engaging in provocative speculation. Commenting on the prisoners of the dungeon of the house of pride (1.5.51), Shepherd writes:

> These lines tend to blame wasteful people rather than inherently corrupt institutions. As such they are relevant to the particular mission of Redcrosse, whose individual project it is to learn the correct self-discipline which will prepare him to fight the dragon. That fight will take place outside the context of courts. Thus the narrative suggests that social problems may be solved by individual effort and self-control. The corruption of court is a transitory affair. In this way the narrative inverts the real situation, in which court is both powerful and permanent, and as such provides a fantasy that is pleasurable and necessary to those who distrust what they depend on.   (36–37)

Even in such a comparatively simple passage, there is a progress to demonstrate—in a very old-fashioned way—from text to speculation. How does each sentence lead to the next? Why does Shepherd use the verb *suggests* in the fourth sentence, rather than *says*? In our profession, the standards for argumentation are widely assumed and yet disparate and diverse. A few minutes with such a passage will serve to introduce and set course standards for the "task" of interpretation.

Next to the work of professionals, we must lay the work of our students. Student writing—not only graded papers but also preliminary drafts, journal entries, and invention exercises—must come before the class for discussion. We must make sure this happens, even when our students have taken Freshman Writing and Introduction to Literary Methods. The question is, Where am I going to find the time to do all this? A question to be asked—as I do at the end of this essay.

Gap 3 is familiar. Students often fear the speculative step, for there is nothing beneath their feet that they themselves do not build. As we set up our models, tasks, and standards, we need also—by reading aloud and performing interpretation on our feet—to introduce them to the pleasures of being negatively capable. If speculative interpretation is to be a serious focus of a Spenser course, it is crucial that teachers put forward their own experiences as readers and writers.

All three gaps raise the issue of "critical literacy." As described by Linda Flower, the critically literate person questions sources, looks for assumptions, and reads for

> intentions, not just facts . . . [such literacy] may also mean coming into political or social consciousness and questioning both authority and the status quo. And it may even mean rising to a reflexive questioning of one's own assumptions and responses as a reader and one's own assumptions and assertions as a writer.   ("Introduction" 5)

It was once widely assumed that critical literacy—indeed, the speculative skills in general—just can't be taught. On the contrary, we now understand that such literacy grows as a writer develops from novice to skilled interpreter. Speculation, after all, is an act by which we *transform* knowledge into another form, and work by researchers such as Marlene Scardamalia, Carl Bereiter, and others suggests that such transformational abilities are part of a process of development that includes practice and learning. It is simply backward to bemoan students' lack of preparation in the style of Allan Bloom's *The Closing of the American Mind*, as though their growth should be complete by the time we get them. We can't, of course, do everything for our students—at some point, they will either read or not read the Bible, the *Iliad*, and Chaucer—but we can try to make them desire critical literacy and regard *The Faerie Queene* as a crucial means to it.

Speculative interpretations are common in student papers—but they are often confined to the conclusion of the essay. Kim Massih, after writing a fairly conservative literal interpretation of appearance and reality in book 1, closes her essay this way:

> Throughout *The Faerie Queene* we are faced with symbols, and we must learn whether or not to trust them. Spenser's poem teaches his readers to look beyond the surface, because an allegory does not simply state an argument but casts shadows over the truth and tests readers to see whether they can attain the true meaning. Our task, then, is very much like that of Redcrosse.

Clearly, Massih felt that the only place for this sort of thing was the getaway paragraph. Thus the rushed quality, as though the writer slipped these promising ideas in at the last moment, hoping they wouldn't be noticed. I felt obliged to write, "This should have been your thesis paragraph." Drafting exercises, exploration journals, freewriting, clustering, and other nonlinear, nonthetical forms of writing can help identify speculative potential in a student's thought and help avoid the end that should have been the beginning.

Ethical interpretation operates at a further remove form the literal; the ethical speculator meditates on the significance of his or her speculations in the world of ideas and action. Because *The Faerie Queene*, like *Paradise Lost*, advertises its own ethical and moral importance, it makes a natural object for—and a good opportunity to teach—such meditation. Christine Donohue engages in ethical criticism in her essay on Spenser's ambivalence regarding allegory:

> In "A Letter of the Authors," Spenser labels [allegory] "doctrine by ensample," understanding that readers generally find allegory an effective and enjoyable way to learn a lesson. However, Spenser is also

uncomfortable with using pleasure to deliver doctrine because it goes along with a world where "all things [are] accounted by their showes, and nothing esteemed of, that is not delightfull and pleasing to commune sence." But instead of rejecting allegory, Spenser ends up perpetuating this socially inculcated system of reading. That's a paradox in two ways. At its worst, allegory simply reinforces old prejudices. At its best, it could reveal how superficial allegory is, and the irrationality of the narrow-mindedness that makes allegory popular.

By her last two sentences, Donohue is contemplating the nature of allegory. Her speculations, though still relevant to the "Letter of the Authors," also address wider ethical and philosophical issues. Melissa McCullough, who (riskily) adopts the persona of Queen Elizabeth, engages in strenuously ethical criticism:

> Mr. Spenser . . . I am offended by your treatment of the female characters in *The Faerie Queene*. As a woman who must battle men for my rightful place as ruling monarch, I do not enjoy reading anything which gives men the dominant importance while holding women to a moral double standard by which men are allowed to be imperfect but women must be flawless. Might I suggest that you rethink your views on women and women in power, especially when you desire support from a woman in power?

It is worth noting that the fictional frame leads McCullough to leave the strict confines of the text and view it from without—that is, from an ethical standpoint.

Ethical interpretations address what poets and poems actually do in the world, the values they propagate, the beliefs they imply. A student's critical literacy comes into play, as do his or her awareness of current events, background, tastes, and personal standards of right and wrong. Donohue is surprised to find Spenser uncomfortable with the moral ambiguities of allegory; McCullough is clearly angered by the implications of Spenser's "sexism." Greg Dennison is disturbed to discover that "whenever Redcrosse loses his dominant male sex role, it is also a loss of faith," suggesting that for Spenser "sex roles are not only ironclad: they are divinely ordered."

Ethical speculation sometimes involves identifying inconsistencies and contradictions. Again, students hesitate, assuming that "readings against the poem" are in bad faith. But as students think about their thoughts (that is, as they interpret ethically), they discover some rewarding quandaries. Jeannine Fallon notes that "Spenser's poem implies that nature can be both protector and predator; accordingly, human beings must both love and fear nature in order to survive." Stewart Fyfe points out that "in order to show why evil is dangerous, Spenser is forced to show how attractive it is." And there is the playful reader who, like Michael Billings, enjoys revealing ethical problems:

> Sansfoy, who "care[s] not for God or man a point" (1.2.12), is a rebel with no place in any institution or reason to defend one. Sansjoy, who nourishes "bloudy vengeaunce in his bitter mind" (1.4.38), and Sansloy, "Without Law," represent dangerous behaviors—think of the potential class-conflict overtones in vengeance and rape. The struggle against the Sarazin brothers is less a struggle against anti-Christian impulses than against socially disruptive forces.

So the issue is not that higher levels of speculation don't exist in our Spenser papers but that such interpretation is fitful, intermittent, and even furtive. Again, a process model elaborated in class can help students develop critical and writerly habits that guide them to their own interpretive ambits.

I have picked and chosen among three views of teaching. The process movement, nearly thirty years old, emphasizes the interdependence of writing, reading, and thinking. (If we take process seriously, we *will* use writing to teach Spenser.) Recent approaches deemphasize the instructor as fountain of truth; to them I owe my call for the nonthetical alongside the thetical. Yet I have also envisioned a very active teacher doing some very traditional things. I still believe that, especially with Renaissance texts, there are skills, information, and sensibilities that students will never get anywhere else if not from the teacher. Why pretend this isn't so? Perform interpretation yourself. Make cultural literacy an issue. Bring your class into the teaching as well as the learning. Remember that "doctrine by ensample" is not dead.

That recalls the question to be asked—How am I going to find time to do all this? No teacher does "all this." Teachers experiment, select and reject techniques, and, course by course, build something new. Again to paraphrase Toby Fulwiler, the decision to teach Spenser with writing involves a trade-off: either decide to invest more hours of work in the course (a choice Fulwiler rightly believes most of us will not make) or decide to make room by sacrificing coverage. In my survey course I choose, or am forced to choose, both: I do work harder (grading journals, finding professional models, scheduling conferences and small-group sessions), and usually I have to drop a major text later in the course (one year it was *Volpone*; the previous year *The Duchess of Malfi* fell). All I can say is that the benefits—I think of Ed McDow and Gretchen Wise—lessen the grief of sacrifice.

NOTE

[1]All quotations from *The Faerie Queene* are taken from the Norton edition (Abrams).

"The Form and Gait of the Body":
Physical Carriage, Genre, and Spenserian Allegory

Theresa M. Krier

Need allegorical interpretation be dualistic? Is allegorical reading necessarily a matter of leaving behind sound for sense, rind for pith, sensuous appearance for abstract essence, gaudy rhetoric for austere philosophy? Renaissance theorizing about allegory certainly encourages such dualism in both the writing and reading of allegory, although its emphasis on forms of secrecy in allegorical discourse allows it to save rather than to transcend the text. But students in our day are encouraged in ways of reading allegorically that neglect the enticements of secrecy and emphasize instead a narrow dualism, particularly if they come to *The Faerie Queene* through the heavily glossed editions and excerpts available. Characteristic notes to book 1, for instance, are full of citations from Scripture and identifications of Duessa as the whore of Babylon but necessarily sketchy on how such elements function in the narrative. And if we open A. C. Hamilton's edition, with its treasure trove of commentary and its spirited, subtle argument against formulaic and reductive reading, to the episode of the Redcrosse Knight's battle with the dragon, we find that even Hamilton offers, as part of a running annotation, excerpts from the criticism proposing, for example, that the dragon's fire "expresses God's 'euer-burning wrath' . . . against sinful man"; that the fire the dragon breathes forth, which flashes in the knight's beard, may be linked "to the metaphor of sin as fire and the beard to the *fomes peccati*, the corruption of man's nature"; that the fire symbolizes "both the difficulties encountered by a Christian and the purging of sin" (148).

These proposals, presented in this format of marginal notes, are as may be. I want to suggest that we think of them less as right or wrong than as premature and deracinated, especially for pedagogical purposes. Notes are a partial, inevitable, necessary solution to the difficulties of reading Spenser, but they also, inevitably, help create problems in reading. If the history of allegorical interpretation can be understood as a series of contests or mediations between rhetoric and philosophy (J. Whitman 3–10), then in these extracts-turned-marginalia, philosophy seems to win, appropriating Spenser's rhetoric without having earned the conditions that would make such statements true. They all too easily imply that allegorical reading is a matter of moving from certain textual details, isolated without explicit reasons, immediately to a conceptual schema based on unarticulated assumptions about the establishment of conditions of intelligibility for the allegory. It's the very establishment of these conditions that is at issue in any one allegorical reading. Not to let students in on this fact—that allegorical reading is a process asking time, space, and the willingness to dwell in some interpretive neighborhood adjacent to both poetry and philosophy—is to leave them with the dissatisfied sense that allegorical interpretation is arbitrary and authoritarian; it is to exclude them from the invitation to venturesome reading that Spenser's poem offers.

Of course time and space for such interpretive engagement are difficult to find in most teaching contexts; none of us fully escapes the productivity model that structures education in this century. It is possible, though, to shift our attention, and that of students, to conditions of intelligibility that students may already bear as interpretive contexts; it is possible as well to save the appearances of the text, so that allegory comes to seem, to new readers, less arbitrary in terms both of their own capacities and of the poetry that they read.

Angus Fletcher argues that "[v]irtue, the positive ideal of moral allegory, needs to be given its original sense of 'power,' and moral fables need then to be reinterpreted as having to do chiefly with polarities of strength and weakness, confidence and fear, certainty and doubt" (*Allegory* 295). Moral fables have had to do with polarities of strength and weakness from the time of Prudentius's *Psychomachia* in the early fifth century, and power in this sense preeminently characterizes allegorical romances of the Middle Ages and the Renaissance, built as they are of tales of chivalric heroism, concerned as they are with prowess and with the achievement of ideal strength and goodness (Tuve 42–58). For students, many of whom will have read Marie Borroff's translation of *Sir Gawain and the Green Knight*, or Chaucer's *Knight's Tale* or *Wife of Bath's Tale*, or Shakespeare's *Henry IV, Part 1*, these categories of strength and weakness, confidence and fear will make fine sense. For Spenser's moral fables, we might slant these matters in the direction of the strengths and weaknesses of the body (thus going against the grain of a good deal of criticism and teaching practice): the body's posture, its carriage, its stance or stature in any one episode; we might ask what kinds of movements a creature makes, how it inhabits space, how it establishes itself in relation to the great elements and objects of the world—sun and stars, earth, waters, light. In short, we might consider how a creature is at home in the physical world, for it is through these things that Spenser represents a character's strength or weakness relative to the world (Tuve 370–71).[1]

To read with these questions in mind is, in the language of one familiar paradigm, to shift from spiritual to moral levels of allegory; it is also to shift from the primacy of theological terms of interpretation to the terms of chivalric romance, the données of which Spenser allegorizes with endless inventiveness. To read this way with students is to ask them to adduce conditions of intelligibility based on genre elements with which they may be familiar, so that allegorical interpretation is understood to be not the arbitrary hypostatization of an abstracted meaning but a flexibly coherent process of meaning making that emerges from their own historical understanding.

Book 1 offers many self-evident instances of the relation between physical carriage and moral significance. Duessa's seven-headed beast "Came ramping

forth with proud presumpteous gate" (8.12).[2] Orgoglio sees Redcrosse and
"gan aduance / With huge force and insupportable mayne, / And towardes
him with dreadfull fury praunce" (7.11). Lucifera's arrogance is easy to read
in the lines "So proud she shyned in her Princely state, / Looking to heauen;
for earth she did disdayne, / And sitting high; for lowly she did hate" (4.10).
And the seven deadly sins, being personifications in procession, show their
respective natures in every detail of bodily shape, carriage, and deportment.
But it is the Redcrosse Knight who deserves the closest look here.

Redcrosse's early career—before the house of Holiness in canto 10—alter-
nates between episodes of impetuous chivalric enterprise, with their bold,
forward assertiveness, and episodes in which he simply goes to pieces
morally, spiritually, and physically. The most famous instance must be his
erotic liaison with Duessa, when he forfeits both his upright posture and
the firm shape of his armor and finds himself "Pourd out in loosnesse on
the grassy grownd" (7.7). But there are also noteworthy moments when
he loses his nerve and flees the light of day. He bolts from Archimago's
hermitage:

> At last faire *Hesperus* in highest skie
> Had spent his lampe, and brought forth dawning light,
> Then vp he rose, and clad him hastily;
> The Dwarfe him brought his steed: so both away do fly.
> (2.6)

He flees the house of Pride in shock and fear, before full daylight:

> [He] early rose, and ere that dawning light
> Discouered had the world to heauen wyde,
> He by a priuie Posterne tooke his flight,
> That of no enuious eyes he mote be spyde:
> For doubtlesse death ensewd, if any him descryde.
> (5.52)

In Despair's castle, the hero is found in the deepest, darkest room, hidden
from "heauen's chearefull face" (8.38). For a knight-errant, Redcrosse shows
an unusually compelling and atavistic drive to escape the conditions of visibility and of unabashed relation to the light-giving objects of the heavens—
for these would also be conditions of self-recognition.

Running counter to Redcrosse's alternating chivalric displays of prowess
and his various failures of nerve is a series of mythic, natural, and/or legendary figures in whom radiant heroic energy is presented as spectacle, as the
natural eloquence of bodily, psychic, and spiritual integrity. This is how
Spenser depicts Phoebus (5.2) and Arthur (7.29–34). Images in which the
interior plenitude of an ideal selfhood issues in bodily poise and splendor,

they exist to contrast with the hero's movements toward a more radically human depletion and shame. They also awaken or intensify the reader's wish for such easy energy, opulence, and poise. To awaken this wish is a Sidneyan way of awakening a form of wonder, the capacity to marvel at characters beautifully exemplary of heroic ideals.

The contrast of bodily poise, integrity, and brilliance, on the one hand, and erratic awkwardness and flight, on the other, pervades the whole book, but is strongest in canto 5, where we see a potentially gorgeous heroism depleted in a moral allegory precisely about strength and weakness, confidence and fear. The gold flourisher, the sun, presides over the canto's opening:

> At last the golden Orientall gate
>   Of greatest heauen gan to open faire,
>   And *Phoebus* fresh, as bridegrome to his mate,
>   Came dauncing forth, shaking his deawie haire:
>   And hurld his glistring beames through gloomy aire. . . .
>
>   (st. 2)

This jubilant and self-delighting sun is not only the slightly exotic Phoebus, whose literary associations are brilliant enough, but the sun of Psalm 19, "which is as a bridegroom coming out of his chamber, and rejoiceth as a strong man to run a race," as Hamilton notes (75). Classical and biblical allusions reinforce one another in a description the keynote of which is a gravity-defying triumph over gloom. The diction is dominated by images of radiance, leaping, dancing, light in motion, the effortless jubilation of energy expended and dispelling the "gloomy aire" of a palpable darkness. This figure of Phoebus presents the measure of an ideal bodily joy from which Redcrosse will descend and functions both as an eikastic image that might awaken desire in the reader and as a critique of misdirected chivalric heroism.

Dispositions of the body in the subsequent battle between Redcrosse and Sansjoy work against the buoyant *virtù* of Phoebus. Encased in heavy armor, the knights represent the opposite extreme from Phoebus's naked, joyful glory. He came forth "dauncing" and "shaking his deawie haire"; they are "armed warily" (st. 4) and bear "instruments of wrath and heauinesse" that dent the "yron walls" of their armor with blows like "yron hammers" (st. 6–7). Given the optimism with which Phoebus imbues the start of the canto, and the initial alignment of Redcrosse with the dawn as he prepares his "sunbright armes" (st. 2), these subsequent shifts from light and lift to oppressive weight and joylessness make important points about the bodily as well as the spiritual orientations of knight-errantry. Indeed, a thick stupefaction overcomes both fighters; murkiness and obscurity come to permeate the canto; Spenser ends with Redcrosse stealing away from the house of Pride in the dark, shrinking from "heauen wyde" (st. 52). This downward plunge in the canto's structure may leave the reader with an urgent wish for the candor and joy expressed in Phoebus's carriage, but without the means to that end.

We get such an imaginative means in canto 7 with the eikastic figure of Arthur, a hero of capable imagination in whom radiant heroic form perfectly manifests both his moral *virtù* and his allegorical association with magnificence:

> At last she chaunced by good hap to meet
> A goodly knight, faire marching by the way . . .
> His glitterand armour shined farre away,
> Like glancing light of *Phoebus* brightest ray . . .
> Athwart his brest a bauldrick braue he ware,
> That shynd, like twinkling stars, with stons most pretious rare.
>
> (st. 29)

Again Spenser evokes the vigor and loftiness of Phoebus-like energy, of mobile light; the "twinkling stars" of the stones on his baldric suggest the naturalness of his visibility to others and his easy orientation toward natural objects, especially toward heights and lights. In this Arthur contrasts with Redcrosse, who still finds himself regularly hiding out from the "heauens wyde."

It is of course the grace made effectual through Arthur, as well as through Una and the house of Holiness, that enables Redcrosse to rectify his passions and put on the new man; his fused spiritual and physical strengths are liberated to engage with the very physical, chivalric-romance challenge of the dragon. Such liberated prowess transfigures the hero's pattern of alternate chivalric assertion and undisciplined withdrawal and gives him access to an Arthurian, sunlike sublimity. This battle (canto 11) we seem to find entirely too easy to allegorize quickly, and so it is to this ultimate contest facing the knight that I wish to turn, in order to see how attending to bodily carriage and form might animate an allegorical process of reading, one that gives primacy to features of the chivalric-romance genre.

Of the dragon himself, it is notable that the form and gaits of his body contrast with the knight's not only in the obvious matters of size and monstrosity but more especially in the relation to natural objects. The dragon's movements are always a cruel bodily domination of these natural objects and elements, for example, the tender air. Spenser comes back to this detail repeatedly. When the dragon spreads his wings, "With which whenas him list the ayre to beat, / And there by force vnwonted passage find, / The cloudes before him fled for terrour great, / And all the heauens stood still amazed with his threat" (st. 10). Or again (to cite just one more of several instances):

Himselfe vp high he lifted from the ground,
And with strong flight did forcibly diuide
The yielding aire, which nigh too feeble found
Her flitting partes, and element vnsound,
To beare so great a weight. . . .   (st. 18)

The knight, for his part, shows throughout most of his three-day battle
a transformed combination of chivalric aggression and a literal humility
or lowness as he surrenders to the natural objects that heal him with grace,
the tree of life and the well of life. This pattern, as I have suggested, is
a transformation of his earlier, more chaotic alternations into a rhythmic
ebb and flow honoring the body's needs. Moreover, Spenser is at pains to
emphasize not only heroic wrath but new and momentary achievements
of physical grace, exaltation, energy: "Both horse and man vp lightly rose
againe, / And fresh encounter towards him addrest" (st. 17); unhorsed, Redcrosse "can quickly ryse / From off the earth" (st. 23); on the morning of
the second day's battle "he vpstarted braue / Out of the well, wherein he
drenched lay" (st. 34), and the dragon marvels that the knight is so "fresh"
(st. 35); when stung by the dragon, Redcrosse "can him lightly reare" (st. 39);
on the morning of the third day he "freshly vp arose . . . / All healed of
his hurts and woundes wide" (st. 52).

These immersions of the knight in the well of life and the waters beneath
the tree of life have always been understood allegorically and, truly enough,
as actions of grace, grace through baptism and communion. But to say as
much hardly accounts for the rhetorical charge of the stanzas describing
this well and *this* tree and their effects on the knight. To emphasize the
rhetorical vividness of the natural object—for example, the bounty implied
in the doubling of "fruit and apples," the color saturation of the "apples'
rosie red" and "pure vermilion" (st. 46)—may seem to undermine the spiritual
sense of grace. But perhaps this allegorical problem can be approached
another way, and the sensuous rhetoric not abandoned but rescued for allegorical interpretation, if once again we consider interpreting chiefly in the
spiritual sense.

Natural objects everywhere in Spenser's work can have bodily form and
gait, behavior and effects; it is partly for this reason that they can sometimes be moral agents (Tuve 108–12). From his first works to his last, Spenser
particularly attributes these features of carriage and gait that signify to flowing water, to streams and rivers. The greatest instance in *The Faerie Queene*
occurs in book 4, when the Thames and the Medway celebrate their marriage in an enormous procession that is also their flowing, a passage in which
Spenser celebrates, among many other things, the gait of the rivers, their
forward momentum and elegant glide. These movements come naturally
to rivers, with a poise that is, alas, not naturally accessible to human beings;
we can achieve such poise only after a struggle, and only briefly. This is a

central point about the Thames in *Prothalamion*, the greatest of Spenser's
river poetry outside *The Faerie Queene*. The speaker of *Prothalamion* is
full of anxiety, "sullein care," "discontent," and the awkwardness of all
human circumstances (lines 5–6). His walk along "siluer streaming Thames"
(11) is the nearest human approximation to the enviably steady and assured
glide of rivers, and it is his proximity to this poise that might "ease" his
"payne" (10). We may even suggest that the unity of *Prothalamion*—long
a vexed issue and better thought of as fluid than as architectonic—arises
in part from a quiet emphasis throughout on the human gait of walking
and on the support that the streaming river offers other forms of life. The
"bricky towres" of the temple "on the *Themmes* brode aged backe doe ryde"
(132–33). And the river carries its swans with the most delicate and buoyant
of touches:

> So purely white they were,
> That euen the gentle streame, the which them bare,
> Seem'd foule to them, and bad his billowes spare
> To wet their silken feathers, least they might
> Soyle their fayre plumes with water not so fayre.
>   (46–50)

These swans float to their destinies as human brides without effort and without anxiety, thanks to the literal carriage of the river and in contrast to the
speaker's more human carriage. The poem doesn't claim to resolve the
speaker's personal difficulties, but its tone is soothed by the end not only
because of its epithalamic celebration but also because of the steady support
and gait of the river, which is assimilated complexly to time and to poetry
in the miraculous refrain, "Sweet Themmes, run softly till I end my song."

The flowing waters of *The Faerie Queene*'s well of life and tree of life, less
broad and magnificent than the Thames, are nonetheless similarly supportive, and this natural, perhaps magical support is the agency of grace to the
knight in his battle. It is telling that Spenser uses "virtue" here in its sense
of strength or internal efficacy: "Of auncient time there was a springing
well, / From which fast trickled forth a siluer flood, / Full of great vertues,
and for med'cine good" (11.29). Moreover, Spenser offers a multitude of
interpretive possibilities for the action of the well here, as if to insist that
we loosen the reins of our allegorical-reading temptation to reify meaning,
that we entertain both a spiritual or theological sense and a moral sense,
as well as the possibility of some unknown, magic "secret vertue" of the
kind that natural features in romances are known to abound in:

> I wote not, whether the reuenging steele
>   Were hardened with that holy water dew,
>   Wherein he fell, or sharper edge did feele,

> Or his baptized hands now greater grew;
> Or other secret vertue did ensew. . . .
>
> (st. 36)

If flowing water does indeed suggest both natural poise and natural support, this may explain why Spenser adapts the Gospel of Nicodemus, with its oil from the tree of life (Hankins 119). Spenser insists on the balm's flowing abundance:

> From that first tree forth flowd, as from a well,
> A trickling streame of Balme, most soueraine
> And daintie deare, which on the ground still fell,
> And ouerflowed all the fertill plaine,
> As it had deawed bene with timely raine. . . .
>
> (st. 48)

The knight's immersions in these healing liquids suggest a new and harmonious intimacy with objects and elements, here a rectified association with bodies of water. These had earlier been the ominous site of his dalliance with Duessa, and Redcrosse had resembled them by being "poured out in loosnesse."

In just the same way, canto 11 offers a new alignment of knight and sun. At the start of canto 5, the sun had danced forth brilliantly at dawn, a glamorous figure; at the end of the canto, the knight had fled the light of heaven, and the identification with the sun's light, exaltation, and dash had shifted to Arthur. But in the battle with the dragon, Spenser restores a full parallel between Redcrosse and the potent, masculine sun, between the hero's nocturnal drenchings in healing fluids and the sun's nocturnal immersions in the ocean, between Redcrosse's dawn risings and the sun's own risings and settings, like this one:

> Now gan the golden *Phoebus* for to steepe
> His fierie face in billowes of the west,
> And his faint steedes watred in Ocean deepe. . . .
>
> (st. 31)

The renewed alignments of hero and waters, hero and sun are consequences of the actions of grace; Redcrosse has become the Pauline new man *and* has discovered a refreshed identity as natural creature. This makes sense, of course, in the book that is Spenser's greatest fusion of biblical allegory and chivalric-romance allegory. My suggestion is that all of us who are students of Spenser can apprehend the high imaginative complexity of his sensuous allegorical praxis if we forgo the temptation to ascend from immersion in the text.

This Spenserian allegoresis, moreover, creates the theoretical space for a critique of our post-Coleridgean allegorical reading. Coleridge's polarization of allegory and symbol—the one a set of abstract, rational, systematic ideas, the other organic, radiant, sensuous, containing color and depth—seems almost impossible to resist once it has been suggested; from Coleridge on, this polarization involves a privileging of "symbol" and a resentment toward "allegory" with its apparent demotion of the text. The extraordinary valence of symbol in this pairing suggests that the term accrues to itself all the tactility, mysteriousness, and allure of which allegory is denuded. But my suggestion, following Rosemond Tuve, is that allegory and symbol, like philosophy and rhetoric, are more often entangled and even interchangeable in Spenser's work than we can easily see. Moreover, though it can't be argued extensively here, I think that we find it difficult to get beyond these categories because they are gendered: they match our powerful binary categories of masculine and feminine, categories that in Spenser's work are often fluid and multiple rather than opposed.[3]

No one has yet been able to describe Spenser's allegory fully. Perhaps no one can, given its enormous profuseness, variety, and flexibility. We clearly need to take as a primary principle that his allegory is always complex, first in that its senses and levels are multiple and overdetermined, second that, even in a single episode or figure, allegory is a constant shape shifter, slippery, elusive. But while these features are often threatening to readers, another principle of his allegory may help to counter the risks of such excess: Spenser's allegory may sometimes refuse the dualism of Renaissance allegorical theory and of our own time-pressured teaching habits. It requires not that the reader transcend the body of the text like a pure Socratic lover ascending to a greater, more intangible truth but that the reader surrender to the sensuous details of the verse and to the historically contingent genre elements of the narrative. This is to suggest a shift, as I said at the outset, from attending chiefly to theological horizons of meaning, as we so easily do when teaching book 1, to attending to the moral horizons of chivalric romance. One virtue (in Fletcher's sense) of this shift is that it doesn't deny the truth of spiritual interpretations as do those with which I began. A second strength of this shift is that it allows us to distinguish among the multiple spheres of generic significance of Spenser's rich allegory. So, for instance, we could discriminate among the alarmingly proliferating dragons of book 1: Lucifera's and Duessa's dragons may best be understood as biblical in provenance, the one on Arthur's helmet is an English-romance dragon from the Matter of Britain, and Redcrosse's great culminating foe in canto 11 is biblical and romantic in derivation as in allegorical significance; this is why he is such an apt enemy for the hero of this book. Third, if good accounts of allegory grant its enigmatic and challenging secrecy or reticence, as I think they must, then my assay to articulate a paradoxical-sounding rhetorical allegory takes allegorical secrecy not chiefly as a code that needs cracking in order for the reader to interpret any one detail but as gradual disclosure. We understand significance by taking in the sequence of the story and by familiarity with the genre's conventions—processes that take time.

Still, Spenser's allegory is never going to yield itself entirely to rational understanding, not so much because it is enigmatic in its very nature but more truly because it is so open and multiple, copious and abundant. We can say of it what Spenser says of his efforts to catalog the creatures of the sea: "For much more eath to tell the starres on hy, / Albe they endlesse seeme in estimation, / Then to recount the Seas posterity" (4.12.1).

NOTES

[1]The title of this essay, like my present aims in reading, comes from Emerson in *The American Scholar*: "I ask not for the great, the remote, the romantic; . . . I embrace the common, I explore and sit at the feet of the familiar, the low. . . . What would we really know the meaning of? The meal in the firkin; the milk in the pan; . . . the glance of the eye; the form and the gait of the body. . . . Show me the sublime presence of the highest spiritual cause lurking, as always it does lurk, in these suburbs and extremities of nature" (78).

[2]Quotations from *The Faerie Queene* are taken from Hamilton's edition; those from *Prothalamion*, from Oram et al.

[3]For Coleridge, see, for example, *The Statesman's Manual*. In many of the passages I have cited depicting characters' stances toward natural objects, Spenser clearly suggests the masculine character's relation to a feminine object of nature—for example, the dragon's cleaving of the "buxome aire," the eroticism of the sun's immersions in the sea, the apples of the tree of life. At 1.11.50, when Redcrosse has fallen into the balmy stream under the tree of life, he "lay as in a dreame of deepe delight, / Besmeard with pretious Balme"; the description must seem odd in its context unless we take it as indicating the rectified relation not only of hero to nature but also of masculine to feminine. As David Miller reminds me, it does this partly by rectifying the hero's relation to dreaming, since dreams in book 1 mediate the relation of masculine to feminine. In a pattern that runs parallel to the solar imagery already discussed, the narration takes us from Redcrosse dreaming of the false Una brought forth by the graces, through Arthur dreaming of Gloriana, to Redcrosse in canto 11 dreaming "of deepe delight"—presumably, as Nohrnberg observes (197–98), the deep delight of his betrothal to Una after the battle, which realizes in rectified (and waking) form the content of his earlier dream. Such inflections of gender are a matter entirely apt to my subject of the relations between rhetoric and allegory but too extensive for the present occasion; they are worked out at more length in a study in progress on Spenser, Chaucer, and the maternal.

Challenging the Commonplace: Teaching as Conversation in Spenser's Legend of Temperance

John Webster

Book 2 may seem an unusual place to start students on Spenser's *Faerie Queene*, yet its Legend of Temperance offers certain pedagogical advantages over other books. Because it is (like book 3) largely secular, it allows me to skirt apprehensions my students have shown about the theology of book 1. At the same time, like book 1 but unlike book 3, book 2 has a narrative coherence that supplies new readers with at least the illusion of the beginning, middle, and end structures with which they are already most familiar. My main reason for teaching book 2 to undergraduates, however, has been that it offers a relatively uncomplicated stretch of poetry in which students can engage Spenser in something like an interactive conversation, reading and responding as the poetry inventories, questions, and evaluates received wisdom about what constitutes "temperate" human action. Students may or may not come out of book 2 with a fully Spenserian view of temperance (I, for one, have not), but—if the poetry has worked for them—they will better appreciate the difficulty of commonplace wisdoms and may even take with them something of Spenser's patient habit of analytic and imaginative thought.

My aim, then, is to teach book 2 as conversation, but before I describe my pedagogy, I'll first summarize my view of the book, a view that starts from Spenser's frequent problematizing of the ethical commonplaces that encode the culture's traditional wisdom.[1] In ordinary conversation, commonplaces—or what we also call adages or sayings—tend to locate recurrent human issues (each a "common" "place") and are invoked by speakers in specific speech situations to assimilate new and particular events to existing paradigms of ethical behavior. The strategies commonplaces offer for this assimilation run from advice with respect to action ("A stitch in time saves nine"—that is, act now), to explanation ("Misery loves company"), to encouragement ("This too shall pass"), to consolation ("There are other fish in the sea"). What matters most in reading Spenser, however, is that for all their formal simplicity, commonplaces (and the wisdom they encode) are in fact intensely problematic, both because they so briefly epitomize their wise-ness that one may not see the full or proper scope of the help they are invoked to provide and because, even when properly understood, they may not fit the situation to which we apply them (as, for example, with "Untroubled night, they say, gives counsel best"—used by Una and Redcrosse to justify their decision to go with Archimago in 1.1.33).[2]

Thus if people generally use commonplaces to summarize moral thought, in Spenserian allegory their function is often just the reverse. My classroom term for them is *rubric lines*, since, like a rubric identifying a chapter in a text, commonplaces in *The Faerie Queene* frequently mark a starting point for reflection about whatever allegory the poetry is at that stage developing.[3] An example from book 2 occurs when Guyon, responding to the deaths of Amavia and Mordant, defines the role of temperance as to "measure out a meane, / Neither to melt in pleasures whot desire, / Nor fry in hartless griefe and dolefull teene" (1.58). Coming at the end of the heartrending story of Amavia's and Mordant's deaths, his moralizing tone prompts my students to modern condescension and disdain.

But while in the narrative that commonplace has its normal function of summarizing a situation in traditional terms, in the developing allegory its function is to introduce the question of whether a temperance defined as a process of finding means between extremes will actually work. Spenser is not infallible, I tell students, but neither is he a moralistic simpleton, and they need to take care not to confuse the apparent moral certainty of the narrative voice with the poem's final judgment about moral issues. Rather, readers should see commonplaces of this sort as opening gambits for the poem's conversational strategies. For canto 1's commonplaces, the allegorical issue actually only emerges in canto 2's house of Medina, where Spenser explores the notion declared in Guyon's commonplace by imagining a world fully governed by a temperance of means, picturing its peacemaking strength but insisting on its limitations as well. Medina thus does reign, but only by histrionic suppression of extremes and conflicts throughout a dinner party that rivals anyone's memory of the worst family gathering ever.

In structural terms, in fact, cantos 1 and 2 introduce a pattern of action and challenge that governs the book's first seven cantos. In canto 4, for example, no sooner does the palmer deliver his moral summary of Phedon's fate (st. 34–35) than Atin arrives out of nowhere to heave "a thrillant dart" of challenge to its explanation of Phedon's dilemma (st. 46).[4] Similarly, Guyon's victory over Pyrocles's wrathfulness in canto 5 suddenly unravels when Guyon moderately agrees to unbind Occasion, an act that immediately leads to a new outbreak of wrathfulness. Even the inconclusiveness of canto 6 suggests the same revisionary strategy, when Guyon's ostensibly climactic battle to subdue Cymocles is suddenly ended by Phaedria's intervention through commonplace pleadings ("Such powre haue pleasing words: such is the might / Of courteous clemencie in gentle hart," the narrator opines of Phaedria's success [st. 36]). In each of these episodes, the poem reaches an apparent narrative and moral resolution, as if its meaning were (or were about to be) whole and clear, only to then raise challenges to that resolution in such a way as to invite renewed questioning of the issues involved.

If the immediate question raised in the early cantos concerns whether "Moderation in all things" is sufficient advice, however, the larger issue concerns whether temperance should be understood in terms of suppressing passion at all. Spenser's choice of Acrasia as Guyon's enemy provides the framework for this wider conception, for Aristotle uses *akrasia* to denote not a failure of moderation but a failure of will.[5] For him, the *akrates* is the person who knows the right choice in a given situation but who cannot find the resolution to make that choice and carry it out. The word's derivation—from the Greek *krates*, meaning "strength, power, might, or dominion," combined with the negative prefix *a*—focuses attention on the powers of will necessary to make moral choices and to sustain them in action: when you know what is right, will you or will you not have the power or strength of will to do it? One way to describe the limitations of the early cantos' commonplaces of temperance is to note that the poem proceeds there as if the will to temper the passions of the soul could be sustained without any broader understanding of psychological power: Anger is wrong—so don't do it. Lust is wrong—so don't do it. What is not acknowledged is that the task of controlling passionate energies itself takes energy and that the energy for resistance can only be maintained through a clear understanding of why one would finally want to resist at all. Then as now, "Just say no" is not sufficient advice, because it fails to acknowledge the deeper issues of motive and purpose that will have led to the problem in the first place.

Without a convincing sense of why one would want to suppress and channel the inner energies of the mind, then, the powers that temperance requires will prove impossible to sustain, and Guyon's visit to the cave of Mammon now raises that issue directly. For when Mammon offers Guyon first riches, then realms, power, ambition, the love of honor, even the chance to succor the damned, he effectively proposes a whole range of goals that human beings normally invoke to motivate the governing of their inner passions, and when Guyon rejects them all, the issue of what will replace them necessarily arises. No mind can keep suppressing its passions once it has rejected the validity of its reasons for doing so, and consequently when Guyon collapses "in deadly fit opprest," powerless as he leaves Mammon's cave to sustain himself or his quest any further, his failure seems just as inevitable as will be the return early in canto 8 of the temporarily suppressed but still undefeated Pyrocles and Cymocles.

Cantos 1–7 thus enact a survey and interrogation of the cultural wisdom with respect to temperance as moderation; succeeding cantos now propose instead a temperance of purpose informed through God's grace. The transition is the opening to canto 8, where, with a "senseless" Temperance stretched out on the ground, Spenser invokes new commonplaces having to do with God's relation to humankind ("And is there care in heauen? and is there loue . . ." [st. 1]). Even here, though, he does not merely offer "faith in God" as a formulaic alternative to Mammon's secular motives. Instead he offers us Arthur and Alma as metaphorical means through which to reflect on human will in its secular as well as theological dimensions. Consequently, in canto 9 we enter Alma's house of the Soul only to find that it is the body itself, and as we survey the powers that lie within, though we begin with the purely physical, we soon ascend to the mind, to the rooms of imagination, of wisdom, and of memory. Here, as Arthur and Guyon peruse their respective histories, Spenser invites thought about how we as human beings use study and understanding to construct a moral basis for our actions. One establishes that basis, or ethical background—the suggestion is—through an education in one's relation to one's social order, to that order's history (looking backward) and to its destiny (looking forward). That the human mind has these resources at all is both by the grace of God and explanatory of it: Christian humanist education works through the gifts of God's creation in such a way as to enable us to construct a sense of purpose and meaningfulness that will be far more powerful as a basis for action than are any of those many motives figured in cantos 1–7.

In the end, then, Spenserian temperance has little to do with "means" or moderation, a fact that will explain Guyon's resolute destruction of the Bower of Bliss in canto 12. For while a moderating temperance would have to leave something of Acrasia's garden standing or at least lament the bower's lost beauty, a temperance of power informed by purpose sees no room for compromise. For just as Aristotle's *akrasia* is no mere matter of too much or too little of what would otherwise be a good thing, neither is the bower's self-absorbed purposelessness a mere matter of excess. Rather, Acrasia's images of impotent art and sexuality figure a powerlessness in the face of moral choice that needs not moderation but wholesale replacement. Allegorically, after all, the Bower of Bliss is only a state of mind in the first place —either you are in it or you aren't. Moreover (and for the same reasons), those who won't make the choice won't lose the bower: "Let Grill be Grill, and haue his hoggish mind," Spenser says as he ends the book. Acrasia and her bower will live on for anyone willing to have her.

Those, then, are the issues of book 2 as I see them, but how does one teach this revisionary, interrogating Spenser? Since the real power of Spenser's poetry for me is its ability to involve readers in a continual sifting of the culture's wisdom, lecture alone has never worked well. Moreover, my students have generally found Spenser hard going. Book 2 is long, things often seem to happen for no good reason, and its archaic language threatens more often than it seems rich with interpretive resources begging to be explored. And then, too, the book's hero presents his own problem: Guyon is a pretty dull guy. Past mistakes have supplied responses to many of these problems. I used to try reading the book in a week, for example, but no one ever seemed to get straight about anything; I now take two weeks and assign only two cantos of reading at a time. On my university's scheduling, that gives me eight fifty-minute class meetings. That amount of time never exhausts the subject, but (as trial again has shown) it has been about as long as my new readers can sustain their enthusiasm. And though during these weeks students read everything in book 2, I no longer try to cover it all in class. Instead I go very slowly with some cantos and leave others (generally 3, 10, and 11) to general summary. Most important, some sort of writing in each day's work now forms the backbone of my teaching. On the one hand, writing assignments encourage students to interact directly with the poetry; on the other, they provide me with both an outline for daily discussion topics and a class full of students primed to participate.

Since I see Spenser's use of commonplaces to originate and direct the poem's ethical discourse as a relatively easy entry point, I direct my first class toward showing students that while commonplaces (aphorisms, sayings, adages, saws) seem simple their role in ordinary language is actually rather complex. But though my aim will be to show students that commonplaces offer conceptual space in Spenser's allegory to interrogate traditional wisdom, my method won't be direct. Instead, before class I'll write "He who hesitates is lost" or "Know thyself" on the board and begin by asking students for expansion. What do people mean when they use such an expression? Is "He who hesitates is lost" true? Always? How does one know? And so on. Then, having started thought about commonplaces, I'll ask students to contribute examples, asking especially for contemporary versions, discussing whether and how more recent ones like Nike's "Just do it" qualify. I'll list contributions on the board, and—especially after we explore some of the contexts in which these commonplaces could be false or inappropriate—I'll ask them to consider why people say these things at all. Throughout, my point won't be to denigrate commonplaces but to show how frequently people use them as shortcuts to summarize thinking about what are often rather complex situations.

These issues raised, I'll then move to temperance, first asking students to write for five minutes on something easy like "What temperance means to me." Exercises like this work well to direct attention to particular issues; I don't collect them, but I will ask three or four volunteers to read aloud. This is rarely sage and serious, since modern English has made temperance largely a matter of beer and chocolate cake. The very narrowness of our modern view, however, provides contrast from which to recover the virtue's earlier broad importance. I comment on this narrowness and ask students to imagine how one could see temperance as Spenser (and Aristotle before him) did—as a virtue essential to any right action at all. Their immediate sense of the virtue generally is denial: "Just say no." But once students have had a chance to think a bit—and after we've talked about the limits of that new commonplace—I introduce Acrasia, supplying etymological background and moving finally to the proposition that while some aspects of temperance have (just like our modern notion) the relatively small scope of self-control before the dinner table, in its larger sense temperance will be relevant whenever a choice of action, of any kind and any dimension, presents itself. What is strength of will anyway? Where does it come from? How can it be sustained? What diminishes it? How might its loss lead not just to lazy dissolution but even to suicidal depression?

At that point, having established an anticipatory conceptualization of the book's major issues, I'll conclude the first day by assigning cantos 1 and 2. I'll no doubt say something to set a context for reading, but I'll also hand out a writing assignment consisting of three questions, the first just to help students focus on the narrative line, the second and third to start them thinking about how Spenser unfolds and explores his commonplace wisdom. I'll explain that the writing need not be formal (I'm really asking for coherent reading notes, not a "paper"), should be no longer than two pages, and will be handed in; I add that I will skim the assignments to get a read on how well people are coming to terms with the difficulties Spenser's text presents, and I will grade them plus, check, minus—but only to encourage attention, not to judge what's "right" or "wrong." At this point I'm asking for effort rather than insight. Skimming, of course, also asks much less from me and allows me to return the papers overnight. As for questions, the following would be typical:

1. Briefly, what happens at the fountain? Who kills whom, and why?
2. In the context of today's class discussion, how helpful are the commonplaces Guyon offers in stanzas 57 and 58 in explaining the causes of the disaster that surrounds him? How much of what he says about pleasure and pain and the mean between them seems true? Does any of it seem false? What would *you* have said (not said?) if you were he in that situation at the fountain?
3. Assuming the dinner atmosphere at Medina's to be typical of daily life there, how would you characterize her house as a place to live? What would be positive for a life under her rule? What might be negative?

If my first day's object was to raise general issues of temperance and of complexities inherent in commonplace wisdom, following days aim both to involve students in the interrogatory structure of cantos 1–7 and to help them see how Spenser's language—the puns, the pronoun mixing, the loosely constructed syntax, the ambiguous modifiers, the playful orthography—gives room for interpretive perspectives on the passing narrative. I often begin a class with five or ten minutes of having students read aloud—sometimes singly, sometimes together—because the archaisms and strange spellings seem much more easily deciphered when one tries to pronounce them. But I spend most time with student responses to the day's questions, for, ideally at least, I will have formulated those questions so as to provide a sense of structure for subsequent classroom conversation. Thus question 1 is intended largely to get things going (though I've been surprised at how difficult many of my students have found even the narrative line). But it also supplies materials for question 2's discussion of Guyon's canto 1 declarations that Amavia's problems result from a failure to "fare . . . atweene" (st. 58) joy and grief, pleasure and pain. That discussion will be lengthy, both because its answer is by no means obvious and because students need to see that the issues involved are foundational to the whole book. For while the principle of the golden mean makes sense in the abstract, it is problematic in particular cases. Exactly how does one find the "mean" between joy and grief or between pleasure and pain? Guyon's theory promotes an ethics of compromise, but what would the midpoint between pain and pleasure actually be?

The problem is in the logic of language: though pleasure and pain (or joy and grief) are in some sense oppositional, they are not really endpoints on a single scale of feeling, so it is difficult to see what "faring atweene" them would be, unless it were having no feeling at all. And even if Guyon's real point is only that you shouldn't indulge in too much grief or too much joy, how would you know in a particular set of circumstances what would be too much? If, after a year-long quest for him, your apparently rescued husband has just died at your feet, leaving you and a newborn child alone and defenseless in the middle of nowhere, how much grief would be reasonable? Does reason even enter into the matter? Can you always just tell yourself to straighten up and get a grip?

These are the issues I'll raise through student discussion, but at some point someone will usually start looking pained and wonder whether, as clever as all this is, Spenser could ever have meant any of it. I want that challenge to arise; if it doesn't I'll bring it up myself, since it provides a transition to question 3. For in my view the house of Medina confirms Spenser's interest in the logic of Guyon's commonplaces by literally representing a "faring . . . atweene" extremes, offering as it does so a picture both comic and sobering. My students' responses to Medina's place have always been particularly interesting. Some students accept without challenge her values of peace at any cost; others note that the price of peace here is an unstable atmosphere of repressed anger, everyone forced onto their best (if not very good) behaviors like children at Sunday service.

My contribution will be to facilitate a dialectic between student experience and Spenser's text. A big part of doing that will be in directing attention toward particular sections of canto 2: "How do you know?" is my most frequent question—what can you cite in the text to warrant your claim? My students always need help with this. They are pretty good about impressions, but they are also quick to move to, and stay with, a level of generalization that leaves the text behind. So I'll keep after them about the dinner, where I focus on the language that reflects the limitations of the "peace" Medina has imposed and on the fact that no real progress has been made, no issue resolved. And I'll ask whether, and if so how, the superlatives with which Guyon later describes Gloriana ("great and most glorious," "all heauenly grace / In chiefe degree," "so great excellence," "rare perfection" [2.40–41]) are consistent with earlier commonplaces forbidding extremes. Finally, I'll also direct them to the comic dimension of the canto's opening fight, where, after picturing Guyon as a ship boldly faring between "two contrary waves," and projecting his victory ("So double was his paines, so double be his prayse"), the narrator suddenly reverses his field and reformulates the battle in terms that render all three knights indistinguishable: "Straunge sort of fight, three valiaunt knights to see / Three combats ioyne in one" (st. 24–26). The shift is as comic as Medina's later intervention is melodramatic, and it's certainly of a piece with the general confusion that reigns here.

But while I certainly will be working at the specifics of the poetry, I won't be fully able to predict where the classroom conversation will end up on any one day. For if I claim that Spenser's is a poetry of conversation rather than a poetry of didactic instruction, then I'll want to allow students room to think and talk about the poem's problematic moral issues on their own terms and not just on mine. Thus as we describe what happens at Medina's I'll also be asking students to imagine real-life situations in which the same moderation-suppression strategy might be tried. Why do people do this? What's in it for them? What are the costs? What are the alternatives?

By the end of this discussion I'm well launched into the book; what I do from here on continues to use student writing as the basis for class discussion but will vary the format. I may, for example, again give three take-home questions, but this time I'll break the class into discussion groups of four to six and assign each group a question. I'll give them fifteen to twenty minutes to compare their written responses and to synthesize a group position; we will then reconvene to spend the rest of the hour presenting the views they come up with. My role with group work of this sort is largely to moderate, but I may also play Atin, challenging claims, proposing counter-examples. In either case, again the goal is to realize in the classroom the problematics engendered by the poetry.

Or, with a different set of cantos—probably cantos 5 and 6—I'll introduce my "what-why" assignment. Again this asks for writing, but it is much more open-ended in the responses it solicits. I introduce the assignment by pointing out the obvious: that, whatever Spenser has written, it could have been otherwise and that reading well requires readers to start both noticing where Spenser makes particularly significant choices ("whats") and thinking about why he makes them ("whys"). In stanza 11 of canto 6, for example, one might notice that after first describing Phaedria's island as "waste and voyd," Spenser ends the stanza with Phaedria's showing Cymocles the "faire" land's "plentifull great store"—a contradiction at the narrative level yet perfectly sensible allegorically: what is waste and void from a moral point of view is fair and plentiful enough when Phaedria's doing the looking.

Such wordplay is, of course, a great Spenserian pleasure, but because my new readers have never learned to see it on their own, I help them focus on linguistic surface features by asking them first to locate three whats for each canto they read and then to supply an accompanying why for every what. Class becomes easy: I just ask students to volunteer whats, then throw the question of why open to the class. When students run out of steam with one suggestion, we simply move on to the next. To be sure, some whats and many whys are pretty fanciful, but even that helps, since it allows the class to work on ways of discriminating between different hypotheses.

Throughout the poem the class will do a lot of close reading; when cantos 9 and 10 raise issues of education's role in fostering a temperance of purpose, however, I will spend at least one day in more general conversation. We'll start from the poem: one study question will ask students to imagine Arthur's and Guyon's texts as if they constituted an entire curriculum and then to reflect on how such a curriculum would correspond to a modern college student's program. Especially as issues of gender and cultural origin have grown more visible at my university, my students have responded well to such questions about the role of literature and history as ways to establish and maintain a personal sense of purpose. But I will also raise questions about the cultural limits of Spenser's particular argument; for though modern American culture has deep affinities with the English Renaissance, we quite obviously owe much to many other sources, and thus the specific contexts of Tudor history and humanism that Arthur and Guyon use to construct their senses of identity and purpose cannot finally be ours.

At the same time, if the texts Spenser imagines as central to the defining of identity can't supply modern American readers a complete sense of identity and purpose, what should we make of his more general argument that action must be literarily and historically educated if it is to be fully moral? Does this not remain a tacit assumption underlying college curricula everywhere? Should it? And if so, how can this ideal of humanities education—at my university, at least, a dimly understood concept at best—be realized? Are there particular texts or subjects or even lines of inquiry that we can now agree on as necessary to the ethical commitments we must make? Are traditional texts (the canon, in effect) no longer necessary? What (indeed) about *The Faerie Queene* itself?

One reason I like this line of inquiry is that it nicely sets a general context within which discussion of canto 12 can sum up the whole of our two weeks' work. My first question for canto 12 will in fact reach back to the very first lines of the proem. For the issue raised there, almost forgotten for much of the book, is of the relation of this poem, and of the public's perception of poets as "idle" and useless fantasizers, to the surrounding culture: "Right well I wote most mighty Soueraine, / That all this famous antique history, / Of some th'aboundance of an idle braine / Will iudged be, and painted forgery." The focus for study questions here will be two: I'll ask students first to find specific lines that describe "art" in canto 12 (many of which, of course, are dyslogistic) and then to think about the paradox implicit in the way Spenser seems to attack artfulness. When Guyon destroys the quintessentially artful bower, after all, he's destroying not just Acrasia's realm but a world of Spenser's own fantasy. Stanzas 76–80 are especially erotic and especially "art"-ful. Does Spenser destroy his bower just to cover up with a tacked-on moralism his own need to indulge in sensual (some would say pornographic) poetry? Questions like this give room to return to book 2's crucial matter of purpose—how one establishes it and what having such a sense of purpose seems to license. In the end, I think, Spenser shows himself quite tolerant of any art (like any other action) so long as it is clearly subordinated to a properly educated (and therefore moral) purpose; but at the same time, he also seems singularly unsympathetic to any art that he feels is not.

Raising questions about the purposes that motivate art thus offers ways to work through canto 12's paradoxical representation of an art that apparently takes aim against itself, but it also leads to a second issue, that of whether Spenser's temperance of purpose is finally one we want to accept at all. For if book 2 argues that temperance should be an active virtue grounded in an educated and resolute understanding of rightful purpose, Guyon's uncompromising destruction of Acrasia's bower in stanza 83 implicitly asks readers to contrast Spenser's new concept of temperance with the earlier and largely discredited temperance of means. Do we in fact want to think that all actions—however extreme—can be justified by claims to high moral purpose? What happens when the purpose someone claims is one we wouldn't ourselves accept? In the long view, after all, one person's high moral purpose has often turned out to be another person's persecution—how will one know which is which? Outside the poem, Spenser used just such a sense of high-minded purpose to rationalize participation in a brutal, bloody effort to impose English culture on the Irish—an effort that now, four centuries later, seems worse than wrong. Would a temperance of moderation—whatever Cymoclean muddles it might have led to—have provided a more "moral" outcome? Especially where moral absolutes seem impossible to agree on, won't a temperance of toleration always have undeniable value? Won't we in fact have to find ways to accommodate both these notions of temperance?

Thus the general direction, and some of the means, by which I teach book 2. It is hard, however, to describe what one does in a classroom or why one thinks one does it. Moreover, though I have in fact done all the things I outline here, I've rarely done them twice in the same way, and I know that I'll change most of them, some drastically, the next time through. Perhaps the only thing that stays constant for me, in fact, is the metaphor of conversation. For because that concept implies a poetry that shifts dynamically as it progresses, when students can imagine themselves in an interactive relation with the poem, they also can resist the impulse to dismiss or accept Spenser's allegory at face value. Instead they can be ready to challenge the commonplaces that in spite of their "simple shew and semblant plaine" (2.1.21) nevertheless mark out for the responsive reader a path to the conceptual center of Spenser's *Faerie Queene*.

NOTES

[1] I use *commonplace* in its modern sense of moral dictum; that sense derives from the more general *loci communes* of classical and Renaissance rhetoric but actually differs considerably. For its Renaissance sense see my entry for "Logic" in *The Spenser Encyclopedia* (ed. Hamilton) and my introduction to *William Temple's Analysis of Sidney's* Apology (Temple 13–26).

[2] All quotations from *The Faerie Queene* are taken from the Smith edition.

[3] Quilligan's term for such lines is "threshold texts"—places at which to enter the poetry (*Milton's Spenser* 62). Quilligan cites 2.1.57 as an example: "The strong through pleasure soonest falles, the weake through smart."

[4] For a reading of Atin's challenge, as well as background concerning Tudor theories of poetic organization, see Webster, "Methode" 36–42.

[5] See *Nichomachean Ethics* 3.9–12, 7.1–10. Aristotle discusses two different virtues that can be translated with the English word *temperance*. The first concerns the "self-controlled" person (*sophron*); the second concerns the "morally strong" person (*enkrates*). These two concepts are by no means equivalent, and one useful description of the dynamic of book 2 would be as a resolution in Christian humanist terms of these models for temperance. I don't normally provide these terms for undergraduates; they haven't needed the Greek to see that the issues of temperance are conceptually complex.

"Painted Forgery": Visual Approaches to *The Faerie Queene*

Clark Hulse

We have all felt the impulse to fire up the projector and show our Spenser classes every slide we can find of Botticelli or Raphael or, if we have been reading Roy Strong, the allegorical portraits of Elizabeth I. We may be less than certain, though, about the exact point of this exercise. Perhaps our slides illustrate Renaissance cultural or aesthetic principles in which Spenser's poetry also participates. Perhaps—though less likely—they clarify the dense allusions of a specific passage in *The Faerie Queene*. The only thing we can be sure of is the sheer pleasure of seeing colored light stream through celluloid.

A certain restraint is in order when we connect *The Faerie Queene* with the visual arts. It is unlikely that Spenser had ever heard of Botticelli or seen works by Raphael, although he makes a passing reference to Michelangelo in his letters to Gabriel Harvey. It is even doubtful that Spenser had seen most of the allegorical portraits of Elizabeth, even though they come from the same milieu as *The Faerie Queene* and share some of its motives. Nor can we assume that painting and vision are the same thing—an issue continually disputed in the history of art—or that every passage in *The Faerie Queene* that strikes us as "visual" is thereby "pictorial."

I do not mean to deny that there are connections between the arts or that those connections should be explored in the classroom—quite the contrary. There are few better ways to approach *The Faerie Queene* than through the visual arts, if one does so with some regard for what the plausible connections might be. And the way to find those plausible connections is not to roll out massive iconographic, epistemic, or period-style frameworks to place between the poem and its students before they have begun to explore it but rather to ask the poem to tell us what it has to do with the visual arts.

The poem's response to our question is likely to be rich and nuanced, leading its readers on an aesthetic excursion of some magnitude. For in asking what the narrative art of *The Faerie Queene* has to do with the visual arts, students must consider the poem's own art, the structure of the poem's metaphors, and the ways in which the poem reflects or imitates both sensory and supersensory reality. In short, the approach to *The Faerie Queene* through the visual arts leads directly to a discussion of its central aesthetic and ideological questions. Allowing students to puzzle over the passages where the poem aligns itself with the visual arts gives them the chance to work through and re-create within themselves Spenser's logic of representation.

This visual analysis—at first concerned not with actual pictures but rather with Spenserian concepts of picture and of portrait—can begin just before the poem itself actually begins, that is, with the last dedicatory sonnet, addressed "To all the Gratious and Beautifull Ladies in the Court" (assuming that the dedicatory sonnets are placed before the poem, as they are in the 1596 and subsequent editions, and not at the end, as in the first folio of 1590):

> The Chian Peincter, when he was requirde
> To pourtraict *Venus* in her perfect hew,
> To make his worke more absolute, desird
> Of all the fairest Maides to haue the vew.[1]

Spenser is alluding here to the story told by Pliny about Zeuxis of Chios. Commissioned to create a picture of Venus to adorn a temple, Zeuxis has the courtesans of Crotona parade past him naked. He chooses the best body parts from among them—a leg here, a breast there—and assembles them in his design for the likeness of Venus. This story, repeated endlessly in Renaissance aesthetic treatises, was a touchstone for theories of mimetic representation. Supplied with that minimal information, students should quickly work out what is at stake in the stanza: how the artist represents an unseen divine object in physical and sensory terms; whether the limited and imperfect features of the flesh can really be combined or transformed into "absolute" art; and how art can simultaneously be "absolute" and "desird" (for "desird" seems momentarily adjectival before resolving into a verb). These are questions easier to pose than to answer, and any further investigation will likely focus on the gendered nature of the issues: how the male artist turns a demand into a desire (note how "requirde" rhymes with "desird"), how the aesthetic and religious are transformed into the sexual, and even how the noumenal wholeness of the goddess is controlled by being cast into mortal flesh and divided into the separate pieces that are subjected to the male view.

With these or similar questions out in the open, the discussion can proceed to Spenser's next stanza, to see which of these possibilities he ratifies, which he denies, and which he simply ignores:

> Much more me needs to draw the semblant trew,
>   Of beauties Queene, the worlds sole wonderment,
> To sharpe my sence with sundry beauties vew,
> And steale from each some part of ornament.

As Spenser applies the Zeuxis story to his own situation, he creates a stanza that is a model for the kind of reading that we have all been taught so well by Paul Alpers in *The Poetry of* The Faerie Queene. The first clause of the second stanza seems to lead us back in the direction of the word "requird" in the first: as Zeuxis needed to portray Venus, so Spenser needs even more to give a true semblance to "beauties Queene." But with the third line of the stanza, we see a different grammatical structure emerge: to make his portrait, Spenser needs much more "to sharpe my sence with sundry beauties vew" in order to "draw the semblant trew." That is, we now read as if there were a comma after "needs" and no comma after "trew."

The shifty syntax releases a centrifugal swirl of speculations. Why is he more in need: because his object is much higher even than Venus or because he as an artist is inferior and unworthy? Does the insistence on "trew" after "semblant" raise the possibility of an art of the false semblant? If we assume "beauties Queene" is Elizabeth, how did we make that leap? If she is the "worlds sole wonderment," has she become the object of a universal gaze, and if so, is it still erotic? Is the phrase "sharpe my sence" similarly erotic? How has he evaded the potential comparison of the court ladies to courtesans? What sense of the illicitness of his own artistic activity makes Spenser describe his poetic imitation as stealing? If all he takes are "ornaments," how can they successfully portray the transcendent beauty of his queen? And is Spenser himself setting out to imitate nature directly, as Zeuxis did, or to imitate previous artists such as Zeuxis?

I will not preempt discussion by answering these questions. Suffice it to say that the licit possibilities of the opening stanza are actualized in the second, the illicit possibilities are momentarily shrugged off, and the two stanzas together express concerns that are raised again and again in the poem. Most especially they appear in two similar pictorial references in the proems to Spenser's several books. The first of these comes in the proem to book 2. Spenser's readers have followed Redcrosse Knight through the bypaths of book 1. They have encountered the good and evil described in the dedicatory sonnet embodied in the visible illusions of Archimago and Duessa and the veiled truths of Una and have seen the difficulty that each presents to mortal understanding. Spenser now pauses at a new threshold

and directs toward himself and his own poem the questions that have thus
been raised:

> Right well I wote most mighty Soueraine,
>   That all this famous antique history,
>   Of some th'aboundance of an idle braine
>   Will iudged be, and painted forgery,
>   Rather then matter of iust memory,
>   Sith none, that breatheth liuing aire, does know,
>   Where is that happy land of Faery,
>   Which I so much do vaunt, yet no where show,
> But vouch antiquities, which nobody can know.
>
> (bk. 2, pr. 1)

Spenser pushes to the surface his only half-submerged doubts about the
adequacy of representation by imagining a skeptical reader who challenges
him about the veracity of his poem. In my experience, students share this
skepticism about mimesis, not only because of the dedicatory sonnet but
also on the basis of their experience with modern and postmodern literature,
and they are likely to seize on the problem posed by Spenser's hypothetical
reader. Once separated from historical records and observed reality, poetry
enters the realm of poetic imagination. But what then is the poet imitating
besides fancy and illusion, "th'aboundance of an idle braine"? A metaphor
from painting again focuses Spenser's fear: is his poem simply a "painted
forgery"? As with the dedicatory sonnet, students attuned to gender issues
will see that the phrase "painted forgery" has sexual resonances as well, for
"painted" suggests equally the work of the visual artist and the work of cosmetics. The false body of the poem, and with it the image of the Faerie
Queene herself, may be no more than the tricked-up copy of a prostitute, designed to stir the base desires already circulating in the idle brains of the poet
and the male reader. Such a poem would be no more than pornography.

The second reference, in the proem to book 3, takes up this fear and directs
it toward the specific problem of the representation of Elizabeth. Spenser
does so by turning again to the precedent of the Greek painters Zeuxis and
Praxiteles:

> But liuing art may not least part expresse,
>   Nor life-resembling pencill it [Elizabeth's chastity] can paint,
>   All were it *Zeuxis* or *Praxiteles*:
>   His daedale hand would faile, and greatly faint,
>   And her perfections with his error taint:
>   Ne Poets wit, that passeth Painter farre
>   In picturing the parts of beautie daint,

> So hard a workmanship aduenture darre,
> For fear through want of words her excellence to marre.
>
> (bk. 3, pr. 2)

All the implications packed into that clipped phrase "painted forgery" are now unpacked into something approaching a mimetic system. The painter has a "daedale" hand, that is, one reflecting both the ingenuity of Daedalus and his skill at mimesis (for Daedalus imitated the flight of birds in his escape from Crete and, according to Vergil, carved the bronze doors of the temple of Apollo at Cumae). As all the arts are mimetic, so each has its ancient masters, and Zeuxis and Praxiteles are invoked here as Homer or Vergil might be in a passage about poetry.

Yet even as he compares the arts, Spenser asserts a hierarchy among them. As we might expect, poetry is said to be superior to painting in the work of "wit," the depiction of the emotions or the invisible soul. But Spenser also claims that poetry is superior in painting's own realm, the visible, and is better able to picture "the parts of beautie daint." This claim is on the surface puzzling, unless we recall that the beauty to be depicted is the chaste beauty of Elizabeth; it is an unseen beauty. The putative superiority of the poet resides precisely in his supposed ability to depict more than the flesh, to depict the transcendent. But this assertion of superiority recoils on itself, for the distance between the visible and invisible may be so great that art may fail to bridge the gap. A depiction of the physical body alone would raise again the specter of lascivious art. Yet if the artist reaches for more, he runs a double risk, not only of producing an art that is morally corrupt but even of corrupting its transcendent object through the mimetic process.

When Spenser turns, in the next stanza, to find his own place in this mimetic system, he is both humble and daring:

> How then shall I, Apprentice of the skill,
>   That whylome in diuinist wits did raine,
>   Presume so high to stretch mine humble quill?
>   Yet now my lucklesse lot doth me constraine
>   Hereto perforce. But ô dred Soueraine
>   Thus farre forth pardon, sith that choicest wit
>   Cannot your glorious pourtraict figure plaine
>   That I in colourd showes may shadow it,
> And antique praises vnto present persons fit.
>
> (bk. 3, pr. 3)

He begins with all the ritual phrases of artistic abasement and belatedness: he is an apprentice, humble and "Lucklesse"; artistic glory "whylome" did reign in such divine wits, but that was long ago. He approaches his task not freely but under constraint. He's stretching. But presume he will; what is constrained perforce must be, if not through his power then through hers. After all, that "choicest wit" Sir Walter Ralegh has depicted her glory in his *Cynthia*. Her royal pardon can clear away the inherent corruption of art, and the very things in art that were the sources of corruption can instead be the sources of its virtue and strength. The gap between the glorious object and the sensory media of imitation means that Spenser cannot depict her "plaine." Instead he will "in colourd showes . . . shadow it." The line is saturated with visual wordplay. "Color" and "shadow" in Renaissance art theory occupy the same place that "style" or "figure" does in Renaissance rhetoric. They make up the third part of the artistic process, which follows after invention and composition or disposition. It is the part most distant from the conceptual grasp of the imagination, the part most involved in the physical appeal to the senses. In short, color and shadow are the outward, potentially deceitful show through which a figure is seen. But that deceitfulness is here purged away or else embraced as the price of art, and Spenser's poem is at last free to proceed.

There is so much in the sonnet and the two proems that one might well pause and ask if these formulations are unique to Spenser and his poem. Needless to say, they are not, although he deploys them with unique skill. Together the stanzas express most of the key dilemmas and possibilities of Renaissance mimetic theory, both regarding imitation per se and as it redounds with political and sexual valences. I find these stanzas a convenient and unexpected place to set up for students the terms of Renaissance aesthetic theory and a place from which students can set to work in finding how various theorists have addressed these questions. Students may be directed immediately to Sidney's *Defence of Poetry* or to recent secondary works such as my own *The Rule of Art*, which analyzes the language of comparison between the arts; Ernest B. Gilman's *Iconoclasm and Poetry in the English Reformation*, which discusses Spenser's suspicion of the mimetic process; or Kenneth Gross's *Spenserian Poetics: Idolatry, Iconoclasm, and Magic*.

Equally, this discussion introduces terms by which we can address basic questions about the uniqueness of Spenser's poem. In an immediate sense, the bodily metaphors of the sonnet and the proem can be linked to the very ideas of a poem's being named after the Faerie Queene and having a "body" composed of several "parts." In *The Poem's Two Bodies*, for instance, David Miller sees the proem to book 2 as a droll aside leading toward the contemplation of the singular and doubled body of Gloriana and the curiously rhetorical-allegorical-sexual body of Alma's castle. Nancy Vickers's classic article "Diana Described" delineates how Petrarch and other sonneteers, by "picturing the parts of beautie daint," could simultaneously glorify and control the noumenous female. Building on Vickers's analysis, Elizabeth Cropper shows how sonneteers conflate aesthetic and sexual discourses to use the portrait of a beautiful female as a metaphor for the artistic beauty of their own works. After applying Vickers's and Cropper's analyses to

Spenser's proem, one can then look at its unique position, both inside and outside the body of the poem. The theoretical discussion about the visual and mimetic nature of the poem is thereby held in a marginal position, and the process of self-accusation and purgation is kept apart from the body of *The Faerie Queene* itself, lest Spenser "her perfections with his error taint."

This may all seem a roundabout introduction to a slide show, but some such discussion of Renaissance mimetic theory and how it bears on the poem is likely to take place in any course, and, if the discussion is sufficiently probing, it will touch on Spenser's notions of what his poem has to do with painting. The key point of strategy here is to have some discussion precede the slide show, so that a method for reading the visual images will already be established. Students of literature are, in my experience, often intimidated by their first contact with visual images. They think they don't have anything to say about them or, rather, don't think that it is appropriate to say what they think. But any reasonably articulate literature major is ready to say a great deal about visual images. This is not simply a matter of imposing a literary-critical vocabulary on the image. Rather, precisely to the extent that there was a shared vocabulary between literary theory and artistic theory in the Renaissance (and, increasingly, in postmodern literary theory and art theory as well), the poems and visual images demand that they be talked about in similar ways and are fully capable of showing the attentive reader or viewer the limits of that shared or comparative vocabulary. Poems and pictures have their own answers to the questions What do you have in common? How are you different? Once we have asked these questions and listened to the answers, *The Faerie Queene* can appear as a critical commentary on Renaissance painting fully as much as the paintings serve as a guide to *The Faerie Queene*.

Take, for instance, the allegorical portraits of Elizabeth, beginning with the famous Ditchley portrait (see fig. 1, p. 26). Viewers will instantly grasp the central fact of the image: that the figure of Elizabeth appears immense, not because of the scale of the figure within the frame but because of its relation to the map beneath her feet and the background of sun and storm. The association to Spenser's principles of mimesis should also be quick. This is not Elizabeth "plain" but Elizabeth "colourd" and "shadowed" to depict her glory. As much as Spenser's proems, this is a work concerned with the inexpressibility of its subjects. Once the central dislocation from realism has been noted, symbolic details will quickly emerge, such as the whiteness of Elizabeth's dress, the Tudor roses, and the pearls in her hair.

Spenser's comparisons of pictorial and poetic rhetoric will likewise have prepared students for another startling feature of the painting, which is that it is conceived of less as a window through which we see Elizabeth than as a surface on which she is written. On the right margin of the painting is a sonnet, mutilated when the canvas was trimmed. The text, which can be found in Strong's *Gloriana*, *The English Icon*, or *Tudor and Jacobean*

Portraits, cannot be fully made out, but its main terms are clearly those of the painted image. Elizabeth possesses the heavenly glory and grace of the sun and the divine power of thunder. The thanks of her subjects flow to her as rivers flow to the ocean. Comparing poem and image, we are reminded that Elizabeth's full nature appears not through the bodily image of the bejeweled queen but only through the interaction of figure, map, background, and inscriptions. If words and visual images each have their limitations, they can through such juxtapositions challenge those limitations, show what is invisible, and say what is beyond words.

As Spenser promises in book 3 to portray Elizabeth "in mirrours more then one," so the Ditchley portrait is just one of the guises under which Renaissance painters "shadowed" her. The Rainbow portrait, probably commissioned by the Cecil family and still in their possession (fig. 2, p. 27), likewise suggests the divineness of the queen. The inscription "Non sine sole Iris" ("The rainbow cannot appear without the sun") either identifies Elizabeth as a messenger bearing peace from its divine source or even identifies her directly with that divine sun. The painting *Queen Elizabeth and the Three Goddesses,* at Windsor (fig. 3, p. 28), painted some three decades earlier, plays on a more elaborate and familiar divine identification. Juno, Minerva, and Venus, who strove to win the golden apple of beauty in the Judgment of Paris, here concede the contest to Elizabeth, who holds the apple metamorphosed into a royal orb. Allegorically she combines sovereignty, wisdom, and beauty in her person, and, grouped with the two ladies-in-waiting behind her, forms the principal member of a group of three modern graces. In creating the sensory image that conveys these abstractions, the painter enacts that same process Spenser attributed to the "Chian Peincter" in his sonnet to the court ladies. He depicts the parts of multiple bodies, both "absolute" and "desird," in his search for the "semblant trew" of the "worlds sole wonderment."

The portraits of Elizabeth produced in England usually reflect the influence, if not the control, of the crown (see Strong's works and John King's *Tudor Royal Iconography*). But those probably produced abroad likewise operate through a political aesthetic that is simultaneously earthly and ethereal. One of the most impressive portraits in large is the Sieve portrait in Siena (fig. 4, p. 29), painted by a descendant of the great Quentin Massys of Antwerp (Rodríguez-Salgado 86–87). We have no evidence that either the painter or the painting was ever in England, but admiration for Elizabeth was widespread in Europe (see Constance Jordan's *Renaissance Feminism: Literary Texts and Political Models*), and Spenser's poem views her in an international as well as a domestic context. I do not discuss the painting at length here, since Julia Walker does so in the following essay in this volume. Suffice it to note that the column to Elizabeth's right is decorated with scenes from Vergil's *Aeneid* that have dynastic implications for Elizabeth and for England's imperial claims. The painting, like Spenser's poem, approaches its subject by a chronological layering, so that the artist can "vouch antiquities" without constraining his wit. The result is that both works show how "antique praises vnto present persons fit."

This reciprocal process of reading the poem through pictures and reading the pictures through the poem extends to portraits of other "present persons" as well. I have found that students appreciate seeing a rogue's gallery of prominent Elizabethans. Portraits of Ralegh, Burghley, Sidney, Leicester, Essex, James of Scotland, and Philip of Spain give a vividness to our accounts of the poem's composition, reception, and historical allegory. These portraits often seem far more "realistic" than those of Elizabeth, but they will yield to the same sort of reading that *The Faerie Queene* suggests for the Ditchley, Rainbow, or Sieve portraits.

Take, for instance, one of the portraits of Ralegh in the National Portrait Gallery (fig. 5, p. 30). He appears suave, handsome, and well-dressed, as befits a member of the court of Gloriana. But quickly the snapshot effect dissipates as the picture surface reveals its signifying details. The limp, delicate, almost boneless right hand, like the hands in both the Ditchley and the Sieve portraits, reminds us that the image before us is dictated as much by period styles and workshop techniques as by observation. Likewise the pearls at Ralegh's ear may recall for us those in Elizabeth's hair in the Ditchley portrait. In the upper left is a crescent moon, which, since the painting is dated 1588, may refer to the crescent formation of the Armada. Hovering face downward, it may also allude to Ralegh's poem *Cynthia*, perhaps suggesting that Ralegh is a kind of man in the moon who needs the reflected sunlight of royal favor if he is to shine.

Like the portraits of Elizabeth and like *The Faerie Queene* itself, the painting is an approximation of its subject, a set of conjectural images aimed at bringing to our senses the multiple aspects of Ralegh's identity. The ornate and glistening surface of the painting, like the metaphoric surface of the poem, is both a lure and a distraction, a bait that draws us toward Ralegh's inner nature and yet threatens to arrest us at the door. The inscription to the left of Ralegh's head, reading "Amor et Virtute," is a later addition, but it captures the metaphoric nature of the painting. Presumably meant to allude to the virtuous passion with which Ralegh adored Elizabeth, it can summarize as well the simultaneous sensuality and transcendence of its own image.

The general principle I am espousing through these examples is the avoidance of any simple referentiality between *The Faerie Queene* and Renaissance pictorial images, in favor of seeing poetic and pictorial arts as parallel forms with common purposes. This principle is clearly operative in Spenser's proems, which use visual metaphors to mark the boundaries between the inner world of poetic fiction and the outer world that calls itself reality. As boundary markers, the proems serve as Spenser's free space for reflection on the most general problems of representation as well as on the specific problems created by his juxtapositions of the visible and the invisible. But the issues of representation raised in this way are obviously not confined to the proems and spill over to the body of the poem, and so likewise our analysis of the visual dimension of *The Faerie Queene* must reach into the narrative itself. Specifically, it must take up the *ekphrases* that punctuate every book of *The Faerie Queene*, the elaborate pictorial scenes that Spenser uses to dramatize his poetic principles in the interior of the poem.

The most important of these *ekphrases* are the fence and gates of the Bower of Bliss (2.12), the "clothes of *Arras* and of *Toure*" in Malecasta's castle (3.1.34), and the "goodly arras of great maiesty" in the castle of Busirane (3.11.28). One can see instantly that all three appear in sites of sexual violence, and hence all three recapitulate the aesthetic of pornographic transcendence I have already sketched out. Particularly successful and subtle is Spenser's description of the gate to the Bower of Bliss, in which was "ywrit" (as if sculpting were writing) the "famous history" of Jason and Medea. Carved in ivory is the ship carrying the lovers away from Colchis:

> Ye might haue seene the frothy billowes fry
> Vnder the ship, as thorough them she went,
> That seemd the waues were into yuory,
> Or yuory into the waues were sent;
> And other where the snowy substaunce sprent
> With vermell, like the boyes bloud therein shed,
> A piteous spectacle did represent,
> And otherwhiles with gold besprinkeled;
> Yt seemd th'enchaunted flame, which did *Creüsa* wed.
>   (2.12.45)

Spenser's stanza anatomizes a process that is simultaneously visual and intellectual, as our minds see the ivory of the gate metaphorically, as representing the waves under the ship, at the same instant that the eye sees it for what it is, artistic material cunningly wrought. Likewise the red ("vermell") and gold decorating its surface are simultaneously inert pigments and the blood and flames of Medea's crimes. The entire metaphoric process of poetry is here cast into visual terms and arrested before our eyes, so that we may see ourselves seeing. And in that process of seeing, we are implicated, as if by nature as well as by art, in the matrix of gendered violence that the episode of the Bower of Bliss unfolds. It is, indeed, a gendered violence that art here seems to partake of by its very nature.

As dazzling as this stanza is as a revelation of Spenser's symbolic practices, it reveals yet another artistic process that is simultaneously pictorial and poetic. For this stanza, like the other *ekphrases* of the poem, compresses and encapsulates the narrative action in a way that throws the peculiarly poetic dimensions of storytelling into relief. It sketches out the entire long "history" of Jason and Medea, which in the *Argonautica* of Apollonius Rhodius is the matter of many books. It then compresses that history into a few lines, first by picking out two key incidents, the murders of Medea's brother and of Creüsa, then by focusing on details that are both peripheral and salient—the color of blood and the brilliance of fire. The narrative is "pictorialized" through this compression and selection, in contrast to the techniques of extension and elaboration by which Spenser's poetic narrative normally proceeds. The same narrative processes can be traced in the *ekphrases* of book 3. The depiction of Venus and Adonis in the tapestries of Malecasta's castle demonstrate the operation of the salient "pictorial" detail. The tapestries at the castle of Busirane, by contrast, emphasize the amassing of "many faire pourtraicts, and many a faire feate" (3.11.29), by which the matter of an epic is compressed into nineteen stanzas.

Again, these "visual" features of Spenser's poem are not poetic renderings of actual paintings. Rather, they are explorations of the common purposes and common methods of poetry and painting. If we look at Renaissance narrative paintings, we can see the same features running, as it were, in reverse. Titian's stunning *Rape of Europa* (fig. 6, p. 31) selects the same salient detail that Spenser does to encapsulate the entire narrative. Europa has mounted the back of the docile bull, but as it wades into the sea, she suddenly realizes that some dangerous power controls both the beast and her:

> Ah, how the fearefull Ladies tender hart
> Did liuely seeme to tremble, when she saw
> The huge seas vnder her t'obay her seruaunts law.
> (3.11.30)

Like Spenser, Titian focuses on Europa's moment of confusion and terror and on the bull's surge of force. As Leonard Barkan puts it, "The painter devotes himself exclusively to the terrors of the abduction, with no reference to wedding or triumph to balance the fears associated with transformation and sexuality" (*Gods* 201). Flung across Jove's back, Europa is half ecstatic, half losing her balance. Her arm shields her, but her knees are open to the cupids above her, and to the backward glance of the bull. Spenser endows his reader with a resistance to erotic violence through the figure of Britomart surveying the tapestries of Busirane. In contrast, Titian has positioned Europa's body so that the viewer is inscribed in the rape. In the near distance (fig. 7, p. 32), Europa's companions scream for help, but the majestic sweep of the far background hints at the vastness of the forces at work here and the futility of human fear.

Titian achieves a superb compression in this painting. By placing it in a series of mythological canvases (which Titian himself called his *poesie*), he achieves narrative extension as well, comparable to Spenser's "many faire pourtraicts and many a faire feate" of love. To the same group with the

Europa belong his other great Ovidian works of the 1550s: *Venus and Adonis, Perseus and Andromeda, Danae and Jupiter, Diana and Actaeon,* and *Diana and Callisto*. The bodies of mortals and deities intertwine, echoing and mirroring one another from canvas to canvas, as the themes of desire, violence, and transformation similarly echo from scene to scene, creating patterns of interlacement akin to those of romance.

Titian's technique of grouping multiple canvases can be contrasted with that of a Renaissance book illustrator who must somehow cope with the narrative extension of poetry within a single illustration. Particularly relevant are the illustrations to the 1584 edition of Ariosto's *Orlando furioso,* which employ a "ribbon" composition of sequential scenes running from the front to the back of the scene to capture the narrative sequence of the poem. In the illustration to canto 33, for instance (fig. 8, p. 33), Bradamante views the frescoes in the castle of Sir Tristram, exactly as Britomart would view the tapestries at the castles of Malecasta and Busirane. In a sequence of panels running across the wall from upper left to lower right, the engraver depicts the inset narrative—in effect, the *ekphrasis*—of Ariosto's poem. On or out the back wall, like an inset narrative, runs the main narrative of the canto, beginning at the lower left and twisting its way up and back to the top center.

To these can be added other programmatically grouped images that take on narrative elaboration. In *Literature and the Visual Arts in Tudor England,* for example, David Evett proposes Raphael's Vatican *logge* and Primaticcio's gallery at Fountainebleau as analogues to Spenser's art. "Reading" such images as narratives makes more evident the comparably elaborate and subtle narrative techniques of *The Faerie Queene*. To speak in structural terms, the images enact a process of dilation and compression along a horizontal, or narrative, axis that gives temporal extension to a medium too often assumed to lack any narrative or temporal dimension. Likewise, the process of metaphoric illuminations and opacities that Spenser's poem so often exhibits, and that so often disrupt or divert narrative flow, can be thought of as a vertical, or symbolic, axis intersecting the horizontal axis of narrative. This vertical axis is the narrative equivalent to that focus on the "instantaneous" single scene that characterizes the pictorial arts of the Renaissance. While later aestheticians such as Lessing would claim that the narrative and the pictorial, the temporal and the visual are somehow mutually exclusive, no such exclusion seems to be sustainable within Spenser's aesthetics. Taken together, the horizontal axis of narrative and the vertical axis of the visual image generate separate and complementary modes for investigating art, modes that can be used simultaneously to "read" Renaissance pictures and to read the "visual" elements of *The Faerie Queene*.

At the beginning of this essay I speak against the deployment of massive iconographic, epistemic, or period-style frameworks at an early point in one's approach to *The Faerie Queene*. I do not in that breath mean to deny out of hand the existence of a zeitgeist or the potential meaningfulness of such terms as *mannerism* or *the age of correspondences*. On the contrary, I have tried to emphasize how Spenser's *ekphrases* act as mediating elements that reach out from the poem to its cognitive and ontological frames or indeed even act as the poem's inward agent of cognitive framing. But such frames are contingent rather than absolute structures, and they arose in the minds of Renaissance poets and readers in response to specific dilemmas in the process of representation. It seems to me wisest, therefore, both as a general epistemological principle and as a specific pedagogical strategy, that inquiry should begin not by delineating the solution but by creating or re-creating the dilemmas in the minds of one's students and perhaps in one's own mind as well. The frameworks will then arise, as if by themselves and as if anew, as shelters from the hard rain of questioning. Derived this way, the frameworks retain their true appearance as hypotheses, as propositions, and as projections of yearning and desire. The labor of literary criticism can in turn be dedicated simultaneously to skepticism and to the preservation of the often alien mystery of its objects of inquiry. It can, in sum, be a labor of restraint amidst the rich feasting of the eye.

NOTE

[1]All quotations from *The Faerie Queene* are taken from the Roche edition.

From Allegory to Icon: Teaching Britomart with the Elizabeth Portraits

Julia M. Walker

When I teach *The Faerie Queene* in any context other than a senior seminar —British Literature I, Introduction to the Epic, Sixteenth-Century British—I focus on the Britomart narrative in books 3, 4, and 5. After teaching all of book 1 and cantos 1, 7, and 12 of book 2, I assign cantos 1, 2, 3, 9, and 12 of book 3; cantos 1 and 6 of book 4; and cantos 1–7 and 9 of book 5. (If pressed for time, I do only canto 7 of book 5 and provide a lavish context through storytelling.) While this approach has some obvious drawbacks (the slighting of the garden of Adonis being the worst), there are many benefits: I can stress the development of the woman warrior from Camilla through the Italian epics; the students can follow one narrative through the tangle of Ariostoesque plots and cast of thousands, appreciating the scope of the latter while keeping their sanity; and the students, enabled to bring up themselves the question of whether Spenser is actually doing what he says he's going to do with the image of Elizabeth and therefore in the poem as a whole, allow me in turn to raise questions about closure and book 6.

In both the letter to Ralegh and the proem to book 3, Spenser speaks of figuring forth the public Elizabeth in the invisible Gloriana and the private woman in the virginal Belphoebe. I start with the phrase "mirrours more then one" in the proem and suggest that this ambiguity (also discussed in Diana Henderson's essay in the present volume) in conjunction with the title of that particular textual mirror—the Legend of Britomart—allows Britomart to emerge as the unnamed third image of Elizabeth. Like Elizabeth, Britomart is the motherless daughter of a king, and the Protestant Spenser would have argued that she was also sisterless, whereas Belphoebe has both a mother and a sister and no father, and we know nothing of Gloriana's background. From the beginning of the Britomart story, therefore, Spenser is telling us one thing and showing us another—an important principle of interpretation. After a brief lecture on the practical political and philosophical problems facing a female monarch in 1558, I show a series of slides of portraits, stressing the progression from the generic female figure to the allegorical figure to the much more subtle and complex statements of the Siena Sieve portrait (see fig. 4, p. 29). The Sieve portrait, employing as it does the intertextuality of Petrarch and Vergil, is clearly even more of an exercise in thesis-and-support reading than the allegorical *Elizabeth and the Three Goddesses* (fig. 3, p. 28) and *Elizabeth and Pax*. When the students realize this, they are hot to read the Armada portrait, the Ditchley portrait (fig. 1, p. 26), and finally the Rainbow portrait (fig. 2, p. 27).[1] After seeing what can be done with a public image in painting—which they generally had assumed to be a less complex medium than poetry—they turn to the poetic allegory as both careful and deeply suspicious readers, picking up on all the references to painting in the book 3 proem. Having seen what one series of portraits can accomplish, we can look for visual representations of political, social, and sexual identity as we move from the early descriptions of an allegory of female fears in cantos 1 and 2 of book 3 (with Britomart's inability to read either the Venus and Adonis tapestries or the mirror image of a male knight), through the allusions that link her with both Dido and Aeneas, on to the rescue of Amoret and to Britomart's partial reading of Busirane's walls, to the mirroring meeting with Artegall, the transformation of imagery in Isis Church, and the battle with Radigund—a representation every bit as radical as that of the Siena portrait—concluding with Britomart's complex statements about women's rule and her line "farewell fleshly force" (5.7.40).[2] We look next at Mercilla, as safely iconic a figure as any in the later portraits. Allowing—even encouraging—the students to read Britomart as an Elizabeth figure gives them the opportunity to formulate many complex questions about art, and especially about poet-artists who discuss the goals of their works. They see that painting and poetry can have more than a metaphoric connection, and they realize that no artwork of any kind can be taken out of its social and political context.

Suggesting that the royal houses of Renaissance Europe were "consciously . . . intensifying the mystique of monarchy" because rulers were "assuming more and more of a messianic role in an age which had witnessed the breakdown of the universal church and the shattering of the old cosmology," Roy Strong argues for the consequent importance of images of the monarch (*Gloriana* 11). Recent work on the Siena Sieve portrait and the Rainbow portrait has established in impressive detail just how true this intensification had become for court artists in the last years of Elizabeth's reign (Goldberg, *Endlesse Worke*; Belsey and Belsey; Jordan, "Representing"; D. L. Miller, *Poem's Two Bodies* 147–53). A comparison of three portraits gives us a clear measure of how radical was the shift from Elizabeth's image as a generic royal virgin to her representation as a unique icon of female power. In *Queen Elizabeth and the Three Goddesses*, we see an allegorical revision of the choice of Paris, with Elizabeth holding both the orb and the elevated position. Juno and Minerva are painted in postures of defeat—the former turning away, having lost a shoe, the latter beginning to turn and holding up her palm in acknowledgment of a greater power. Venus, however, is at rest with Cupid at her side. The face-off between Elizabeth and Venus raises the issue of the queen's personal life, balanced then on the margin of her public image (Windsor Castle, in the middle background, serves as a reminder of her public place) but certainly not a real question, even if posed allegorically. In the Siena Sieve portrait, Elizabeth's public image is so firmly established that it may be represented by details—the globe with England uppermost, the imperial column, the medallion with the crown of the Holy Roman Empire, the court scene in the upper right corner. The sieve—icon of virginity since Petrarch's story of Tuccia, a vestal virgin who defended her maligned chastity by carrying water in a sieve from the Tiber to her temple—provides the central image of the painting, but visual allusions to both Vergil's story of Dido and Aeneas (the other nine medallions are scenes from book 4 of the *Aeneid*) and the negotiations over Elizabeth's possible French marriage (the short man in French dress is being blocked by a figure who is probably Christopher Hatton, an opponent of the match) provide subtexts that offer a clear statement of either policy or caution: look at the Dido story and consider what happens to successful queens who become involved with foreign princes; look at the Aeneas story and consider the personal sacrifices that must be made for one's country. Neither reading suggests a wedding. Nor does the virginal mask of youth of the Rainbow portrait suggest a bride. Here we see a goddess, her beauty and icons of power deliberately represented as beyond the boundaries of reality. The serpent of wisdom on her sleeve, the crescent moon on her head, wing-shaped lace springing from her shoulders, her dress covered with the eyes and ears of prudence, Elizabeth herself becomes the sun without which there is no rainbow. The association between the masculine sun and the male monarch has here been completely represented, but in the process all contact with reality has been rejected and Elizabeth is presented as a collection of powerful icons.

Spenser's Elizabeth portrait surpasses all the painted panels, however richly encoded with meanings, because it is a changing image, one altered by confrontation with physical and political realities. Because the epic portrait is linear, it presents its central figure to the eye only gradually, as the veil of allegory is withdrawn by the poem's narrative to reveal the image of a virgin whose dynastic motherhood is merely fictive. When we view the forty-five-year narrative of Elizabeth's portraits, we see many parallels between the allegorical narrative and the queen who turned her virginity from promise of physical motherhood into an icon of national motherhood. With the example of her sister, Mary Tudor (whose marriage to Philip of Spain was so unpopular), and with a legal system in which the female monarch could be recognized only as a sort of honorary male, Elizabeth might well have been as indecisive as Britomart seems in the opening cantos of book 3. Elizabeth's own policy, mirrored by her portraits, relied heavily on dynastic power's being gradually transformed from the literal to the iconographic. That Britomart's story follows the same pattern of development is, I suggest, no accident.

After making the connection between poetic representation and painting in the book 3 proem (Clark Hulse discusses this passage in his essay in this volume), Spenser begins his own complex word picture. In books 3, 4, and 5, Spenser shows us one thing with the story (the action) and tells us another with the narrative (the way in which the story is worded). The poetic story—the (hi)story of Elizabeth's "ancestor" Britomart—is foregrounded by the proem and by the generic expectations that accompany Spenser's invocation of Ariosto, only to be gradually erased by the narrative of these three books.[3] If the story and the narrative were consistent, we would find a wedding in book 5; instead we lose sight of Britomart as she bids farewell to fleshly force and to the fiction of dynastic motherhood, finding instead the image of Mercilla. Using as pigment the fiction of a dynastic epic and framing his portrait with allusions to two epic couples—thus overgoing the painter of the Sieve portrait—Spenser offers to the queen a text that mirrors her own multivalent image (Gent 46, 47; Yates, *Astraea*).

The multiple images of Elizabeth—monarch, virgin, mother, warrior, lover, goddess—are daunting enough to make any artist "fear through want of words her excellence to marre." Monarchy and dynasty are inextricably linked, but to avoid any suggestion of failure on Elizabeth's part, Spenser must find a way to transcend the dynastic paradigm. By setting up the complex metaphor of portraiture and mirroring, Spenser offers his own text as "mirrours more then one" in which Elizabeth can see herself. No less graphically than the Siena Sieve portrait in its depiction of Dido's love-inflamed death, Spenser—through Britomart's struggles with various manifestations of fleshly force—undertakes to figure forth the sexual as well as the political implications of Elizabeth's radical transformation from queen and virgin to Virgin Queen.

Beginning very much "in the middle of things," book 3 opens the epic-within-an-epic that continues through books 4 and 5. In canto 1, the reader knows the secret of Britomart's identity but not her story. When she looks at the Venus and Adonis story in the tapestries and fails to understand it, Britomart's chastity is a mere absence of sexual knowledge, painted without the confusing complexities of her real history, as we learn in canto 2. Britomart's problems, revealed to us in increasingly complex images, have been neither assuaged nor displaced by her transmogrification from a weak, sick girl into a successful knight; they have merely been placed below the level of her immediate consciousness—for Britomart, although an allegorical figure, represents both the physical and psychological elements of the female—unlike the simple allegory of *Elizabeth and the Three Goddesses*. In the Castle Joyous, Britomart misreads the allegory and is wounded because of her failure to remember sexual lessons she has already learned.

This failure, produced by denial, goes far to explain the lies Britomart tells to Redcrosse at the beginning of canto 2. Denying the reality of her girlhood, she gives Redcrosse a tale that conflates the childhoods of Vergil's Camilla and Tasso's Clorinda—significantly, two women who live and die not only as warriors but as virgins. After this lie, the narrator gives us the real story of Britomart as a young woman looking in her father's mirror. When we realize that her Amazon childhood is a fiction, we also realize that Britomart's desire for a male-defined identity has grown out of, not been manifested within, the mirror vision. Like Elizabeth, Britomart also sees "mirrours more then one": first the mirror of romance and then the mirror of public policy in which a ruler may see his enemies. After first seeking in vain for her own face, Britomart thinks again and looks once more to see that which might "to her selfe pertaine" (st. 22). According to the narrative of stanza 23, the particular "that" for which Britomart looks is a husband (lines 5–6). What she sees is Artegall.

Spenser's language in stanza 23 figures forth vividly the psychological construct we now call the unconscious; Britomart is not actively seeking, or thinking about, a husband, but the idea is in her mind. Britomart—while seemingly unaffected—is actually the unknowing victim of Cupid's secret arrows, wounded in the arena of public policy that is the mirror, while the reader is told that she is unaware "that her vnlucky lot / Lay hidden in the bottome of the pot" (st. 26). "Unlucky lot"? This phrase and the description of "the false Archer, which that arrow shot / So slyly," is the language with which Vergil speaks of Dido. Dido became "unlucky" when the gods placed her in a position where her private emotions became a threat to the public good. By using the mirror, an instrument of public policy, for private (however heedless) pleasure, Britomart may have placed herself in a similar situation—or her status as her father's (unsuitable) female heir may have so placed her.

After her mirror vision, Britomart falls ill and speaks "fearefully," arguing with her nurse that it is not love from which she suffers, describing what she has seen in the mirror with negatives (st. 38). Britomart goes on to detail her ills in terms more sensuously realistic than allegorical (st. 39), describing symptoms closer to the particular discomforts of the menstrual cycle than to the "ulcer" she diagnoses in herself. The vision of Artegall generates in Britomart physiological and psychological reactions, both unpleasant—the first, however, necessarily and naturally linked to female sexuality, the second a sign of conflict over that sexuality. At the end of the canto, we are left with the word picture of Britomart consumed by the cruel flame of a love that is somehow wrong, once again bringing to mind Vergil's Dido.[4] Britomart, shot by Cupid's arrow, feels the physical response to her vision of Artegall, suffers from bad dreams, tells her female confidante of her pain, is told by Glauce that what she feels is only natural, is not entirely comforted by this, seeks comfort in the church, and remains the victim of burning love. Dido turns for comfort to her sister, Anna; both narrative and story in book 4 of the *Aeneid* form a pattern that Spenser's poem shadows. Anna argues that love should not be viewed as unnatural, and Dido thus goes to the temple to seek confirmation of this; but her state of mind is such that she cannot benefit from whatever religion might offer, and unhappy Dido still burns with ill-fated love. The problems raised by such a reading, however, seem—initially at least—even more troubling than the problem it lays to rest. But Spenser does not confine Britomart to the paradigm of Dido; he allows her to follow in the footsteps of Aeneas (Gross 154). Guided by Glauce, Britomart finds Merlin in his cave. After hearing the dynastic history, Britomart—like Aeneas—is changed and pursues her destiny with vigor.

Britomart arrives in Merlin's cave still shadowing Dido, inflamed by an imperfectly understood passion and weakened by a lack of self-knowledge. She leaves somewhat comforted and with a specific goal of public identity, reshaped into the model of Aeneas. Her gender, however, does not conform to the pattern she must follow. Like the artist of the Sieve portrait of Elizabeth, Spenser presents the allusion to a male Aeneas through a female figure, although the tradition of epic romance provides the poet with a solution not available to the painter. Acting at Glauce's "foolhardy" suggestion (3.52), Britomart dons her father's armor and identifies herself with the figure presented to her by her father's magic mirror. That Glauce introduces her suggestion with a catalog of women warriors is, I believe, less significant than her remarks about Britomart's person: Britomart can become "a Martiall mayd" (2.9) because she can be made to look and act like a man, like an Aeneas or an Achilles. But in secret she remains a woman, like Penthesilea or Camilla or Clorinda, women who do not marry but die. This secret, however, is one of which only the reader has full knowledge, for Britomart seems (still) as confused about her sexuality as the others will be who see her in armor. For unlike her literary antecedents, Britomart does not proclaim herself a woman warrior, much as Elizabeth forbore to change the gender of the ideal ruler, choosing instead to find ways to speak of herself, legally and metaphorically, as a man. Indeed, as Andrew Belsey and Catherine Belsey remind us, Elizabeth's pose in portraits often makes graphic reference to portraits of her father (12–18).

Britomart goes on her way through the next seven cantos, meeting with success (her encounter with Marinel in canto 4) and failure (her wound in 1.65), but avoiding the problems raised by her dual identity. Without getting sidetracked into Busirama (or the Busirane Tournament of Interpretation), I would point out that the episode has more to do with Amoret than with Britomart, for all that it falls at the end of her book (Roche, *Kindly Flame* 72–88). At this moment in the poem, Britomart has more in common with most icons than she does with most women and so, again within Spenser's poem, does Elizabeth. Britomart's private, female self is now a secret, placed outside the bounds of representation by circumstances, by other figures in the poem, and most of all by herself, just as Elizabeth's public image as nonvirginal female was displaced by herself in lines such as those she wrote to Parliament in 1563: "though I can think [that marriage is] best for a private woman, yet I do strive with myself to think it not meet for a prince" (Neale 127). In canto 12, Britomart is less a private woman than a prince, and every time she comes close to gaining a realization of her female self—as in her first encounter with Artegall—she is diminished, weakened by secrets, by fear, by "secret fear." Yet both the story of the poem and the tradition seem to argue that she must accept—nay, achieve—the realization of that private female identity. Britomart's presentation as a conflation of the figures of Dido and Aeneas therefore constitutes the middle ground that will keep Elizabeth—married to no man but to a nation—from taking offense at the literal implications of the dynastic references. This would explain why Britomart does not recognize Amoret's sexual fears as her own. It does not, however, explain how we are to read Britomart's sexuality.

As long as Britomart's sexuality is located within the paradigm of dynastic epic, we must read it realistically. If, however, we see the dynastic construct as a fiction, as the poetic equivalent of an iconic symbol in a painting—such as the miniatures on the pillar in the Sieve portrait—we can look beyond this foregrounded image to the main figure. The image adds richness to the central figure, as the globe in the Sieve portrait adds a cosmic dimension to Elizabeth's monarchy; but the globe in the portrait does not suggest that Elizabeth literally rules the world. Neither does the fiction of dynasty mean that Britomart is going to marry and have children. As the eye moves beyond the globe in the portrait, so does the reader move beyond the suggestion of dynasty within the poem. By choosing to begin Britomart's odyssey of self-knowledge with a literally untrue but metaphysically and psychologically significant mirror image, after calling attention to Elizabeth's mirror images in the proem, Spenser is reminding us of the complexity of this image: mirror of truth, mirror of vanity; mirror as text, text as mirror. The image of the mirror becomes the portrait of a multivalent image: Elizabeth.

How, then, can we read Elizabeth looking into the textual mirror/portrait of Britomart's quest? By watching Elizabeth watch Britomart turn herself from a woman looking for a husband to beget a dynasty into an icon figuring forth the elements of just rule to achieve immortality. If Britomart is one of Elizabeth's mirrors, what happens when Britomart comes face-to-face with her own mirror vision? In canto 6 of book 4, Britomart sees not a mirror vision but a flesh-and-blood Artegall. Significantly, much of this canto's vocabulary reflects for us the mirror scene in book 3, as the two knights mirror each other's actions. But it is even more important, I believe, that between Artegall's and Britomart's recognition scene and its extension in the conflicted wooing of stanzas 40 and following comes Scudamour's plaintive inquiry about Amoret. Instead of reading this as a comic incursion in a long-delayed love scene, I suggest that it serves as a reminder to the reader of a larger pattern being sketched out, as Britomart's quest is not completed by finding Artegall. Both the conventions of dynastic epic and society's conventional resolution of women's lives—they marry princes (of one sort or another) and live happily ever after—militate against easy recognition of Spenser's revisionist strategies. He uses the reader's expectations as pigments applied to canvas, softening the contrast between his narrative and his story. As we can see by looking at Elizabeth's public portraits, there are no icons or patterns of representation immediately identifiable as those of a female monarch. Elizabeth's court painters had to rely on recognizable icons in new context: a phoenix jewel, an ermine with a lacy crown around its neck, a sieve associated with an imperial crown, a single pearl where a codpiece should be. Just as the court painters force us to reread those icons, so Spenser leads us through recognition into revision.

I here raise more strongly my suggestion that we suspend our belief in Spenser's dynastic intentions, what I call his dynastic fiction. If we look at the poem in the way Spenser has taught us to from book 1 on—with structure and composition as functions of meaning—we see neither wedding nor nursery in Britomart's journey. For the meaning of her quest we must look to Isis Church and to her dream. Britomart's dream is the crucible in which the major elements of her mirror vision, her victory in the house of Busirane, and the hermaphroditic Venus of book 4 come together; heating this crucible is the tension between two types of allegorical reality (or nonreality)—the dynastic reality of English history and the iconographic reality of Elizabeth's reign. Through her dream, Britomart fuses the two fictions into one; she becomes mother not of a dynasty of Englishmen but of a dynasty of virtues.

That Isis Church is intricately related to her other significant adventures is made immediately clear. What Britomart sees in the Isis statue forms a palimpsest of iconography with elements of those other statues: the statue of Cupid, which she has seen, and the statue of Venus, which she has heard described. Her dream is a prophecy of what might be if she continues to follow the path the poem has set for her; it is a warning. To say that Britomart, in her dream, identifies with or becomes the Isis statue is too easy. Most critics concur with Hamilton that the female pronouns of these stanzas refer to both Britomart and the idol/goddess she is becoming. This presents no serious problem until we come to the point where the crocodile is beaten back by "the Goddesse with her rod" (5.7.15). Britomart, whose dream appearance is so carefully described in stanza 13, has no rod. Britomart and the idol are two separate figures, their separation emphasized by the narrative, in which all other female pronouns refer to Britomart (except "her rod"), whereas Isis is always called "Goddesse" or "Idole."

In a sense, Britomart's dream of bringing forth a lion tells Britomart nothing she did not already know. But, like the Siena Sieve portrait of Elizabeth, it presents to her unavoidable connections between events she has perceived separately and over a long time; thus her reaction is the most significant part of the entire episode: she awakes "full of fearefull fright, / And doubtfully dismayd through that so vncouth sight" (st. 16). True, when the priest gives his dynastic reading of the dream, Britomart is "much . . . eased in her troublous thought" (st. 24), but the dream that the priest is reading is not the dream Britomart has. The "misreading" is not the priest's fault, for he can only read what Britomart recounts, "As well as to her minde it had recourse" (st. 20). What the narrator is telling us with this line is that Britomart does not or cannot report the whole truth of the dream.

Britomart denies what she has dreamed just as she denied what the mirror vision offered her.

This denial takes concrete form in canto 7 of book 5. When Britomart fights with and kills the Amazon Radigund, she subdues the part of female power that can, by its exclusionary nature, be read as a threat to male empowerment. But because of Artegall's lapse she is unable simply to place herself within the male-dominated paradigm of the dynasty. Artegall, like the crocodile of her dream, has been humbled by a woman. Britomart awoke from her dream "dismayd" by her "vncouth" union with just such a figure. She must find a place for herself within the poem, but that place cannot be with Radigund, whose female power threatens the natural order and continuity of life, as did the rule of Mary Tudor; nor can it be with Artegall, whose male power has been compromised by defeat at the hands of one woman and rescue at the hands of another. Like Elizabeth, Britomart in the closing stanzas of canto 7 feels responsibility for the larger social order without being able to find any place for herself within that order. Spenser foregrounds this disordered order with a reference to Homer: "No so great wonder and astonishment, / Did the most chast *Penelope* possesse, / To see her Lord, that was reported drent, / And dead long since" (st. 39). Britomart's wonder, astonishment, and uncertain fears are indeed greater than Penelope's, for—as Spenser here cleverly reminds us—it is Britomart who has been out having the adventures *and* remaining chaste while Artegall has donned woman's clothes and done the very woman's work of Penelope and her ladies, with none of the Greek queen's strength or cleverness but through his own failure. Here, I suggest, Britomart is presented as greater than both Penelope and Odysseus—an androgynous image not unlike the Dido/Aeneas allusions of book 3—while Artegall is both less powerful than Penelope and more wretched than the king disguised as a beggar.

What can Britomart do when she is confronted with such a vision? How can she privilege—or even repair—such a society? Any action she takes will further violate the order of a male-dominated universe, an order already damaged by Radigund. To help this society, Britomart must place herself outside it. Her questions to Artegall in stanza 40 also question the justice of a society that can both define roles of sex and power and then make those roles inaccessible to one who is ambiguously placed by circumstance. As closely as he dares, Spenser is depicting the predicament facing Elizabeth when she ascended the throne. In stanzas 41–43 Britomart deals with her situation in much the way Elizabeth came to terms with hers; in stanzas 44–45 the poet provides, as did Elizabeth, a rhetorical smoke screen that will prevent the radical action from threatening the sensibilities of the established order.

After asking her five questions in stanza 40, Britomart answers herself with the only solution available to her: "Then farewell fleshly force." The literal, fleshly level of dynastic empowerment is no longer a possibility; there remains only the power of the icon. In stanzas 41–43 Spenser presents his most carefully crafted conflict between narrative and story. The story restores Artegall's male garments, outlaws female rule, and returns Artegall to the action of the poem, leaving Britomart "sad and sorrowfull." The narrative, on the other hand, shows us a Britomart who never relinquishes, and indeed adds to, her control of the action. In stanza 41 all the active verbs are Britomart's; Artegall is presented only in the passive. The difficult action of stanza 42 mirrors the policy of Elizabeth when she found herself on the throne, following the rule of a wrong-thinking woman. She must privilege her own position without changing the position of all women; she must privilege the male-dominated social order without losing the means of empowerment. She must, as Spenser openly admits, be both Gloriana and Belphoebe, public queen and private virgin. She must, in fact, be both in one; she must be Britomart as she has been so complexly presented in books 3, 4, and 5. The female power that Britomart "restores" to men's subjugation is that of dynastic reality, linked to physical force, to blood, and to the "secret feare" of sexuality, but Britomart is no longer a dynastic figure. She has instead become a "Goddesse" (st. 42) to be adored for her wisdom, far removed from the physical girl of book 3, canto 2, and very close to her final representation as Mercilla in book 5, canto 9. Britomart of book 5, canto 7, the narrative tells us, changes the "forme of common weale" by "restoring" women to "mens subiection"; and yet it is the men who needed to be "restored." Stanza 42 constitutes a double negative of story and narration that cancels itself out. In stanza 41 Britomart restores Artegall's private person to his place in the social order. In stanza 43 Britomart restores Artegall's public person to a position of control: she frees the other captive knights and makes them "sweare fealty to *Artegall*." But Britomart is still giving the orders; her actions are still presented in the active voice, the men's in the passive. As did Elizabeth, she limits the power of other women but not her own. At the end of stanza 43, Artegall—ultimately still the object acted on—leaves "Vppon his first aduenture, which him forth did call."

In stanza 44 we find the rhetoric of romance—functioning much as do the rhetorical and visual allusions to Petrarch in the Sieve portrait—masking the overt statements of political power. Britomart recognizes that the social order depends on establishing the honor of the knight of justice. Having done so, Britomart departs from the scene and from the poem. When she bids farewell to fleshly force she finally achieves what she has been striving for since her first sight of Artegall in the mirror: a way "her anguish to appease" (st. 45). She renounces the physical world and her place in it as a woman; by privileging iconographic lessons of Busirane's house, the temple of Venus, and Isis Church above the discourse of dynastic prophecy, Britomart moves out of the poem as a fleshly force so that, like Elizabeth, she may appear as an icon of justice.

In the Isis Church dream, Spenser begins to depict Britomart's identity as a dynastic mother; but the vision of that identity, compounded of past and present knowledge and of dynastic prophecy, is somehow wrong and leaves her "doubtfully dismayd." She becomes not the mother of a fleshly force but an icon, a "Goddesse," which has neither sex and both sexes—both Dido and Aeneas, both Odysseus and Penelope. The offspring of an icon must be an abstraction—not flesh and blood but public policy. As for the larger pattern of the poem, this iconic representation explains why we look for an end-of-book set piece built for Britomart and find instead Mercilla's court. In book 5, canto 9, stanzas 27–34, representation of Mercilla is a palimpsest of the iconography of Britomart's mirror vision and quest, a surface as densely inscribed and as far removed from fleshly reality as was the Rainbow portrait from a monarch in her sixties. The flesh and blood Britomart of book 3, canto 2, has become an icon of justice, reinscribed as the perfectly allegorical Mercilla, who can be read openly as a representation of Elizabeth. As Spenser anoints the historical wounds left by Mary Stuart's execution with the balm of Duessa's trial, he is also giving us the closing vision of his linear portrait, the Elizabethan mirror trick begun in book 3. We are faced with the reality of a poem that gives us not a dynasty of Englishmen but a dynasty of ideas, of virtues. Britomart's dynasty has become a fiction that is first deflected and then transcended by the complex icon of political reality that is Spenser's portrait of Elizabeth in the last years of her reign.[5]

NOTES

[1]The three slides necessary for this approach are *Elizabeth and the Three Goddesses* (fig. 3), the Siena Sieve portrait (fig. 4), and the Rainbow portrait (fig. 2). For a full examination of the portraits of Elizabeth, you will need the family of Henry VIII (c. 1543–47), Elizabeth (c. 1546–47), the Coronation portrait, a couple of early "generic" portraits from the 1560s, *Elizabeth and the Three Goddesses*, *Elizabeth and Pax*, the Phoenix portrait, the Siena Sieve portrait, the Armada portrait, the Ditchley portrait (fig. 1), and the Rainbow portrait. The best sources for plates are Strong, *Gloriana* (a revised edition of his 1963 *Portraits of Queen Elizabeth I*, it constitutes the single most exhaustive study of the topic). See also Strong's *The Cult of Elizabeth* and Pomeroy's semiotic gloss on the work of Strong and Yates, which has a fine selection of color plates.

[2]All quotations from *The Faerie Queene* are taken from the Hamilton edition.

[3]The story-narrative distinction is set forth in more detail in Genette's *Narrative Discourse*. I am indebted to Mary Nyquist's use of this distinction in her excellent article "The Genesis of Gendered Subjectivity in the Divorce Tracts and in *Paradise Lost*."

[4]See Bono 61–77 for a discussion of what she calls the Venus-within-Diana paradigm of Dido, used by Spenser to represent Elizabeth. In a discussion of the Sieve portrait Jonathan Goldberg argues, "even though [Elizabeth] is in the position of Dido in the painting, her destiny fulfills the model of Aeneas" (*Endlesse Worke* 156).

[5]A greatly expanded version of this essay appears as "Spenser's Elizabeth Portrait and the Fiction of Dynastic Epic" in *Modern Philology* (90 [1992]: 172–99).

Handling Elizabeth

Anne Shaver

One of the many pleasures of teaching *The Faerie Queene* to new students is that they come to the text unburdened by traditional interpretations. It is a simple matter, then, after showing them what Spenser says in his letter to Ralegh about praising Queen Elizabeth and about representing her two selves in Gloriana and Belphoebe, to lead them directly to the court of Mercilla (5.9.25), a maiden queen in whom Spenser has clearly represented a third aspect of Elizabeth. Here students are treated to a shocking sight: the tongue of a poet who dared to criticize his queen, nailed to a post. I suggest to them that another of Spenser's avowed purposes in writing the poem—"to fashion a gentleman or noble person in vertuous and gentle discipline"— might also apply to the queen, if he could get away with it.

Beyond this, all that is needed to set up a search is a brief exposition of cultural norms: Renaissance veneration of hierarchy, including gender hierarchy; the negative attitude toward women on top, epitomized in John Knox's *First Blast of the Trumpet against the Monstrous Regiment of Women*; the British tendency to have tales of courtly love end in marriage (Lewis, *Allegory*); Spenser's own celebration of woman as wife in his *Amoretti* and *Epithalamion* as well as in *The Faerie Queene*, especially in his ending the Britomart and Artegall story with the ferocious heroine's total acquiescence to the social role prescribed for her. (Compare Julia Walker's reading of this passage in "From Allegory to Icon," in this volume.) The courtly equation of Elizabeth with Cynthia/Diana, the virgin goddess of the moon, also gives Spenser access to the iconography of other, more dangerous aspects of the deity, aspects embodied in the Diana who appears in the poem, her foster child Belphoebe, and the Amazon queen Radigund.

Although this approach works most thoroughly in a seminar where there is time to read the entire poem, it has recently proved effective in a course on romance in which we read books 1, 3, and 6 as a sequence, and it even works as a way of reading just the redaction of book 3 provided in *The Norton Anthology*, if augmented with a little storytelling from books 4 and 5. The students enjoy looking for encoded criticisms of the queen to such a degree that they almost forget to complain about the difficulty of the language. They find that Spenser expresses quite a lot of disguised disapproval and covert teaching by trivializing the female characters who avowedly or fairly obviously represent her, including several evil maiden queens some of whose negative attributes she shares, and by representing as most acceptable several versions of ruling women who support male supremacy. What follows is a description of what they and I have found so far, by no means meant to be exhaustive. In fact, I was recently surprised to find in the

Spenser Encyclopedia entry on Pastorella that even this sweet, silent maiden might be a negative comment on the queen (Hamilton et al.)

In the letter to Ralegh, Spenser declares that Gloriana, the queen of faerie land, represents "the most excellent and glorious person of our soueraine the Queene" and that faerie land represents her kingdom.[1] If that is so, then the way she is represented implies that she is more a glorious function than a person. Even her role as presiding monarch is blurred. Although Spenser tells Ralegh she initiates the adventures that structure the first three books of *The Faerie Queene*, in the poem he revises those beginnings to diminish her ceremony and control. According to the letter, Gloriana exercises her power to assign the dragon fight to Redcrosse because she made him a rash promise in typical medieval fashion, while Una is again typically reluctant to accept such a "clownish" and untried young knight. But when Una tells her version of the story to Prince Arthur (1.7.46–48), she admits to no such reluctance and tells the prince she is in love with Redcrosse. Thus in book 1 Spenser changes what began as a royal assignment into a personally motivated quest, and he does the same in books 2 and 3.

In book 2, Sir Guyon is not dispatched by Gloriana to destroy Acrasia because a palmer brought a bloody-handed babe to court, as the letter to Ralegh says he is. Rather he encounters the baby in the forest, where it is paddling in its dying mother's blood beside its father's corpse, and Guyon vows heartfelt fierce revenge against the enchantress whom the baby's mother accuses of causing the carnage. In book 3, Gloriana does not send Scudamore to rescue Amoret from Busirane because a groom bewailing her capture appears in court; rather Scudamore loses Amoret just after their wedding and sets out to find her on his own. In the poem, then, the role of the Faerie Queene is diminished just a little; she is not as much the heart and power behind the heroes' quests as the letter to Ralegh declares her to be. That she never appears in the text in all her courtly glory in some ways adds to her mystique, as does her being the goal of all Prince Arthur's heroic efforts, but the single appearance she does make is not reverently presented. David Norbrook calls Gloriana's appearance to Arthur in an erotic dream-vision, "a characteristic Spenserian alienation effect" that "momentarily undermines a simple identification between faery legend and the historical Elizabeth" (115). Since the poet explicitly equates the two queens, however, the sexual promise of the pressed grass rather undermines the virgin whose political supremacy depended on her refusal to take a husband. Spenser shows appropriate caution in that Arthur does not achieve his trophy bride before the poem ends. Elizabeth enjoyed playing courtship games and might well have been flattered by the sexual glamour attributed to Gloriana in this episode, but it was always dangerous to try to pick a husband for her.

The second character in whom Spenser deliberately figures forth his queen is Belphoebe. He writes to Ralegh that she represents Elizabeth not as a queen but as a private person, "a most vertuous and beautifull Lady." Belphoebe has many more appearances than Gloriana's single moment; moreover she appears in even fleshlier flesh, unmitigated by the veil of dream. She is a virgin, the adopted daughter of Diana, and she is the only nubile woman in the poem whose refusal to love a man is not punished. Not only is her self-sufficiency condoned, it is praised, but in the midst of praising it Spenser never ceases to plant seeds of contradiction.

Belphoebe's first appearance in *The Faerie Queene* is fairly straightforward (2.3.21–42). It seems only fitting that the royal huntress should scorn lowborn Braggadochio, the would-be knight on a stolen horse, and Trompart, his opportunistic squire, and should disappear into the forest with a ferocious shake of her boar spear when Braggadochio, inflamed rather than awed by her beauty, tries to embrace her. There is no faulting Belphoebe the private person here; on the other hand her privacy is invaded by the poet in a manner much practiced and parodied by Elizabethan poets. Spenser anatomizes Belphoebe in a Petrarchan blazon while Braggadochio peeps from the bushes, subjecting majestic femininity not just to the reader's invasive gaze but to the gaze of a churl. Even though the passage is one of the most reverent descriptions of a female body ever to come out of the tradition, there are still enough clichés (ivory forehead, cheeks like roses and lilies, hair like golden wires) and enough mention of intimate body parts (eyelids, hams, knees, snowy breast and dainty paps, legs like two fair marble pillars) to link these ten stanzas firmly to the voyeuristic pleasures of the genre, so that the eye-arresting Vergilian half-line "Was hemd with golden fringe" that ends stanza 26 both leaps modestly over Belphoebe's pubic triangle (it describes the hem of her short dress) and suggests it mightily (Montrose, "Elizabethan Subject" 327).

Voyeuristic invasion gives way in book 3 to implied criticism of Belphoebe's behavior. The power of her beauty infects Arthur's squire, Timias, whose gentle manners and heroic acts have made him a sympathetic character. He sickens for love of her even as she cures his physical wounds. "She gracious Lady, yet no paines did spare, / To do him ease, or do him remedy," except that she will not become his lover. "To him, and to all th'vnworthy world forlore / She did enuy that soueraigne salue, in secret store" (3.5.50).

The story of Belphoebe and Timias continues in book 4 when her unavailability turns to outright anger at his attentions to another woman, an episode traditionally interpreted as representing the trouble between Elizabeth and Ralegh over his marriage to Elizabeth Throckmorton. The problem is Spenser's divorcing the lady from the queen. Whether or not an aging belle would prefer that her young favorites remain bachelors, a patriarchal ruler of either sex is likely to require that an important subject consult her before forming a liaison that is as political as it is private; the crux here is that Belphoebe is not a queen but a forest nymph, so that her anger with Timias for his attentions to Amoret when she herself is unavailable to him seems irrationally and personally selfish. Belphoebe and Timias are later reconciled, but not until he suffers a forest exile and madness ironically patterned on those of Lancelot and Tristan, whose reconciliations with their beloveds are passionately sexual, while his with Belphoebe only means that he will be allowed to hunt chastely with her and her nymphs again.

Gloriana and Belphoebe are the characters Spenser designates to represent his queen; therefore it goes almost without saying that their diminishment exists simultaneously with awe-inspired praise. Yet by allegorizing Elizabeth in two parts the poet makes her actions in each partial avatar seem less acceptable. Gloriana means "glory in my generall intention," says Spenser to Ralegh, but she is so disembodied that it is clear the glory she means is not her own but the glory earned by her knights and especially the glory sought by Prince Arthur. Her appearance to the prince in a sensual dream could simply represent the limits of his understanding—after all, it was *his* dream—but it also suggests the poet's discomfort with women in power and his need to present a woman of any rank as essentially sexual. Thus Gloriana is both a nonbeing and a seductress, while Belphoebe, representing the other half of Elizabeth, is disturbingly and solidly physical at the same time that she is sexually unavailable, so that she is made to seem responsible for the passion she then repudiates with ego-destroying anger.

The misleading synopses of the letter to Ralegh stop with book 3, but it is clear that figures throughout *The Faerie Queene* also represent Elizabeth: most specifically, poet-punishing Mercilla in book 5. The central event of the Mercilla episode is the execution of Duessa, a.k.a. Mary, Queen of Scots, in which Mercilla's reluctance to condemn the sorceress reflects Elizabeth's historical delay in sentencing her cousin. Mercilla is trivialized not through sexuality but through an odd mix of ferocity and weakness. Faced with condemning Duessa, Mercilla bursts into tears; it is not at all clear whether she voluntarily condemns Duessa or acquiesces reluctantly to the advice of her male counselors. Spenser interprets Mercilla's tears as reflecting her gentle nature (5.9.50; cf. Craun's discussion in this volume), but he also presents her grotesque punishment of the poet Malfont as the act of a "gratious Queene" (st. 27). Further, although her court is said to be the locus of "ioyous peace and quietnesse alway," where justice cannot be swayed by bribes or threats (st. 24), it is also the home of cowardice, for when a champion is sought to rescue Belge from the monstrous Geryoneo, Arthur volunteers because Mercilla's knights fall silent out of "cowheard feare" (10.15).

The goddess Diana is also inevitably an image of Elizabeth, however varied Spenser's iconographic intentions in his uses of her. When Diana exercises her Olympian temper out of all proportion to the provocation, creating immediate harm with lasting repercussions, it is no stretch to read her actions as reflecting the relations between a powerful queen and the courtiers whose ambitions and projects she could so easily stop short. Her disgust with a lazy nymph creates the fountain whose sloth-producing water will put

Redcrosse in Orgoglio's power (1.7.5); her protection of another nymph's chastity results in water too pure to wash a baby's bloody hands (2.2.9). Her anger when Venus, like Acteon, interrupts her bath is absurd, since Venus is not a presumptuous mortal but her sister goddess (3.6.19); her subsequent nurturing of Belphoebe results in a superhuman creature who will hurt a good man. Her anger at Faunus for another Acteon-like trespass causes her to destroy Arlo Hill (7.6.54). That the goddess is not a particularly sympathetic presence in *The Faerie Queene* must be in part what the poem says about the queen: under the praise and the expressions of awe remains the conviction that women should not have power over men, since both their sexual attractiveness and their irrationality make them dangerous to masculine—and thus human—enterprise.

The female characters who directly represent Elizabeth—a goddess, a quasi-supernatural virgin, and two queens—all wield such power. There are three other queens who invite comparison to the historical monarch, because like her they are unmarried. It is remarkable that in Spenser's poem, all the maiden queens except Mercilla, whose grateful acceptance of Prince Arthur's help feminizes her, and Gloriana, whose role as his inspiration makes her useful to male enterprise, are villains whose power must be resisted or destroyed. The first is Lucifera, self-made queen in the house of Pride (1.5). Spenser partly dissociates her from Elizabeth by making her a usurper, but neither her narcissistic self-contemplation nor the fatuous behavior of her courtiers nor the crimes of pride punished in her dungeon unmake her queenship. Lucifera does not pursue evil actively; instead she misuses and trivializes her power in being so self-involved, so vain and proud that she does nothing to prevent the nastiness around her. Thus her courtiers' transgressions seem to be her fault.

Perhaps because she might recall the actual maiden queen, Lucifera is not stripped of her usurped glitter the way the disguised sorceress Duessa is stripped of her usurped beauty in book 1 (8.47–48). Lucifera's unmasking is deflected onto her house and onto the overweening pride of her courtiers. The house of Pride is too tall to be steady, its veneer is the thinnest golden foil, and not only are its lower parts built on sand but they conceal a noisome and well-populated dungeon. Its prisoners are all rulers, but only the queens are defamed as sexual transgressors: Semiramis, guilty of incest; Sthenobia, a suicide for unrequited passion; and Cleopatra, the mistress and downfall of Antony, herself a suicide (1.5.50). There are strong implications in this episode that woman's rule is itself a transgression and firmly tied to sexual appetite: although Lucifera is a maiden queen, her castle's "nether parts" are a place where the pride she represents is translated into female sexuality and therefore punished. Although the house of Pride seems about to fall of its own fragility, Redcrosse does not bring it down. The best he can do is escape.

The maiden queen offered to Guyon in book 2, canto 7, is likewise invulnerable and can only be resisted. That Philotime, Mammon's daughter, is part of the booty the money god uses to tempt the knight of temperance is unremarkable, because rich woman as prize was and is such a well-established patriarchal notion. Although Mammon's larger world is in a way the obverse of the house of Pride in that it appears "dusty and decayed" when it is really gold underneath, the person and court of Philotime are as superficial as Lucifera's. Philotime does not claim false parents, but she does counterfeit beauty with cosmetics, "Thereby more louers vnto her to call" (st. 45), so she has her share of sexuality and false glitter. Her courtiers are not as aimless as Lucifera's; in fact, their scramble to climb her golden chain of hierarchy makes them seem quite energetic in comparison. Her lying father describes her as "The fairest wight that wonneth vnder skye, / But that this darksome neather world her light / Doth dim with horrour and deformitie" (st. 49). Even in a context in which huge wealth is deceptively dirty, the maiden queen is presented as falsely beautiful, inviting comparison with Duessa's filthy lower body, Lucifera's lower dungeons, and her own subterranean world, all dangerous to proud men in search of honor.

In some ways Spenser's least powerful maiden queen is Radigund, queen of the Amazons (5.4–7). She, at least, can be destroyed. She also has a weakness her more emblematic counterparts do not share: she is romantically susceptible to men. Radigund is legitimately the queen of Amazons, as Elizabeth is of England; not until Britomart beheads her and gives the rule of her decimated realm to men is the idea of usurpation mentioned. Then it is applied not to Radigund but to the entire Amazon nation, indeed to all the female sex, when Britomart "The liberty of women did repeale, / Which they had long vsurpt; and them restoring / To men's subiection, did true Iustice deale" (5.7.42). This generalization could have been aimed at Elizabeth as well, in hopes that she would name a suitable male successor. Also like Elizabeth, Radigund hampers the activities of men. If the historical queen did not go so far as to force her courtiers to wear women's clothes and to spin, her political caution and financial close-fistedness limited a good deal of the warring and exploring that many of them wanted to do. A king's exercising the same powers to limit activity would also be frustrating to ambitious men, but a male monarch would not be so quickly seen as an emasculator. A stubborn woman on the throne of an absolute monarchy in which feudal entitlement was fading while rank and power were becoming available to men of intelligence, courage, and persuasive powers must have seemed a bitter irony to those who could articulate the situation.

If Spenser was one who could so articulate it, the only way he could dare—no Malfont he—would be through indirection and obfuscation. Two examples of deflection might be that Radigund cannot be Elizabeth because she is killed by Britomart, legendary progenetrix of Elizabeth, and that Radigund, unlike Elizabeth, is destroyed by mishandled passion. Radigund's vendetta against knights is not typical of the general quasi-historical character of Amazon queens; it occurs because she is rejected by a particular knight.

Embittered by Sir Bellodant's refusal of her love, she takes revenge by killing or imprisoning as many knights as she can. Once she has imprisoned Sir Artegall, the knight of justice betrothed to Britomart, she falls in love with him and cannot bear to set him free, even though she wants him to love her of his own free will. Too proud to sue, she pursues him indirectly, through Clarinda, who is not just her lady-in-waiting but also her dear foster child. Clarinda, in spite of the loyalty or gratitude that might be expected of her, wants Artegall for herself, and so she lies to both Artegall and Radigund, representing Radigund's overtures as cruel demands and Artegall's courteous parries as disgusted rejection. This impasse is broken when Britomart arrives to claim her man, giving him back to himself and his quest for justice.

Thus Radigund's passion for men and her death at Britomart's hands separate her from direct comparison to Elizabeth, just as the facts that Philotime is her father's to give away and that Lucifera is a usurper make the two of them different from the historical queen, even though other qualities invite a second look. Radigund's battle gear, sumptuous as any queen's robes, is replete with moon motifs, recalling Elizabeth as Cynthia; Artegall becomes her prisoner not because she is the better fighter but because she is so goddess-like he is paralyzed and because, like any other good courtier, he keeps his promise to a queen. The perfidy of Clarinda, moreover, suggests what must also have been a feature of Elizabeth's court: the uncertain friendships and inevitable rivalries of ambitious women in a man's world ruled by a queen who did not encourage other women but held herself unique.

Finally, all truly virtuous queens and women in positions of power are very different from Elizabeth. They are either married or widowed, and far from preventing male heroic activity, most of them urgently require it, because they are in the sort of distress from which only a male champion can rescue them. Lucifera's virtuous double in book 1 is Caelia, head of the house of Holiness. She is neither a queen nor in distress but would have no meaning if wayfaring Christians like Redcrosse never came to her house; gracious widow, mother of Faith, Hope, and Charity, mistress of Mercy, Patience, Penance, and Remorse, she is nonetheless the servant of men's souls, a way station both to Contemplation, a male aescetic on a mountaintop, and to the renewed dedication to active knighthood required of mortal men.

Meanwhile, the only other queen in book 1 is a cipher: Una's mother silently accompanies Una's father, who emerges from the liberated castle to preside over the celebration and betrothal ceremonies that follow the dragon's death in canto 12. If this royal pair represents our first parents, the queen as accessory to royal ceremony is Eve as she ought to be, helpmeet and rib. A later and much humanized version of Una's mother is Claribell, the mother of Pastorella in book 6, whose passionate response to the discovery that the beautiful shepherdess is her long-lost daughter is lovingly detailed. Claribell is not a queen, though she apparently inherited "Many Ilands" (6.12.4) from the father who tried to use her to cement his relationship with the prince of Pictland; she is the wife of a lord, Sir Bellamour. She humbly appeals to him to acknowledge the daughter born to them before they could be married, and he gladly does so. Their reciprocal love in the Legend of Courtesy blurs gender hierarchy and makes it seem unimportant, but it remains part of the story.

Between books 1 and 4, characters wander in and out of a confusing landscape where normal gender relations sometimes obtain but cannot be depended on. In these books, the female characters presented for approval are usually not personally or politically powerful. The closest to a queen in book 2 is Alma, who rules her own house but who, like the queens of the second part of book 5, requires a hero to rescue her from attack. The closest in book 3 is the fledgling Britomart, while Cambina and Canacee in book 4 are not rulers in their own right, although they do have magic powers. They use these powers to resolve the fight between their brothers, Sir Cambell and Sir Triamond; then each marries the other's brother and dwindles into a chivalric accessory. The only queens in the first part of book 5 are the evil Radigund and the male-identified Britomart; it can hardly be an accident that, as soon as Britomart has killed her rival and given the Amazon land to men, book 5 is full of manageable women and the approved sort of queens.

Mercilla may be problematic as a representative of mercy, but she clearly acknowledges the need for masculine activity on her behalf when she sends Arthur to rescue Belge and Artegall to free Irena. Belge, a widowed queen, has been blindsided by greedy Geryoneo, who approached her with gallant offers of protection only to seize control of the lands she held in trust for her seventeen sons. With Belge's fears creating a foil for Arthur's courage, the prince fights on her behalf, kills the evil steward placed by Geryoneo to oppress and torment her, then does away with Geryoneo himself and receives her passionate thanks. Remember, though, that Belge had once been grateful to Geryoneo. If acceptable gender relations depend on women's being at the mercy of men, then Spenser finds it natural that only the honorable behavior of individual men stands between a woman and disaster.

Honorable though he is, Artegall through his delay has further endangered the very queen he was assigned to rescue. Although he knows that her captor, Grantorto, has set the day of her execution should no champion appear, through his own human weakness, he is trapped in Radigund's prison; then even after he is freed, he is distracted by another adventure. He rescues Sir Burbon from a "rude rout" of "rakehell bands" (5.11.44) in order to free Burbon's helpless lady, Flourdelis, herself a victim both of Grantorto's greed and of her lord's inability to protect her because he has discarded his shield. The morality of this situation is not as clear as Belge's distress or Irena's captivity; apparently Flourdelis has succumbed to Grantorto's persuasions and has betrayed Sir Burbon, exacerbating their vulnerability to the villain's ragged army. Artegall and Talus, his iron squire, scatter the mob and set the royal pair free only to find Flourdelis scorning her shieldless lover; Artegall's response is to preach her a sermon on constancy that has the improbable instant result of shaming her into amazement so that Sir Burbon can ride off with her. Whether she is now completely tamed is unclear; Artegall has done the best he can.

He does the best he can to rescue Irena, too, managing to behead Grantorto in a traditional joust, but before he can help the battered queen sort out her realm, he is recalled to the faerie court to answer the detractions of his enemies, leaving Irena's future safety at risk. Because political allegory occasioned the invention of the three queens of book 5, who are named for the countries they represent (Belgium, France, and Ireland), psychological analysis of them as individual women rather than as kingdoms would be inappropriate. But the tradition of feminizing territories ruled by men reveals an expectation about real women as well, and especially about queens and heiresses: rich, desirable, and helpless, they are prizes to be taken through male entitlement or enterprise and fiercely guarded from the depredations of other men. The relatively traditional feminine behavior of the fictional queens and great ladies of books 5 and 6—Mercilla, Belge, Flourdelis (that chastened flirt), Irena, and Claribell—occurring as it does after the destruction of Radigund and the restoration of male rule over one small Amazon remnant, seems to affirm something more far-reaching: normal gender hierarchy, remembered as existing before Elizabeth's long reign and hoped for after her demise. In spite of Spenser's need, even his desire, to please his queen, and in spite of his admiration for strong women who use their strength to serve and encourage men, Spenser's feminism never encompasses women's rule.

NOTE

[1]All quotations from *The Faerie Queene* are taken from the Roche edition.

"Be Bold, Be Bold . . . Be Not Too Bold": The Pleasures and Perils of Teaching Book 3

Diana E. Henderson

Why tackle the entire third book of *The Faerie Queene* in an undergraduate course? In part, its inclusion on my syllabus for the course Literature of the Sixteenth Century was motivated by its absence in my own undergraduate Renaissance class at William and Mary. Then, I found the severity of the Christian allegory in book 1 off-putting, despite the heroic efforts of Robert Fehrenbach to highlight the fairy-tale fun and energy of Spenser's poetry. Although as a teacher I have adopted Fehrenbach's stance toward book 1, I still find that many students share my undergraduate sense of detachment, even alienation, from the schematic linear allegory, no matter how much I stress its subtleties or contrast Spenser's method to Bunyan's. Book 3 alters the picture.

It is a critical commonplace that Spenser "teaches us to read" *The Faerie Queene* in the first book, beginning with the wanderings through the catalog of trees into the cave of Error. (Elsewhere in this volume, both Judith Anderson and Evelyn Tribble explore the value of this commonplace for teaching book 1.) To the extent that, after a few classes, students have begun to read allegory as both a narrative strategy and a method of personification, surely they have earned the pleasure of reward; my version of reward is to allow further exploration in *The Faerie Queene*, to play the newly learned game rather than abruptly shift to a sonnet sequence or drama. (When I do move on, it is to a work, such as *The Two Gentlemen of Verona*, that allows them to exploit their new attention to allegory as well as their awareness of poetic conventions.) Not surprisingly, when I suggest that reading more Spenser is a reward, the skeptical students are convinced that I truly have lost it—the same conviction that, in another course, greets my enthusiastic profession that "Milton is fun." But by the time we are well immersed, the tonal and thematic differences of book 3 usually substantiate my claim that there is more delight and more currency in Spenser than they had acknowledged.

In this short essay, I mention a number of questions, topics, and classroom strategies that work well with my undergraduate English majors. Rather than present a single reading, I want to suggest how flexible and amenable a teaching text book 3 can be, encouraging study of a wide range of literary and interpretive issues. Each semester I find it crucial to highlight the changes in narrative technique from book 1 to book 3, and thus I devote substantial space here to sketching out this contrast. As we move on, however, I try to vary my emphases as befits the particular class; and so, after confronting narrative method, I will outline ways to use certain passages (the proem, the introduction of Britomart, the lyric laments of Britomart and Arthur, and the house of Busirane) as focal points for various kinds of discussion. Topics I at least touch on, both here and in class, include genre and the rhetoric of desire, the tension between characterization and moral argumentation, and the rise of the author. I choose not to consolidate all these threads of discussion into a monolithic reading but rather to find the play between topics usefully indicative of the texture and functions of Elizabethan literary language. Finally, by sharing some of the limitations encountered and ways to incorporate the book's difficulties into the process of learning, I hope to exempt others from part of my less pleasant labor.

The third book of *The Faerie Queene*, as has often been noted with various degrees of delight and dismay, has a far less linear quest structure than does book 1 or 2, instead presenting a number of narratively incomplete episodes linked through their themes and, sometimes, characters. This difference can be explained as the legacy of Ariosto, as the Renaissance epic-romance technique of interweaving tales to increase pleasure and to convey the author's artful artlessness; but stopping there merely labels and removes the device instead of leading students to understand it. Whereas the reasons for appreciating this technique may have shifted, the method itself continues to please as much as it perplexes. Obviously, one has to read the book in its entirety to recognize the discontinuities as part of Spenser's design rather than as the result of one's piecemeal exposure, and so we do read (though we do not discuss) all of it.

When quizzed, students tend to think this zigzagging, "unfinished" method imitates a twentieth-century sense of the "way things happen" more closely than does a single knight's complete quest. Their assumption prompts further discussion of narrative method. I may enlarge the issue by considering Walter Benjamin's assertion in "The Storyteller" that the old art of storytelling, with its immediacy and tie to a human voice, is coming to an end. For Benjamin this loss is signaled by the rise of the novel; does Spenser's "textuality" anticipate or undermine that observation?[1] Do the differences between books 1 and 3 allow generalization about how stories are told, even by a single author, during the Renaissance? What is at stake in telling a story in a particular way?

For those who have never considered the historicity of storytelling (other than to label some works as "old-fashioned" and recent works as better), this discussion can be revelatory, transforming what seemed tedious about Spenser's style into an intellectual challenge. The narrative technique of book 3 clearly foregrounds the reader's participation in shaping allegorical meaning out of fictional incidents. It makes the students' labor, in other words, not merely a necessity but a matter for discussion and examination. Their self-consciousness thus becomes a useful tool for more direct engagement with the poem (whereas the daunting task of facing a historically remote epic in verse can all too often lead to self-effacement and detachment). Although a delight in density has traditionally been linked with an elitist, esoteric aesthetic, I don't find the association a necessary or dominant one in the classroom. Indeed, in a culture dominated by spectatorship or solo activity, Spenser's complexity provides another model for the student as audience member, a bridge between being a watcher and being a participant (in a subtler, more generalizable format than the talk show).

Nevertheless, when students first find themselves wandering through the woods of book 3, canto 1, shifting directions to follow characters hardly known before and leaving familiar friends such as Guyon and Arthur in the dust (or, more correctly, in hot pursuit of "beauty's chace"), they may become exasperated. Rather than discount that visceral dismay, one can use it as a "hook" to evoke discussion of narrative pacing and logic. Instead of throwing us into the (ironic) linear motion of book 1, where we began canto 1 by "pricking on the plaine" with a hero who is drawn naturally to Error's cave, Spenser here gluts our desire for activity without providing a clear focus; only later does he pull us back to consider motive and meaning. The loose threads of book 2 are raveled, Arthur and Guyon go off on "many hard aduentures," and Guyon is abruptly unhorsed by a knight "that towards prickéd faire." After presenting this battle, Spenser lauds the "goodly usage of those antique times" when swords were crossed "not for malice and contentious crimes, / But all for praise, and proofe of manly might" (st. 13)—but this brief contextualization hardly explains away the preceding comedy or the victory of a woman as "proofe of manly might."

Spenser's seemingly ironic authorial intrusion is followed by a second semi-comic incident, which will finally focus our gaze on the new knight, but in an unexpected way. We are given the chance to stop and think about our own positionality as we are left watching the action with Britomart, the one knight who does not rush off when a beautiful lady, Florimell, streams past with a drooling "griesly Foster" in pursuit. We recognize Britomart as focal, then, only after she has "prickéd" toward our (Arthur's, Guyon's, the reader's) location in the landscape; has defeated, reconciled with, and been left by, the others; and has adopted our own stance as observer. One may compare this circuitous technique for establishing focus—a far cry from the introduction of Redcrosse in the first line of book 1—to cutting-edge cinematography (in film noir or in movies by Spike Lee and John Sayles, for example). The camera follows one figure until her or his path intersects with another and then pans away to follow this second presence. The comparison encourages students to consider the function and consequences of such shifting—not only its demands on the reader but its jarring assertion of the storyteller's control over the world of representation, a refusal to follow the traditional privileging of one character to center perception.

After examining this extreme play with the conventions of introduction (even those that Spenser has earlier adopted), I ask, What does this technique do positively? That is, What is the author shifting our attention toward, and why? In book 3, of course, the choice is not arbitrary; it is the first sign of Britomart's superiority in the moral terms of this book, with its focus on chastity. The emblematic nature of her first action—not to join the chase —suggests immediately the paradox of that virtue, its internal and passive appearance in a world of heroic activity.

The invocation to book 3, which could provide an obvious starting point for discussion, seems to me a better place to go *after* looking at Britomart's stasis in canto 1. This way, we imitate the poem's dynamics, similarly "pulling back" to regard the poet's assertions rather than rushing off in pursuit of the narrative. The proem, a rich passage for close analysis and comparison, extends book 1's address to the "Great Lady of the greatest Isle," Elizabeth, by investigating the possibilities and problems of her representation. (Compare Clark Hulse's discussion of this passage in his essay in this volume.) Sometimes I have students write, as a prelude to discussion, a paragraph of reaction to the proem. As with most other hyperbolic dedications, the praise of potential patrons Ralegh and Elizabeth quite understandably evokes skepticism if not contempt from democratically minded students who value sincerity and directness. Through close reading, I push them to recognize how Spenser stresses the interplay between poetic and societal authority and how he moves from claiming the impossibility of his task in the second stanza to asserting his multiple representation of Elizabeth in the fifth. This reversal is abetted by a shift of rhetorical address away from the two patrons, who are not spoken of in the third person; now *they* are to be licensed by an unspecified audience to allow the poet "A little leave." The syntactic negativity of his request of the queen, "Ne let his fairest *Cynthia* refuse, / In mirrours more then one her selfe to see," masks his presumption that an image of the queen is not only possible but extant; the fear that she may refuse to look at his work—as she refused to see George Gascoigne's questionable pageant of *Zabeta* at Kenilworth in 1575—does not erase Spenser's representation any more than it did Gascoigne's text. Thus we can discuss Spenser's artful manipulation of the shaping power of audience (especially notable in an era of more clearly defined, delimited readership and a centralized court culture) and link his subtle self-assertion with the historical rise of "the author."

The fifth stanza of the proem also elicits discussion of the greater shiftiness of allegorical personification in book 3, for the "mirrours more then one" reflect not only an alternative to Ralegh's image of Elizabeth but also the multiplicity of Spenser's method. The proem implies more order than the narrative subsequently reveals, for in the proem the poet explicitly limits the images to two. Echoing Tasso's double portrait of heroism, Spenser is to represent the queen in two manifestations, regal and personal: "But either *Gloriana* let her chuse, / Or in *Belphoebe* fashioned to bee: / In th'one her rule, in th'other her rare chastitee." Given the primacy and character of Britomart (not to mention the letter to Ralegh, with its implication that book 3 is actually Scudamour's quest), the instructions seem inadequate if not disingenuous, as Julia Walker also stresses in her essay in this volume. They suggest that students be as quizzical about Spenser's attitude toward formulaic personification as they have become about his deference toward authority.[2] These passages again encourage a focus on the narrative rather than on static aspects of allegory.

In discussing the pleasure students derive from book 3, I have not yet mentioned the most obvious appeal: the episodes stress the "secular" problems provoked by desire, problems that usually have special urgency and appeal for young adults. After students have read several cantos, we return to the idea of chastity in the proem, now giving fuller attention to the Elizabethan concept of married chastity to clarify the role of Britomart and the presence of the garden of Adonis at the center of book 3. But in doing so we don't gloss over the problems still inherent in representing heroically what is most immediately perceived as a negative virtue, in that chastity most obviously entails a physical denial or refusal. Belphoebe provides an excellent focus for this discussion, especially since her story both leads into and refuses the fertility of the garden. In my course, the difficulty of defining Spenser's virtues has been introduced earlier, when we read a few passages from book 2 (partly as preparation for a departmental senior comprehensive exam). Hence we read chastity with reference to temperance, most especially Guyon's paradoxical behavior in furiously destroying the Bower of Bliss. That episode makes clear that the knights of various virtues need be neither unchanging nor uncomplicated in their symbolic status. That realization clearly extends to many of the characters in book 3.

Here I stress the rich tension between romantic characterization, anticipatory of the novel in low mimetic moments, and moral argumentation. In this way, Spenser's allegorization of chastity connects nicely with themes raised in my students' required study of Shakespeare's tragedies and Milton's major epic (the representation of Christian patience, the dramatic appeal of evil characters, etc.), but also with the nineteenth-century novels that tend to interest the students more immediately. It allows them to discover a link, often obscured by formal differences, with the related tension between moralizing and ironizing impulses in these later narratives.

Because my course concentrates on Elizabethan lyric poetry as well as on *The Faerie Queene*, I also find book 3 especially helpful in prompting discussion of genre and the rhetoric of desire. The solitary love complaints of Britomart (3.4.8–10) and of Arthur (3.4.55–60) work well to suggest how narrative can frame a love poem in reinforcing or ironizing ways. Britomart's speech, echoing Dorigen in Chaucer's Franklin's Tale (which our majors read as sophomores) and using Petrarchan tropes familiar from Wyatt and Surrey, illustrates Spenser's subtle use of allusions and an unfamiliar notion of poetic originality.[3] Because both lamenters are true lovers, the conventionality of their rhetoric cannot be dismissed as automatically conspiring against sincerity—but neither are the complaints presented as unequivocally admirable. Given that the semester usually concludes with a Shakespeare play in which a would-be sonneteer is mocked (*The Two Gentlemen of Verona*, *Love's Labour's Lost*, or *Romeo and Juliet*), confronting the complexity of lyric-within-narrative here counters the notion that Shakespeare was "not of his age" or was superior because he "saw through" the poetics of his naive contemporaries. Indeed, discussing these lyric laments encourages comparative contextual reading of Shakespeare as well as Spenser.

Later episodes reinforce our observations about the formal laments and the way in which moral evaluations can be inferred from and debated through the rhetoric of poetry. The mockery of Petrarchanism in canto 8's construction of false Florimell is clear to the more perceptive students, based on their earlier reading of sonnets. Comparison with the false Una of book 1 suggests both the murkier allegory of Florimell as Beauty and the difficulty of justifying why artificial beauty is not only not good but not beautiful. Paridell's seduction and abandonment of Hellinore in canto 9 also stresses the dangers implicit in the conventions of love lyric and courtship, using narrative consequences rather than logical critique as "proof." Having attended to these incidents, then, the students are prepared (as much as one can be) when they again join Britomart as an active spectator to the masque of Cupid in canto 12.

One successful strategy for addressing the allegorical indeterminacies of the book's concluding battle is to use the snippets of critical articles on the house of Busirane included in the Norton edition of Spenser. I organize a panel of students, each taking the position of one of the critics, and ask them to consider how they might textually support or qualify their arguments; after brief presentations, we open up the discussion for a class debate. Not only do the students become aware of the communal (or competitive) nature of professional literary criticism, but they also use the skills needed to construct and evaluate their own interpretations in a forum other than that of the paper (in which the process of critical evaluation is often left, understandably but unfortunately, to the instructor alone). This exercise lends itself to feminist critique as well because of the unacknowledged masculinist bias informing many critical readings of this book, in which gender is so clearly at issue (the relation between gender and heroic chastity has invariably been addressed when we analyze earlier passages).

The critical passages in the Norton edition are in some ways too disjointed and brief to promote discussion of how one constructs an argument and decides what evidence is sufficient; if an instructor has time or inclination to use complete articles from A. C. Hamilton's *Essential Articles* or recent feminist and new-historicist essays, I suspect the results would be even more successful. The constraints of class size, time, and my students' unfamiliarity with criticism have so far kept me from expanding this exercise; but as my students are beginning to acquire greater consciousness of their methodological and theoretical grounding, I hope to use this format more extensively in the near future, perhaps supplementing the Busirane panel with one using more recent articles that are not focused on a single episode. Formerly, the students on the panel read the temple of Venus episode from book 4 and discussed it as applicable, but I no longer assign this passage or other anthology passages from books 4 and 5 of *The Faerie Queene*, because the piecemeal effect has diminishing returns. If time permits I prefer to include the Mutability cantos, which provide similar iconographic richness and which work well with *Amoretti* and *Epithalamion*. My inclination, however, is to do more with less in the future. When I tried bits of both book 5 and book 6, I indeed found out what it means to be "too bold."

The boldness of confronting the indeterminacies and intricacies of book 3 still rewards the effort threefold but needs to be tempered, finally, by a sense of limitations. As I hope I have demonstrated, I try to attend to the rhythms of the narrative and use them as guides for analysis. Although I want students to read the entire book and sense the way in which episodes and characters serve as foils and variations, I never attempt to consider all the cantos thoroughly. Given that we have at most six hours of class time for book 3, careful selection is crucial. In working individually with students to develop topics for their ten-page papers, I encourage them to pursue the issues that most engage them and to supplement class analysis as they wish. Depending on the other texts we are reading and the particular interests of the class, I may highlight issues of genre, of gender or authority, of linguistic indeterminacy—but not all, nor with equivalent emphasis, each semester. This approach requires conscious choice on my part: I subordinate not only my desire for coverage but also my desire for thorough thematic discussion; I exercise a willed willingness to concentrate on the richest observations that emerge from the class discussions and panel; and I try to sustain those emphases for the remainder of the semester. If I do not, the challenges of book 3 will strike students as an aberration or a dead end, a glitch in the coherence of their semester. At the same time, the need to understand and yet resist the seductiveness of mastery—in the sense of classification and compartmentalization—becomes more than an issue prompted by Busirane's castle. It can become an allegory of reading for the semester, as I try to substitute for a falsely lucid vision of Elizabethan poetry "mirrours more then one": a mirroring that reflects and represents its subject matter with more complexity than even its own critical glossing can articulate, yet a mirroring that can still be discussed, analyzed locally with care and coherence, and linked with texts and experiences beyond Spenser's castle or my classroom walls.

NOTES

[1] I owe the genesis of this connection to my friend and former colleague Jennie Jackson, who used Benjamin's essay to initiate a narrative-theory seminar. I am also

indebted to Humphrey Tonkin, with whom I studied Spenser in graduate school, and Nancy Coiner, who kindly read this essay in draft. All quotations from *The Faerie Queene* are taken from the Roche edition, although I use the Maclean and Prescott edition in class.

[2]The marginality of Scudamour to "his" quest has often been used to indicate Spenser's sloppy structure of confusion in book 3 but more recently has encouraged feminist reappraisals such as Silberman's in "Singing Unsung Heroines."

[3]Quint and Greene are most helpful for background on Renaissance notions of origins and originality.

Finding the Feminine in Book 4

Dorothy Stephens

Although most undergraduates are as unfamiliar with book 4's recent rise in popularity as they are with its traditionally modest place in Spenserian criticism, they often welcome the opportunity to tidy up the frayed ending of book 3 by reading onward. Yet the Legend of Friendship prolongs the general untidiness by offering inadequate examples of its titular virtue—in Amoret's rape from Venus's temple, Belphoebe's condescending reconciliation with Timias, Britomart's anticlimactic betrothal, the three relentlessly happy brothers and their peasant-crushing sister, the formally orchestrated marriage of rivers, and the textual celebration of Florimell and Marinell's exhausted, unmusical spring. Whereas chastity was a complex virtue in the previous book, friendship seems an illogically subordinate one here.[1]

Books 3 and 4 make a good pairing for a major-authors course (for example, Chaucer-Spenser-Milton) precisely because they do not form one smoothly connected narrative unit, and students will get more out of both books if they can see book 4 as a reevaluation of previous material rather than as simply a continuation of Britomart's and Amoret's stories. I suggest that an exploration of book 4 might begin on the last day devoted to book 3, before the students have read very far ahead. Because the class will have begun to develop a sense of Spenser's method, one strategy is to end the discussion of book 3 by asking them what they expect of "The Legend of Cambel and Telamond, or of Friendship." I do this in the crudest possible way, by summarizing the plot structure of books 1 and 2 (which they may not have read) and asking them to predict or invent several typically Spenserian schemes for illustrating the virtue of friendship with Cambel and Telamond as heroes. We write these down and return to them a few days later, when the students have begun to notice discrepancies between the amicable title and the book's discordant content. The students' inventions generate questions in and of themselves: does the class believe that friendships are ideally opposed to sexual relationships or that the two should coexist? (The reasonable answer to this question may seem obvious, but students have taught me that the issue is often either unclear or threatening to them.) Do they see friendships as fundamentally in need of protection from conflict or as generated in part from conflict? Do they differentiate among various types of friendship? Does gender enter into their definitions of friendship? Having considered their invented schemes in the light of these questions, they will be ready to ask whether Spenser's ideas fulfill, evade, or disturb their expectations.

Meanwhile, I ask students to compare the two endings of book 3: Amoret and Scudamour's joyful hermaphroditic embrace after they have been reunited in the 1590 version and the cancellation of this felicity in the 1596 version, where the two lovers remain painfully separated from each other. Which ending seems most useful? What does each ending enable the poem to do? Briefly, I explain Jonathan Goldberg's argument that Scudamour and Amoret's hermaphroditic embrace in the original ending represents a desirable closure that the poem cannot allow itself or its readers to possess. When Scudamour has the chance to "reclaim his wife" later in book 4, he chooses instead to tell his friends a story about how he originally won Amoret from Venus. "Rereading," Goldberg argues, "is his only prize. We are in Scudamour's place, left with our desire for an ending" (*Endlesse* 66). I ask students, though, whether the hermaphroditic bliss in the stanzas that conclude the three-book edition in 1590 is the same from every character's point of view. It will be enough at this stage for them to see that Britomart does not yet have her Artegall; however, as we proceed through the next book, with its many failed friendships, it will eventually become possible for them to understand that although the cancellation of the hermaphrodite has frustrated one couple's erotic desires without bringing the second couple together, it has allowed the temporary formation of a third couple: Britomart and Amoret.

In this way, we make room for a reading of book 4 that treats the book's sullying of several supposedly exemplary friendships (including those of the four central characters) less as failures of the text to realize its own goals than as opportunities for an alternative set of questions about gender and friendship. What, for example, does Amoret's story—her entanglement with Busirane and subsequent travels with Britomart—mean for readers who do not desire the particular sort of closure that Scudamour desires? And why should we believe that the poem expects us to desire this closure? In book 3, Britomart's labor to release Amoret from Busirane has taken place on the prisoner's behalf rather than in her company, but now not only does the poem give them an additional quest, it gives them a quest together, as friends. The distance between "Amoret" as the sign of Scudamour's proprietary loss in book 3 and "Amoret" as the sign to Belphoebe of Timias's lust at 4.7.35–36 constitutes a space for feminine desire in which Amoret and Britomart may "wend at will" just as Scudamour does, and without his company. This is the promise—and the warning—with which the second version of book 3 ends.[2]

Whether or not the students have decided that the poem thoroughly approves of Britomart's wandering in book 3, it makes sense to ask them to compare Spenser's treatment of that wandering with his treatment of Amoret's divergence from Scudamour. Although book 4, like its predecessor, opens with a maiden seeking her beloved far and wide, it also complicates the picture in several ways. If Britomart's quest for the loss of virginity in book 3 takes her away from her father, it points always toward Artegall—or at least toward his idealized image. Yet the poem's cancellation of the hermaphroditic ending for Britomart's book may well make us reconsider our assumptions about what the goals of Britomart's quest are and about how the poem is asking us to evaluate these goals. Is it possible, for example, that we are being asked not only to contrast Busirane's sadistic treatment of Amoret with Scudamour's loving embrace but also—however obliquely—to compare the two? The image of Amoret melting into Scudamour's welcoming arms oddly echoes a previous image of Amoret welded to Busirane's cruelly phallic pillar of brass. Subtly or not, the hermaphrodite begins to recall Busirane's own idea of a proper relationship between the sexes. Busirane insists that Amoret confine her thoughts and speech to his claustrophobic system of meanings—and if the other demands that he makes are immoral, they nevertheless exert pressure on his prisoner because his initial demand for her rapt attention resembles similar demands made by moral men. But the requirement that women remain sexually constant is at odds with the requirement that they always adapt to masculine social and literary structures.

To give students a sense of this paradox, I assign brief excerpts from the pamphlet wars over the sexes. (Henderson and McManus's *Half Humankind* offers an excellent selection.) Womankind's inherent tendency to wander receives more frequent mention in the pamphlet wars than any other trait does; time and again one reads that women are susceptible not only to sexual inconstancy but to general, all-purpose wishy-washiness. Because their minds are ever-changing, the argument runs, women cannot be depended on for rational thought. Yet most social exigencies during this historical period—except for the protection of virginity and the production of legitimate heirs (two admittedly crucial exceptions)—demanded that most women train themselves into inconstancy. I also show students a passage from *The English Gentlewoman* (1631). While giving advice to newly married couples, Richard Brathwaite spins out a long series of paragraphs beginning "Is he young?" "Is he old?" "Is he rich?" "Is he poor?" "Is he foolish?" "Is he wise?" and in every case, the wife's responsibility is to adjust herself to complement her husband (132). Some stubborn wives or enterprising widows would have resisted the advice of moralists like Brathwaite, of course, but the personal writings of women from Margaret More Roper to Elizabeth Egerton suggest that even these unusually well-educated women found it difficult to shake free of the notion that adaptability was a particularly feminine characteristic. It was not that circumstances pressured women into transgression, in the way that hunger sometimes forces honest people into crime, but that error constituted the unwritten rule. A woman was supposed to find her duty on winding side paths. Her usefulness depended not on whether she was inconstant but on which types of inconstancy she exercised and whether these usurped or buttressed masculine authority. By constantly repositioning her anchors, each woman contributed to the illusion, at least, of constant stability in her larger society.

The trouble was that this desire for women always to adapt, to flow into chinks among the definite and unyielding shapes of men's occupations, made the requirements for *sexual* constancy less coherent. Britomart must wander to find Artegall, and Amoret to find Scudamour, but their wandering exposes them to lustful men. Their journey problematizes the complex distribution of blame and punishment that occurred in the sixteenth century whenever a wife erred. Neighbors' rough music could be almost as severe on the cuckold as on his wife, because he was assumed to have corrected her too seldom, leaving her too much to her own devices. He was culpable precisely because every woman left unsupervised was considered perilously on the verge of becoming morally wayward.[3] When Scudamour and Amoret are separated in an unfamiliar territory, she becomes the stray by definition—the one who must adapt quickly if she wishes to remain "perfect hole" (3.12.38).

Obviously, a woman's ability to adapt herself to the men around her would have dubious social value when extended to her evil—though male—abductor or paramour. "I haue seldome seene an honest woman to haue many frinds that wil take hir part, that wil speake for her, that will quarrell for her, that wil fight for hir . . . ," writes Barnabe Rich. "You may quickely ghesse a Strumpet by her multitude of friendes" (24–25). Although the context of these sentences suggests that Rich is thinking only of male friends (he mentions their gifts of capons and conies, for example), no pronouns in the passage positively indicate masculinity. Yet the text's very assumption that "friends" means "male friends" evades the issue of whether an honest woman will have confidantes of her own sex. The only female acquaintances mentioned in the passage are strumpets who slander the honest woman to bring her to their level, so that one way or another the restrictive boundaries of this particular passage deprive the exemplary woman of female companions.

I ask students to think about Rich's association of friendship with sexual wandering while they read the first canto of book 4, where Amoret has wandered away from masculine protection and into another woman's company. Curiously enough, it is here that *The Faerie Queene* addresses the question of whether a woman should adapt herself even to her abductor. At the beginning of book 4, Amoret does not yet realize that her flirtatious rescuer is female. Britomart's armor allows this passage to do double service as a commentary on relationships between the sexes by converting some of our laughter at the transvestite comedy into a sense of irony about glitches in the patriarchal system. Amoret acts in dutiful accordance with cultural expectations pressing on her from two sides: she should be resolutely self-contained; she should be pliantly grateful. Yet the notion that every man of miscellaneous goodness who saves a woman from torture "Right well deserue[s] as his due-full meed, / Her loue, her seruice, and her vtmost wealth" (1.6) cannot seem anything but misguided in this context; by indicating that strong bonds do not assure sexual parity, the poem tacitly underscores its mistrust of the absolute fusion and immobility represented earlier by the hermaphrodite.

Nothing in Britomart's history of comical aggression toward strange knights has quite prepared us for her infliction of gratuitous anxiety on

Amoret, to whom Britomart speaks "Of loue, and otherwhiles of lustful-nesse, / That much [Amoret] feard his mind would grow to some excesse" (1.7). The motives we are given for the teasing are that Britomart wishes "to hide her fained sex" and "maske her wounded mind." Yet each of these phrases encloses two opposing ideas. In Spenser's grammar, where two nega-tives make a deeper negative and where redundant intensifiers—such as "greedy *Auarice*"— defy our accusations of superfluity, hiding one's feigned sex means that one does an awfully good job of hiding it. But of course the phrase also means, illogically, that Britomart manages to hide her pretense of being male. And if she "maske[s]" her painfully frustrated desires the way that Busirane masques his, she is not concealing but displaying, putting on a show of signs meant to be deciphered. These two phrases' duplicity about Britomart's duplicity suggests that her flirtation is more than just a private antidote and that she halfway intends Amoret to guess what her armor hides. If Amoret hesitates in the face of this riddle, still believing in her rescuer's specifically masculine seductiveness, our own partiality for the other half of the answer (that this knight is really a woman who flirts only to feign) may excuse her.

But then, Britomart dallies more with Amoret than she ever does with Artegall, and it is tempting to say that at this stage of the game, she feigns only to flirt. By keeping her helmet on, Britomart can afford to raise the dialogue to a higher erotic pitch, engaging in a closer intimacy than would otherwise be allowable. This eroticism becomes even more charged in the stanzas in which these two women sleep together after Britomart has re-vealed her true sex; the double entendres of the words "passion," "bemone," and "hard aduentures" reinforce one's initial sense that, when Britomart and Amoret talk about "their loues," the phrase not only points outward to two male objects but encloses a more private exchange between the two women (1.15–16). It is wonderfully odd that the one happy bed scene in the whole poem appears here. While the text declares that each of the women longs to complete herself in her absent mate, the subtext at least momentarily believes in the self-sufficiency of their interaction with each other.

Only parts of this argument will emerge in any given classroom discussion, but my primary object is to introduce the students to a way of reading Spenser that is not based solely on theories of what the text is trying to do. A text may devote the greater part of its bulk to trying to accomplish one set of goals—such as presenting marriage as the greatest possible friendship—while nevertheless drawing much of its strength and offering much of its interest in other ways. I suggest, for example, that it is precisely because of the overwhelmingly negative cultural pressure on women's friendships—superadded to the pressure of romance narrative structure, which tends to deflect and defer the desires of both sexes—that the few female alliances in the poem take on such importance. While some of the poem's voices attempt to circumscribe or constrict relationships among women, other narrative voices seem on the point of acknowledging that these socially marginal alliances provide the poem with a kind of energy found nowhere else.

Britomart's tenacious refusal to "forgoe" Amoret "so light" bears only superficial resemblance to the male knights' attempts to keep hold of female property (5.20). In fact, Britomart is the one who more than once perversely draws their female property back into circulation, withholding women the way that some women withhold favors. By the same token, Britomart and Amoret's wandering in each other's company while searching for their lovers bears only superficial resemblance to the knightly rush for Florimell's look-alike. Spenser's argument for that canto has to be one of the funniest and most profound moments in the poem: "Both Scudamour and Arthegall / Doe fight with Britomart, / He sees her face; doth fall in loue, / and soone from her depart."

Despite Britomart's tenacity, however, Amoret goes "astray" while her friend lies sleeping outdoors (6.36). Perhaps Britomart has been careless, but the more immediate reason for us to read about Amoret's straying is that in the preceding stanzas Britomart and Artegall have fallen in love. Britomart inscribes a kind of epitaph on the monument of her friendship with Amoret: "Ne euer was there wight to me more deare / Then she, ne vnto whom I more true loue did beare" (st. 35). There is not room among the living for this and Artegall too.

Britomart's declaration of love for Amoret in the same passage in which the poem supplants Amoret with Artegall may throw some light on the cave of Lust, where Amoret lies at this narrative moment. Students will be interested in the implications of Amoret's abduction by the character Lust, given Amoret's still unconsummated marriage; and after they have read Scudamour's recollection of his wedding day later in book 4, some of the students may decide that it is interesting to compare or even conflate Lust's abduction of Amoret with Busirane's abduction of her in the midst of the nuptial celebration. But in addition to these approaches, if you want to steer the class into a consideration of less obvious relations in the poem, you will do well to ask them what they make of Amoret's experience within the cave of Lust. In some ways, this is the most masculine of spaces; the monster Lust is shaped like a six-foot set of male genitals, and after raping his female victims, he gorges bloodily on their bodies. Why, then, does the poem have Amoret and Aemylia whisper confidences in the darkness of this particular cave? Why a feminine community here? One incomplete answer is that this cave, like caves in many other romances, figures the interior of woman's body, protected and protecting as long as man remains outside. When Aemylia makes her former life into a story for Amoret, one is conscious of other men besides Lust who hover at the cave's entrance, such as her father and her lover. One also becomes conscious of a slight narrative ambivalence toward her change from a state defined by these men to a state in which, although she is "of God and man forgot" (7.14), she can enter into close communion with another woman. *The Faerie Queene* does not allow many such meetings to happen within its borders, and the very pressures on these meetings—the efforts of the poem to contain them in small spaces, to make us forget about them once they are over or to subordinate them to heterosexual relationships—gives them added power once we have bothered to notice them. Rather than simply applaud a few exceptionally virtuous women or offer men self-completion by helping them appropriate the humanizing effects of femininity, this poem often seems to desire the simultaneously defined and indefinable positions of marginality.

Amoret's sojourn in Lust's cave is an especially important topic for class discussion precisely because the episode will most likely generate more questions than answers. The cave's dark interior encloses obscure self-contradictions. First, although the monster Lust is extravagantly male, students may logically decide that Amoret loses herself to Lust—becomes lustful—while in the company of the sleeping Britomart (7.3–4). How, then, do we allegorize the cave itself? Second, unlike the house of Busirane, the cave of Lust enacts the opposite of violation's wound, when the darkness enables Amoret and Aemylia to develop a brief but intense friendship by emptying out their painful life stories. The cave protects these women's intimate conversation even as it imprisons their bodies.

After Amoret escapes from Lust's prison, Belphoebe peers into the cave's shadows to ask who remains. With eerie spareness, Spenser tells us that she sees nothing and hears only "Some litle whispering, and soft groning sound" (7.33). Griefs shared within the cave have prepared us for pathos here, but the light of moral day requires that our sympathy make distinctions among women:

> Then forth the sad *Aemylia* issewed,
>   Yet trembling euery ioynt through former feare;
>   And after her the Hag, there with her mewed,
>   A foule and lothsome creature did appeare. . . .
>   (st. 34)

As long as the women remained inside Lust's cave, the poem asked us to sympathize with their fear of male invasion from without. Now, however, when the cave empties itself out, a female character absorbs and reemits that element of threat. Daylight transforms the unnamed "old woman"—who saved a grateful Aemylia in the dark by donating her own body to the monster's appetites—into a "Hag" who incurs both Belphoebe's and the narrator's contempt. The burden of disgust has moved from a male rapist to one of his captives. No one defends her; the poem does not refer to her again.

Just what distinguishes the old woman's donation of her body in the cave from Amoret's self-"ouersight" in worrying about a stranger's sobs—or from Aemylia's own captivity to Lust (7.10)? Daylight declares our questions moot by bidding us to believe its loathsome picture of the old woman's true nature and to compare this picture with Aemylia's pure aspect. Yet Aemylia and Amoret emerge from the cave's immoral influences into a confusingly immoral world where dashing young rescuers give sexual wounds and then more or less accidentally leave their rescued maidens to famish, as Timias does (7.26–39; 8.19–21).

The relationships constructed by women who are hedged with threats of violence—Britomart and Amoret, Amoret and Aemylia, Aemylia and the old woman—differ markedly from Amoret's relationships with men after her rescue, and Spenser takes pains to underscore the difference. I ask students to compare Britomart and Amoret's interaction in the first canto of book 4, after Britomart has rescued the young bride from Busirane's tortures, with Amoret and Arthur's interaction after Arthur has rescued Amoret from starvation. In both passages, Amoret experiences discomfort at finding herself alone with a knight who might justly claim a debt of gratitude from her. There is just one difference:

> Thus many miles they two together wore,
> To seeke their loues dispersed diuersly,
> Yet neither shewed to other their hearts priuity.
> (9.19)

Whereas Britomart and Amoret break their silence when Britomart takes off her helmet in canto 1, stanza 13, soon becoming close confidantes, good breeding will not allow Arthur and Amoret to speak more than a few courteous words while circumstances dictate that they sit closely together on a horse. Or rather, Spenser calls good breeding to mind here, though he chooses not to do so in other outwardly similar situations.

The phrase "Yet neither shewed to other their hearts priuity" retroactively deepens the value of that earlier relationship with Britomart. It also retroactively makes Amoret's and Aemylia's mingled, shadowy voices all the more important in that the women's tenuous response to divisive violence has given the poem a means of questioning the restrictions placed on women's public—and private—expression. In fact, the statement that neither Arthur nor his charge "shewed to other their hearts priuity" marks the end of Amoret's conversations in the entire poem, since this is the last line that brings Amoret before our eyes. From here on, she remains silent, existing only in the mouths of other characters, who refer to her as if she were present but who never speak directly to her.

The difference between Amoret's interaction with Britomart and her interaction with Arthur provides one explanation for Amoret's famously uncanny invisibility in the passage where she is reunited with her husband (9.38–10.58). If Scudamour attempts through his oral reminiscences (his story of how he originally won Amoret from Venus's temple) to reconstitute

Amoret as the perfectly whole sign of his proprietary loss, crying up her value within a masculine system of meanings, then instead of interpreting her failure to reappear as her own loss of self, we can read her absence as a resistance to mere contextualization. Within the story, of course, Amoret does want to return to her context upon emerging from Lust's cave; nevertheless, Spenser renders the cave's interior ambiguous for the poem's own set of desires. Just as a wife's body is and is not her own territory, the cave is and is not woman's context. In this passage (as well as in others that students will find for themselves), Spenser opens his text to the possibility of a feminine world not entirely controlled by masculine expectations, and these collusions with marginality fuel book 4 even when the book's more explicitly important friendships have lost our admiration.

Students will readily understand that a text may reshape itself when read from a woman's point of view. Nevertheless, they may need some coaxing to see that, no matter how committed to patriarchy Edmund Spenser was, his poem is not simply the product of a relentlessly masculine mind. Looking at the ways in which book 4 opens itself to the same femininity that its overtly masculine agenda often seems to elide (and one thinks not only of Amoret's wandering but also of Ate's more dangerous grip on the materials of epic poetry), students will begin to realize that the poem's voices are complexly gendered indeed.

NOTES

[1] A longer version of this essay appeared in *ELH* (58 [1991]: 523–44), from which portions are excerpted by kind permission. The earlier article developed a theoretical point that receives only brief mention here, since the present project is designed to help teachers ask their students questions rather than to wrap up one argument for classroom consumption.

[2] All quotations from *The Faerie Queene* are taken from the Smith and de Selincourt edition.

[3] David Underdown discusses the fears enacted in skimmingtons. Karen Newman gives an example of a rough music directed at a cuckold and his erring wife (86–87). A. L. Beier shows that magistrates often assumed a connection between women's geographical wandering and their sexual appetites (7, 25, 55–57).

"That Savage Land": Ireland in Spenser's Legend of Justice

Sheila T. Cavanagh

In the fifth book of *The Faerie Queene*, C. S. Lewis says, "the wickedness [Spenser] shared begins to corrupt his imagination" (*Allegory* 349). Lewis's damning comment on Spenser's involvement in Ireland reverberates in the responses of subsequent scholars (see Aptekar 117; Nelson 26) and students of the Legend of Justice. Even without any historical background, students object to the violence Artegall and Talus bring against enemies. They express understandable indignation that a poem dedicated to virtue suddenly abandons its stated values for the sake of depicting political expediency. When students react this way, it often becomes difficult to discuss what book 5 does accomplish since the class has lost patience and interest.

To prevent this void in my graduate Spenser course and in my undergraduate Renaissance course, which includes *The Faerie Queene*, our class discussions preceding the Legend of Justice relate Elizabethan perceptions of Ireland in the sixteenth century to time-honored practices of portraying the "enemy" as stupid, barbaric, and, inevitably, less than human. While this expanded focus does not justify or excuse Artegall's strategies, it does enable students to formulate a richer understanding of the complex relation between the Legend of Justice and Spenser's experiences in war-torn Ireland. The selections discussed here could also be used to incorporate book 5 into a course on colonial discourse.

In addition to Spenser's text, materials for the course include a packet of readings containing both sixteenth-century writings about Ireland and twentieth-century analyses of colonial and racial discourse. To facilitate the use of these materials in other classrooms, I am here taking as many of my Elizabethan examples as possible from the selections available in James P. Myers's *Elizabethan Ireland*. Well-stocked libraries will provide numerous additional sources.

Since students' initial familiarity with the history of Elizabethan Ireland tends to be minimal or nonexistent, parallels with the political uses of racial propaganda during diverse periods of conquest and war become useful. As Geneva Smitherman-Donaldson and Teun A. van Dijk note, "Discourse is not just a symptom or a signal of the problem of racism. It essentially reproduces and helps produce the racist cognitions and actions of and among the white majority" (18). In accordance with this premise, we examine tabloid literature and current journalistic portrayals of "foreign" peoples as well as Elizabethan responses to other colonial populations. We also explore the avenues by which these texts contribute both to policy and to public reaction. Early depictions of Native American peoples help provide illumination, especially since the two colonial movements shared several key participants (H. M. Jones 173). Space limitations here preclude more than an allusion to these intersections, but selections by Nicholas Canny, Francis Jennings, Howard Mumford Jones, and Tzvetan Todorov help students recognize that Elizabethan writings on Ireland are part of a broader discourse. Placing the Legend of Justice in the context of racial and colonial discourse gives students a valuable perspective on the issues in Spenser's text. Their typical resistance to book 5 gives way to a fresh appreciation of the political as well as the poetic implications of the poem.

In the packet of readings prepared for this section of the course, Edward Said's writings on Orientalism often prove insightful for students. Said presents "the Orient" in terms analogous to those describing sixteenth-century Ireland; the parallel becomes clear when the reader substitutes "Elizabethan Ireland" for "the Orient" in the following passage: "In the system of knowledge about the Orient, the Orient is less a place than a *topos*, a set of references. . . . Direct observation or circumstantial descriptions of the Orient are the fictions presented by writing on the Orient" (177). These travelers', scholars', and writers' creation of a fictive space under the label of "the Orient" helps highlight similar strategies regularly employed either by Spenser or by his English contemporaries in Ireland. In the classroom we continually interweave discussions of colonial discourse with examinations of Spenser's place in the spectrum of Elizabethan "fictions" about Ireland.

Elizabethan colonizers exhibit attitudes and behaviors demonstrating their adoption of the basic tactics for gaining control over a native population: genocide and assimilation. As we read and discuss passages from both Spenser and his contemporaries that illustrate these goals, we also consider the rhetorical strategies these writers call on to create support for both options. We look, for example, at passages that present bestial images of the Irish and of traitorous English settlers, and we consider arguments exhorting the desirability of transforming the unruly Irish into dutiful English subjects.

Such illustrations are easy to find. Sixteenth-century English observers of Ireland repeatedly created tabloidlike denunciations of the enemy perceived to be living there. Edmund Campion (1571), for example, relates the Irishry's purported history of cannibalism: "The Irishe were great gluttons, eaters of man's flesh, and counted it honorable for the parents deceased to be eaten up of their children" (Myers 26). Similarly, Henry Sidney (1567) proclaimed that "I cannot find that they make any conscience of sin" (Collins 25); while Barnabe Rich (1610) pronounced that the Irish "are naturally inclined to cruelty" (Myers 135). Other writers openly equate the Irish with beasts. Giraldus Cambrensis, for instance, whose twelfth-century history of Ireland supplied numerous subsequent generations with their conceptions of the country, maintains that the Irish were known to have physical relations with animals:

It is a fact, that shortly before the arrival of the English in the island, a cow gave birth to a man-calf, the fruit of a union between a man and a cow, in the mountains of Glendalough (Glendelachen), a tribe being especially addicted to such abominations; so that you may be certain that there is another instance of a progeny half-ox, half-man, half-man, half-ox. (85)

Reminiscent of modern tabloids, the early writings of Cambrensis and those Elizabethan writers who followed him in this genre helped create a sensationalized Ireland with only an incidental basis in reality.

The English forces felt highly threatened and vulnerable during the Irish wars: the turmoil seemed interminable and the native inhabitants continually resisted efforts at subjugation. Hence military leaders such as Spenser's patron Lord Grey de Wilton chose increasingly violent means to gain submission, while English writers produced texts to justify the bloodshed. As one essay notes, "If one may have to kill Germans or Vietnamese people for one's country, it will be easier if one has been encouraged to refer to them as 'krauts' or 'gooks,' rather than as human beings with a national identity and heritage" (Greenberg, Kirkland, and Pyszcynski 80). Elizabethan portrayals of the Irish consistently furthered these aims.

Most of these treatises claim that the Irish are so recalcitrant in their brutishness that nothing short of bloodshed could be effective. Rich, for example, claims that the Irish populace vehemently resists changes in their lifestyle: "The Irish had rather still retain themselves in their sluttishness, in their uncleanliness, in their rudeness, and in their inhuman loathsomeness, than they would take any example from the English, either of civility, humanity, or any manner of decency. . . . They have made a vow to be ignorant" (Myers 131).

Rich's belief that liberal use of the sword provides the only possible answer to the Irish problem is echoed repeatedly. Richard Beacon (1594), for instance, praises even unlawful use of the sword:

[Binghame] did forthwith deliver those traitors and rebels to be put to death, without lawfull indictment or condemnation. For seeing himself fallen into the extremities, that either he must spare the lives of open and manifest rebels to the damage of the common-weale, or execute them without indictment or other ceremonies, like a wise governor, two mischiefs offering themselves, made choice of the least. (16)

Similarly Philip Sidney, in his *Discourse of Ireland* (1576), of which only a fragment is extant, firmly states that the sword is the only effective weapon against the disturbances in Ireland:

Truly, the general nature of all countries not fully conquered is plainly against it [lenity]. For until by time they find the sweetness of due subjection, it is impossible that any gentle means should put out the fresh remembrance of their lost liberty. And that the Irishman is that way as obstinate as any nation, with whom no other passion can prevail but fear.   (Myers 36)

Similar sentiments reverberate through Elizabethan treatises concerned with Ireland. Whether justified by supposed Irish bestialness and recalcitrance, the native history of noncompliance, or a myriad of other explanations, the solution is always the same: bloodshed is the only answer.

Ironically, given this emphasis on Irish degeneracy, disconcerting numbers of English settlers adopted Irish characteristics and allegiances. Not surprisingly, these defections deeply disturbed loyal English settlers. As John Davies (1612) exemplifies, the writers who attack this unsettling trend and try to stem the flood of Irish "converts" now emphasize the bestial aspects of the colonizers who defect: "they become degenerate and metamorphosed like Nebuchadnezzar, who, although he had the face of a man, had the heart of a beast" (Myers 161). When Davies claims bestial transformations of the errant Anglo-Irish he also further dehumanizes the native Irish, again diminishing the consequences of killing them. Davies's strategy fits a familiar paradigm: "The settler paints the native as a sort of quintessence of evil . . . insensitive to ethics; he represents not only the absence of values, but also the negation of values" (Fanon 41). From the perspective of Davies and countless military leaders and observers in Ireland, demonizing the Irish population not only helped justify bloodshed but also might help diminish the numbers of English settlers lured into adopting Irish ways of life.

The English hoped, of course, that the conversions would work in the opposite direction. Davies, for instance, articulates the main aim of the colonizing forces: "So as we may conceive an hope that the next generation will in tongue and heart, and every way else become English" (Myers 174). Davies's desire here for cultural assimilation obviously ignores the losses suffered by the native population. Nevertheless, it presents the desire of many contemporary English soldiers and settlers—namely, an Ireland identical to its conquering neighbor and containing a population that gratefully acknowledges their rescue from evil and bestial existences.

This goal accords with the ambition Said identifies with the British presence in the Orient, where acceptance required conformity: "Being a White Man . . . meant—in the colonies—speaking in a certain way, behaving according to a code or regulations, and even feeling certain things and not others. It meant specific judgments, evaluations, gestures" (227). English observers throughout the Elizabethan period express similar attitudes toward Ireland. Ultimately, the only acceptable Irish become those without distinctly Irish qualities.

At the same time, however, this widespread problem of English settlers "becoming" Irish and the proliferation of anti-Irish tracts, especially those emphasizing the "wild" aspects of Irish life, suggest that the English were also grappling with the truth of Stallybrass and White's conjecture that the appalling is always attractive, even while it repulses: "But disgust always bears the imprint of desire. These low domains, apparently expelled as the 'Other,' return as the object of nostalgia, longing, and fascination. . . . '[T]he savage' placed at the outer limit of civil life becomes symbolic content[s] of bourgeois desire" (191).[1] When presented with readings by sixteenth-century English observers in Ireland, students quickly recognize that such fascination permeates these texts. Particularly since Ireland is presented as a beautiful country whose populace has run amuck, writers focus on the strange and "uncivil" much as tabloids might today.

At this point in the discussion, it proves useful to stop and assess the readings presented thus far. Generally, the breadth of theoretical and historical selections does not phase students; rather, they begin to raise related issues from their own experience of the media's perspective on foreign peoples, particularly in those regions perceived as threats to the United States. By cross-referencing materials from the sixteenth and twentieth centuries, students appear to formulate a clearer understanding of the ways that both fictive and ostensibly nonfictive writings can combine to create visions of the "reality" of other countries in order to promote specific political gains. Placing sixteenth-century Ireland into the contexts both of Native American experiences and of more recent displays of similarly charged writing helps make Spenser's works more immediate to the students. Thus, by the time we return to the Legend of Justice, the students have acquired valuable historical and political information to assist their efforts to respond in more depth to the Irish portions of book 5.

A close reading of the poet's work on Ireland also aids this transaction. Spenser's contemplation of the Irish wars in *A View of the Present State of Ireland* details the dilemma of writing a Legend of Justice in such a strife-ridden environment. Itself a regularly maligned text, *View* evinces Spenser's acute awareness of England's repeated failures to calm the situation and his sensitivity to Ireland's beauty and culture.

And while *View* presents a dense text even to scholars, including excerpts of it in a reading packet for students quickly leads them to note the absence of familiar sensationalizing in Spenser's work. Unlike most of the representative tracts cited above, *View* does not attempt to incite support for violence in Ireland through portrayals of Irish barbarity and bestiality. Instead, Spenser presents detailed histories of numerous derided Irish practices, with explications both of their usefulness in Irish life and of the ways in which they provide obstacles to English colonization (see Cavanagh, "Such Was"). He does not rely on tales of cannibalism and filth to make his point. Rather, he outlines the history of the rebellion and bloodshed that plagued the island and offers his proposals for the best means to end the wars, with the stated goal of eventual peaceful cohabitation between inhabitants of both countries

(Renwick, *View* 153). In *View*, Spenser repeatedly stresses the need to inflict violence on the leaders of the rebellion and those whose resistance seems unyielding, yet Irenius asserts that in the overall plan, violent measures should be limited, in the hope that the sword will provide deterrence: "that all the meaner sort, which were also then generally infected with that evil might of terror therof be reclaimed and saved, if it were possible" (107).

Irenius does protest, however, that once the government adopts harsh methods, they must be followed through to their completion; he insists that the rebel leaders must be eliminated before reformation can begin and peace can be assured. He therefore believes that Elizabeth's greatest mistake was to call Lord Grey back to England just as Grey approached what Irenius sees as the brink of success: "not only all that great and long charge which she had before been at quite lost and cancelled, but also all that hope of good which was even at the door put back and clean frustrate" (106). He is equally horrified when John Perrot, Grey's successor, decides to reverse previous strategy by pardoning many of the rebels: "For it was even as two physicians should take one sick body in hand at two sundry times, of which the former would minister all things to purge and keep under the body, the other to pamper and strengthen it suddenly again" (109).

Throughout *View*, Spenser is clearly torn by the pull of political necessity, even as he admires Ireland's bounty. Book 5 of *The Faerie Queene* provides the site where Spenser's concerns with justice, mercy, rebellion, and beauty coalesce. Although the entire legend is not explicitly linked to Ireland, I argue that Ireland serves as the predominant source for the conflicts portrayed in the text. Critics have long seen Artegall as a figure for Lord Grey, and there are strong parallels between the descriptions of Arlo Hill (which refers to Ireland) and numerous scenes in *The Faerie Queene*. Since Spenser personally witnessed the severe crises afflicting justice, close connections between the country and the legend seem appropriate.

As the proem to the legend suggests, Ireland serves as a microcosmic portrayal of a world gone awry:

> For that which all men then did vertue call,
>   Is now cald vice; and that which vice was hight,
>   Is now hight vertue, and so vs'd of all:
>   Right now is wrong, and wrong that was is right,
>   As all things else in time are chaunged quight.
>   (st. 4)[2]

When references to Ireland recur through book 5, they bring that beleaguered country often to the reader's mind, adding realistic poignance to the fictive tale.

The poem comes under considerable attack, however, from critics and students who find fault with the historical parallels and with the English policies Spenser seems to be upholding. Within the context of colonial writings by Spenser's contemporaries, though, the tone of the discussion often shifts. Although the depiction of Artegall's methods may not receive any more approval, the absence of tabloid indictments of the population allows a broader consideration of the relation between justice and policies being presented, especially since the range of other treatises about Ireland demonstrates the typical Elizabethan view of Ireland available in print. While students and scholars may readily disagree with the strategies Spenser presents in book 5, it becomes apparent that his recommendations do not emanate from the same sensationalistic sources that one might expect from him as an Elizabethan settler.

Nevertheless, the destruction of the giant in canto 2, for example, provokes serious denunciation from critics:

> Whom when so lewdly minded *Talus* found,
> Approching nigh vnto him cheeke by cheeke,
> He shouldered him from off the higher ground,
> And down the rock him throwing, in the sea him dround.
>
> (st. 49)

Graham Hough, for instance, finds Talus's intervention reprehensible: "It is in the willingness to settle what is after all a real debate by these brutal and summary methods that casts a slightly malodorous cloud over this and other parts of Book V" (195). With no additional historical considerations, Hough's comments seem unquestionably appropriate. In Spenser's Ireland, however, the giant represents the major perceived threat, that is, the luring of the people away from the cause of justice:

> Therefore the vulgar did about him flocke,
> And cluster thicke vnto his leasings vaine,
> Like foolish flies about an hony crocke,
> In hope by him great benefite to gaine,
> And vncontrolled freedome to obtaine.
>
> (st. 33)

Rich, among others, argues that the Irish are unable to resist such seductions: "But as the throng of fooles, doth euermore exceede the number of the wise, so the multitudes of the rude and ignorant among the Irish, do far passe the number either of the religious or ciuilly reformed" (Myers 140).

Still, if Spenser in *View* is not as harsh on the general Irish population as Rich is, he does nevertheless fear that they can be easily enticed away from righteousness: "besides these evil things being decked and suborned with the gay attire of goodly words, may easily deceive and carry away the affection of a young mind that is not well stayed" (Renwick, *View* 74). In canto 2, he uses Talus to mirror the strategy he recommends to the queen: "her Majesty may now likewise curb and cut short those Irish and unruly lords that hinder all good proceedings" (143). Thus Talus destroys the giant but stops short of massacre, content to intimidate the "lawlesse multitude" when they refuse a truce (st. 52–54).

There are numerous other interstices between book 5 and Elizabethan Ireland, many of which I have discussed elsewhere and which space disallows here (see Cavanagh, "Such Was"). One of the most striking, however, which has long been recognized, is Malengin's resemblance to the Irish kern, or foot soldier. Apart from sharing many physical similarities, this guileful enemy personifies the duplicity and the elusiveness for which the kern were famous. Malengin's deceitfulness, for instance, could fool almost everyone:

> So light of hand, and nymble of his pace,
> So smooth of tongue, and subtile in his tale,
> That could deceiue one looking in his face.
> (9.5)

In a similar vein, Fynes Moryson warns that the Irish could not be trusted either, despite their shows of hospitality: "These wild Irish are not unlike to wild beasts, in whose caves a beast passing that way might find meat, but not without danger to be ill entertained, perhaps devoured, of his insatiable host" (Myers 192). Until Artegall arrives, Malengin has successfully terrorized the countryside, as Samient relates:

> To weet a wicked villaine, bold and stout,
> Which wonned in a rocke not farre away,
> That robbed all the countrie there about,
> And brought the pillage home, whence none could get it out.
> (9.4)

Samient's description of Malengin foreshadows Davies's portrait of the rebels in Ireland:

> As for oppression, extortion, and other trespasses, the weaker had never any remedy against the stronger; whereby it came to pass that no man could enjoy his life, his wife, his lands or goods in safety if a mightier man than himself had an appetite to take the same from him. Wherein they were little better than cannibals, who do hunt one another, and he that has the most strength and swiftness doth eat and devour all his fellows.   (Myers 155)

Malengin's magical metamorphoses and his ability to elude his pursuers also recall the reputation of the wild Irish. Richard Stanyhurst writes that there were "manie sorcerers" in Ireland (Holinshed 67), and Moryson claims that "they are by nature superstitious and given to witchcrafts . . . they use many like incantations when they go to fight" (Falkiner 314–15). Cambrensis notes that the kern are difficult to capture: "And againe these people are verie nimble and quick of bodie, and light of foot, and for their safetie and advantage they seek waies through streicts and bogges" (Holinshed 230).

On capturing Malengin, Talus responds brutally: "That all his bones, as small as sandy grayle / He broke, and did his bowels disentrayle" (9.19). Again, however, this action accords with the principal message of *View* — that is, eliminate the dominant sources of crime and rebellion, and the rest of the population can be left in peace.

Spenser does not always respond so harshly. When he introduces Irena's plight, he illustrates his affection for the besieged country with his gentle description of her vulnerability, "Like as a tender Rose in open plaine" (12.13). The story of Artegall's efforts on behalf of Irena draws extensively from Spenser's experience with Lord Grey. Although Grantorto has not been identified unequivocally, it is clear that Artegall's mission parallels Grey's unsuccessful campaign to bring Ireland safely under England's rule. From the English perspective, the beautiful island had been held captive by its rebels much as Irena languished under Grantorto's oppression. The task facing both Grey and Artegall, therefore, centered on first eliminating the perceived enemies, then implementing a course of reform.

The strategies Artegall uses after eradicating Grantorto closely follow Spenser's suggestions in *View* (11). He sends Talus, for example, out to police the countryside while he engages in a close study of the country's needs (12.26). Artegall's plans for reform are interrupted, however. Like Grey, he is recalled from Ireland before he can complete the task (9.27). Reflecting the Ireland of Spenser's experience, Irena's kingdom remains a site of unsettlement. As a text grounded in the issues of Elizabethan colonialism, the Legend of Justice thus reiterates the continuing frustration facing the English government and settlers.

Looking at recent proliferations of print and television tabloids and their sixteenth-century equivalents does not lessen the brutality of the Legend of Justice. Nevertheless, a set of readings such as that described above enriches the students' experiences of book 5. In our time the enemies of war are generally portrayed as individuals, not peoples. Thus, we have had Qaddafi, Hussein, and the ayatollah instead of "the Irish." *Time* is less likely now to present a piece entitled "How to Tell Your Friends from the Japs," as it did two weeks after Pearl Harbor. Although racism still runs rampant, it operates less overtly in the media. Still, students are acutely, if often uncritically, aware of the lure of the tabloid in our culture. An analytic foray into this familiar territory opens up the realm of politically motivated racial discourse and provides a rich environment for exploring "that savage nation" in Spenser's Legend of Justice.

NOTES

[1]Selections from Jean-Paul Sartre's *Anti-Semite and Jew* are also useful for this discussion.

[2]Quotations from *The Faerie Queene* are taken from the Hamilton edition.

"Most Sacred Vertue She":
Reading Book 5 alongside Aristotle
and Thomas Aquinas on Justice

Edwin D. Craun

Like most other English teachers in these days of television and film court-room dramas (even sitcoms), I look out over rank on rank of aspiring lawyers when I meet an upper-level class. In my small university, a school of law, the only graduate division, swells those ranks, drawing undergraduates dazzled by lawyering. Many of them turn to English as a traditional prelaw major. In my first year of teaching, my three dozen majors wrangled passionately, though not very lucidly, over both books of Thomas More's *Utopia*, and the ablest of them wrote twelve pages on one stanza from the trial of Duessa after reading book 5 on his own (I had assigned the standard brace of books 1 and 3). The representations of public life in Renaissance literature at once engrossed and baffled them. Drawn to think about Utopian laws like that restricting domestic travel or about problematic *exempla* like Artegall's surprisingly light punishment of the homicide Sir Sanglier, they quickly realized that we lacked adequate terms, let alone concepts, for analyzing the functions of law ("deterrent" was about it) or the relation of punishment to crime (it should, of course, "fit"). At the same time, colleagues in the law school were lamenting how positivistic the teaching of law usually was, confined to dissecting case and text, save for the adventurous use of a few novels in courses like Professional Responsibility or Evidence. Where, I wondered, would my students learn to think theoretically about law and justice? Why not in the undergraduate classroom, with its freedom from the constraints of professionalism and its volatile mix of future social workers, doctors, and teachers with future lawyers?

Searching for a way to import an appropriate theory of justice into an English course, I turned first to that Renaissance school text the *Nicomachean Ethics*, which, as the Variorum shows, provides a useful theoretical gloss on Artegall's adventures as justiciar in the first four cantos. For law, equity, clemency, and mercy—and for more sustained, detailed argument about justice—I added the *Summa Theologiae* of Thomas Aquinas, rich in dicta from Aristotle and the Bible, plus Cicero, Augustine, Isidore, Gratian, and others who shaped Western thinking on justice and the law.[1] (Sixteenth-century treatises like William Perkins's *Epieikeia; or, A Treatise of Christian Equitie and Moderation* and Christopher Saint German's *Dyaloges* are either out of print or difficult to obtain, either too narrow or too broad for reading alongside *The Faerie Queene*.)

With these texts in hand, I was joined by a colleague in philosophy, W. Lad Sessions, and together we designed a seminar, Law and Justice: The Christian and Aristotelian Traditions in Renaissance Literature. We began with Shakespeare's *Measure for Measure*. Its locale (the streets, the jail, the judges' chambers) and some of its characters (the madame, the naive young couple, the libertine, the strict judge who goes astray at mid-career) are familiar enough to TV watchers, while the law at issue—that fornicators are to be punished with death—quickly provokes more than enough questions about the functions of law, letter and spirit, justice and mercy, the limits of law. Once our students—majors in English, philosophy, economics, and history—had struggled with these issues, they were receptive (somewhat) to theoretical thinking, first on virtue in general (*Ethics* 1-3), then on justice (*Ethics* 5; *Summa* 2a2ae.57.1-2, 58.1-12, 59.1-3, 61.1-4, and 62.1-7). *The Faerie Queene* came next to last (before that courtroom play *The Merchant of Venice*) because of its successive explorations of justice, equity, and mercy.

Both in the seminar and in my standard course in sixteenth-century literature as it was modified by my experience in the seminar, book 5 was preceded by *Utopia*, read together with the *Summa* on law (1a2ae.90, 91.1-3, 92, 95, 96). So when students in both courses took up Artegall's adventures, they had already thought about the nature and functions of law, especially by anatomizing Raphael's rejection of European law on thievery and the social functions of specific laws in Utopia (the complex of laws on chastity and on labor being favorites). Despite my preference for including a variety of genres, where different representations of public life—the trial, the backstage debates between justices, the humanist diatribe, the survey of rationally designed social practices—can explore a range of juridical issues, *The Faerie Queene* alone can be profitably read alongside the *Ethics* and the *Summa*. I confine myself to that enterprise here.

Artegall passes judgment in four cases (as we would say) and engages in a *Firing Line*-style debate over distributing wealth equally, all without citing a single law. In the first four cantos, only oppressors invoke laws, Pollente and Munera asking passage money "According to the custome of their law" (2.11) and Radigund commanding her messenger to proclaim "My law" to Artegall (4.49). So I have delayed treating law at all until Radigund's proposals and Artegall's assent to them provoke students to ask what a valid law is. The justice of judgments, not the law, dominates the five episodes up to Radegone, set in the uncharted, lawless countryside of chivalric romance with its robber barons and imposters, where Artegall must reason out each person's right in the disputes he encounters. In the absence of positive laws, he must also explain his judgments with principles and terms that all parties will comprehend and, perhaps, accept: "equall things," "his right."

This theoretical language invites the first juxtaposition of literary and philosophical texts: the five adventures with Aristotle's book on justice (5.1-83, with books 3 and 4 forming a helpful prelude on virtue, the golden mean, rational deliberation as the means to a virtuous end) and three of Thomas's *quaestiones* on justice—"Of Right" (2a2ae.57.1, 2), "Of Justice" (58), and "Of Commutative and Distributive Justice" (61). I open discussion with the Case of the Two Brothers, even though it comes last among the five, because it is a simple dispute over property.

Since the text introduces as a conflict over the brothers' rights this dispute over the larger island and the treasure washed up by the sea (4.6), it allows students to begin where Thomas does: with "the right" as the object of justice (*Summa* 57.1, 61.2; also *Ethics* 5.5). Once they see that adjudging the right involves rationally determining some objective standard so as to achieve equality between persons, they appreciate Artegall's position. Even though the father, a man with an eye for justice, "Did equally bequeath his lands in fee, / Two Ilands" of roughly the same size to the two sons (4.7), Artegall cannot exactly achieve a mean between too little and too much by equalizing the two islands that the sea has made disproportionate in size. Even in its most straightforward exemplum of justice, the fictive text has questioned the philosopher's insistence that a numerical mean must be used in justly awarding material goods—in this case, one island to each son. Helped by Artegall's refrain in his judgment ("Your right is good [sayd he] and so I deeme, / That what the sea vnto you sent, your own should seeme" [st. 17, 18]), students are quick to see that, while their justiciar cannot achieve equality of goods in a relationship between people by measuring out those goods in kind, he remains true to Aristotelian principle by finding an objective standard in how the goods were obtained. In this episode, the literary text is closest to the philosophical, its juridical diction inviting the definitions of an Aquinas, its situation (the unequal islands, the treasure chest washed ashore on one island) provoking the reader to think in terms of principles of proportion and a mean between too much and too little. Here the just person's activity is the art of rational calculation, Artegall's art of equality.

To move beyond these basic principles, we explore next Artegall's judgment on Sir Sanglier, the first in a string of the unjust who force their wills on others in ways Aristotle lists in *Ethics* 5.34: plunder (Pollente), theft (Braggadochio), bonds (Radigund). The Squire presents the seizure of his lady by Sanglier as a classic instance of injustice: he is deprived of her by force because the knight "Would not so rest contented with his right"—his own lady (1.17). Students readily approve of Artegall's decision to take the squire's lady from Sanglier: he had taken from someone what was not his own by right. But if justice, as in the Case of the Two Brothers, involves an exchange, reciprocity of some sort, based on an objective, measurable equality calculated by reason, why should not Sanglier's life be taken away for having taken away his lady's life? That such principles work in punishment as well as in property judgments Pollente's death makes clear in the next canto. The punishment of bearing his lady's head scarcely seems proportionate to the crime, even after a professorial excursus on the power of shame in chivalric culture.

But what exactly has Sanglier done and under what circumstances? Thomas's question on injustice (59) is useful at this point, given his careful delineation of the possible causes of an unjust act: ignorance, passion, habit, malice. Materially—to use Thomas's distinction—Sanglier has taken a life, but he has not done so "with malice aforethought and with choice" (Latin *ex intentione* and *ex electione* [Blackfriars ed.]). His lady begged to die and he killed her in a fit of passion, as we say (1.18). Unlike passing judgment in a property dispute, passing judgment on a crime must consider intention and circumstances (for Thomas's *quaestio* on the morality of acts in general, see 1a2ae.18.1). For all this moral reasoning, my students leave dissatisfied with Artegall's sentence. It looks too much like only a neat solution to the dispute over entitlement to the woman, with the Squire riding off with his lady and Sanglier bearing the head of his. Some students are quick to notice that the wrongful seizure is neglected in the sentence; a careful reader of Aristotle, Aquinas, and Spenser would also observe Sanglier's habit of violence and would question whether this can be construed as a fit of passion. Has Sanglier got off lightly? In this episode, unlike the simple property dispute with which we begin, Sanglier's several actions and the complex moral situation insistently raise questions about how just Artegall's judgment is, especially in the absence of positive laws.

Students' disquiet will not be eased by Talus's subsequent punishment of Braggadochio, in which the shaming of Florimell (resulting from conscious choice, I point out, unlike Sanglier's killing of his lady) is punished proportionately by public humiliation: blotting out Braggadochio's arms, shaving his beard, exposing him as a fraudulent justiciar and a thief. Here unjust acts are paid for in kind, an obvious reciprocity, as in Pollente's death for the treacherous slaying of knights. And the punishment clearly acts as a deterrent, again as in Pollente's case, where his head is impaled and placed "on high . . . To be a mirrour to all mighty men" (2.19).

At this point in Spenser's narrative, the work of a justiciar, the work of justice, is clearly, as Aristotle and Thomas claim it is, the work of practical reason. So Artegall's exercise of reason in arguing with the giant of the second canto does not form too radical a departure for class discussion, although the episode is the only one in which distributive justice is at issue.

As a self-designated arbiter of social justice (in contrast to Artegall, Gloriana's "instrument," appointed by the established political authority), the giant claims to seek equal distribution of the community's goods of political power, social force, and wealth. While Aristotle's and Thomas's insistence that the community owes individuals a fair share of common goods compels even my affluent students to take this claim seriously, they are confused and put off by the Giant's and Artegall's arguments from nature. So I focus on the distributor's language in stanza 38, where the apocalyptic rhetoric of making mountains level with the lowly plain to "equalize" them contrasts oddly with his economic program: "And all the wealth of rich men to the poore will draw." The students sense the difficulty of coming up with a standard for fair distribution, let alone with impartial people to apply it. And both Aristotle and Thomas, the students will readily recall, argue that an individual's importance in the community ought to be considered in affixing his or her proportion of community goods: a geometric, not arithmetic, proportion determines what is fair in distributing goods. Furthermore, both agree that how importance is gauged varies according to a community's political organization: amount of liberty in democracy, of wealth in oligarchy, of virtue in aristocracy (*Ethics* 5.4; *Summa* 2a2ae.61.2). In this way, these traditional treatments of distributive justice make Artegall's arguments for social and political hierarchy somewhat accessible.

"But in the mind the doome of right must bee" (2.47). Artegall's rebuke to the giant's attempts to weigh right against wrong crystallizes the justiciar's struggle throughout the first three and a half cantos to apportion fairly the goods and evils in human relations. These judgments require the dispassionate analysis Aristotle and Aquinas advocate, undergirded by "the perpetual and constant will to render to each one his right" (Thomas's definition of justice: Baumgarth and Regan ed. 2a2ae.58.1). Although the violent revulsion Artegall feels when he comes on the headless lady of the first episode suggests that compassion for the victim and outrage at the crime fuel the work of the justiciar, book 5 foregrounds Artegall's struggles to suppress his emotions when he is adjudicating messy incidents. Guyon must pacify Artegall's anger by reminding him that he is "our judge of equity" (*aequalitas* here, not the virtue of equity), and Artegall pities that damsel in distress Munera while she is being dismembered by the unfeeling iron man. So when emotion dictates his actions again in the fifth canto, when in a trial by combat he throws down his sword out of pity for the bloodied Radigund, students know that he has failed as a judge. What they want to discuss is how and why he errs in agreeing to be bound by Radigund's "law," the first specific law he has encountered:

> But these conditions doe to him propound,
>> That if I vanquishe him, he shall obay
>> My law, and euer to my lore be bound,
>> And so will I, if me he vanquish may. . . .
>>> (4.49)

A close reading leads students to realize that Radigund's conditions seem just to Artegall because the parties are to be bound by the same terms; the equality in position is underscored by her parallelism and earlier reference to the law of arms ("try in equall field" [48]). He reasons as a dealer in justice only. At this point the students need to read Thomas on the nature of law and the power of human law (*Summa* 1a2ae.90, 95, 96). Then they will quickly perceive that "my law" is not proper law in traditional theoretical terms. The possessive pronoun alone indicates that it is not ordained for the common good. Recalling Terpine's account of how Radigund's rage against men originated, the students will see this law as a tyrant's tool of vengeance and subjection. In Thomas's article on when the law may bind one's conscience as a just law (96.4), they are certain to find a host of reasons why Artegall has erred. Britomart, by contrast, allows herself only to be bound by the universally accepted law of arms, seeing even the propounding of Radigund's "streight conditions" as an indignity (7.28). Unlike Artegall, who attends merely to the literal surface of a supposedly legal statement to determine its justness and so is entrapped by a "legal wrong" (Aptekar 116; Fletcher, *Prophetic Moment* 233), she considers the intent of the law-giver: to subjugate and shame knights.

These parallel but different responses to a law of dubious justice provide the opening for the students to read about equity (*Summa* 2a2ae.120; *Ethics* 5.105). At a theoretical level, they suggest why equity is a necessary part of justice and why it surpasses a "letter-only" reading of law: it attends to the legislators' intent, to the "meaning of justice," and to the public good. On these grounds equity, as a virtue, may exempt one from a law in a par-ticular case. (At this point I lecture briefly on the lord chancellor's court of equity, which retraversed cases when parties appealed to the ruler's con-science decisions handed down in a court of common law [Knight 269–76; O'Connell 145]. It was responsible, in part, for determining if the appli-cation of a given law in a case violated the intent of the legislators.)

In between Artegall's and Britomart's two judgments of Radigund's law, Britomart's dream at Isis Church surprises us by introducing clemency as the virtue associated with Isis and so, to some extent, with Britomart. As the priest allegorizes Isis's subjection of the crocodile, clemency "oft in things amis, / Restraines those sterne behests, and cruell doomes of his [Osyris's and Artegall's]" (7.22). What does this clemency that operates as a restraint on the justiciar's judgments have to do with equity, which sheds a different light on the same case? Yes, Thomas has a *quaestio* on clemency, too, and students should read it (2a2ae.157) along with that on equity. Both virtues, he argues, function to mitigate punishment, but equity does so by attend-ing to the intention of the legislator, clemency by controlling feeling, specifi-cally the anger at injustice that drives us to punish (2a2ae.157.3). Clemency arises from emotions; nevertheless, like equity, it looks to reason in tem-pering a punishment prescribed by law, but one that seems overly harsh in a particular case (157.2). It is "ruth," students realize, that modifies Brito-mart's desire for vengeance on the Amazons, prompting her to restrain Talus's "piteous slaughter." In this episode, as in the *Summa*, equity and clemency are yoked: Britomart first analyzes, and refuses to be bound by, Radigund's law, and then she restrains Talus's revenge on the crowd.

So far, these central cantos will seem to students what they have often seemed to critics: an object lesson in the superiority of equity and clemency to Artegallian calculations of what is due to malefactors or rival claimants, calculations based chiefly on notions of equality and proportionality in distributing goods and assigning punishments. But what of "the wrothfull Britonesse" killing Radigund, driven by the desire to revenge "her loues distresse," by Radigund's insults, and by her wound (7.34)? Is she swayed by emotions she cannot moderate (as Guyon moderates Artegall's in the third canto)? Or does she deal out in each instance the "true Justice" she is praised for in Radegone: refusal to accept an invalid law according to the light of equity, retaliatory punishment on the malefactor, the sparing of her subjects out of clemency? The narrator juxtaposes these incidents without comment, leaving the classroom open for a free-for-all.

As a last step in reading Spenserian romance alongside theory of justice, I direct my students to that other virtue which, in both discourses, may modify the basic sense of what is right: mercy. Inevitably we juxtapose Mercilla's response to the trial of Duessa, so much maligned by some recent critics (for example, O'Connell 150–54), with Thomas's brief *quaestio* on mercy (*Summa* 2a2ae.30). Quick to see the affinities between Thomistic definition and Mercilla's moral state, the students observe that Mercilla feels compassion for Duessa's suffering and that this drives her to do what she can to help Duessa (*Summa* 2a2ae.30.1); her feeling is all the more intense because she, too, is a woman ruler ("men pity those who are connected with them and who are like them" [Blackfriars ed. 30.2]). Although Thomas considers mercy not in his *quaestiones* on justice but in those on the theological virtues, he still relates mercy to justice, claiming that, as a virtue, this "movement of soul," both of the sense appetite and intellective appetite, is exercised in subservience to reason "in such a way that justice is safeguarded" (30.3). With this in mind, students naturally turn to explicate Mercilla's complex response to Zele's cry for justice against Duessa:

> But she, whose Princely breast was touched nere
> With piteous ruth of her so wretched plight,
> Though plaine she saw by all, that she did heare,
> That she of death was guiltie found by right,
> Yet would not let iust vengeance on her light;
> But rather let in stead thereof to fall
> Few perling drops from her faire lampes of light. . . .
> (9.50)

The "though" clause expresses the perception that qualifies Mercilla's fundamental feeling for Duessa's misery: that the law's penalty of death results from a just process and is Duessa's due.

For all their newly acquired Thomism, students are puzzled by the way Mercilla, a ruler, reacts—the tears she allows to fall, followed by her judgment that Duessa must die (10.4). Where is the mercy so praised by her people, by Arthur, by Artegall? Certainly Mercilla's treatment of Duessa is merciful in Thomistic terms. Without departing from the "doome of right," she does what she can to help her: showing her compassion despite the voluntary nature of her fall and honoring her corpse. Although earlier Mercilla is described as holding the scepter that betokens clemency and as hearing pleas of people "meane and base" seeking justice from the monarch herself (that is, equity), here the text does not mention those related virtues that mitigate punishment when the general law makes the penalty overly severe. She shows not clemency but mercy. "Without griefe or gall" she tempers the "doome a rights" (10.4), mixing virtuous responses in a way that modifies her treatment of the unjust (*OED* "temper" 1–4). Far from the "ethics of rights [subsuming] the ethics of care" in book 5, as Shirley Staton would have it (160) in her pioneering essay on reading *The Faerie Queene* in the light of Carol Gilligan's research, the episode shows Mercilla responds first to human misery, holding both of Gilligan's moral orientations in a dialectic of feeling, perception, and action, as Spenser's syntax nicely conveys ("But . . . Though . . . Yet . . ."). (For a contrasting view of Mercilla's mercy, see Anne Shaver's "Handling Elizabeth" in this volume.)

Interpretive issues, even polemics, bubble up as quickly in the classroom as on this page when Aristotle and Aquinas are read alongside episodes in book 5. A philosopher's definition of "the right" (still a key term in the palace of Mercilla) or of mercy may readily allow students to perceive more sharply what Artegall seeks or Mercilla feels. Yet the very act of glossing a virtue raises the question of whether the virtue is actually realized in the fictive situation and nudges students to close reading, historical inquiry, critical theory. Likewise, philosophical principle (for example, that intent, circumstances, degree of awareness, and habit ought all to be analyzed in determining the morality of an act) can initiate a complex inquiry into a multivalent episode like that of the headless lady, clarifying at least some of the moral issues at stake, although some subversive ambivalences usually remain.

If the complexities of representation can at times subvert theory of law and justice, theory can in turn subvert such easy assumptions as that the just and the merciful are opposed, an assumption stigmatized decades ago by Rosemond Tuve (67) but still very much alive in published readings of book 5. Even more importantly, reading theory and fiction together can enrich and enliven those tags we use day after day when we speak of a specific legal case or social policy, the remnants of the classical education generally prescribed, until the end of the nineteenth century, for those who set out to follow the law or civil service: that punishment should fit the crime, that opportunity should be equal. This symbolic reading can even shame us into considering whole dimensions of justice to which our historical site makes us blind. Unlike Spenser, we lack separate courts of equity and are not confronted by Anabaptists creating experiments in social and material equality.

To weave together a few leitmotifs of this essay, I propose that the Spenserian text provokes us to read in theoretical terms not just by using juridical language but by placing its justiciars Artegall, Britomart, and even Mercilla in a world where they must pass judgment without relying on particular laws. Malfont may have his tongue nailed to a post "by law," but in the trial that meets our expectations for the heart of a book on justice (Stump, "Isis" 88), the laws involved are not promulgated, as are those in the Shakespearean trials of *Measure for Measure* and *The Merchant of Venice*. While many Renaissance readers surely would have recalled the law on treason at this point in the text, its absence shifts attention to the dialectic of right and mercy, to the problem of how to act when the claims of two virtues seem to be irreconcilable but both are daughters of God. Act Mercilla does, and although her actions may not address such controverted points as whether or not mercy is a part of justice—points raised, as the narrator says, by "Clarkes . . . in their deuicefull art" (10.1)—she does realize Thomas's conceptions of how the just and the merciful person performs her functions, even in a highly problematic political situation. Theoretical discourse about justice is "endlesse worke," like the romance narrative of *The Faerie Queene*, but, read together, they may suggest the outlines of a communal moral consensus on justice that largely served as the basis for legal decisions before the seventeenth-century triumph of state-endorsed rules (Millon) and that survives among us in our catchphrases and half-understood social slogans.

NOTE

[1]My thinking on Aristotle's *Ethics*, on Thomas's *Summa*, and on book 5 of *The Faerie Queene* has been greatly shaped by my seminar colleague, W. Lad Sessions of the philosophy department at Washington and Lee. Together, we designed the seminar I describe in the opening pages, and he kindly made incisive comments, local and global, on the first draft of this essay. Lewis LaRue, a Washington and Lee professor of law who audited the seminar, also read the essay with a fine critical eye.

A note on texts of the *Summa Theologiae*: Of the *quaestiones* referred to in this essay, all but four are contained in *On Law, Morality, and Politics*, ed. Baumgarth and Regan. Permission to photocopy these four—on justice, *epieikeia*, clemency, and mercy—may be obtained from McGraw-Hill, the American publisher of the Blackfriars translation.

For the *Ethics* I use the Irwin translation. All quotations from *The Faerie Queene* are taken from the Variorum edition (ed. Greenlaw et al.).

Rethinking the Spenserian Gaze

A. Leigh DeNeef

No recent theoretical or political orientation has more directly affected the curricular and pedagogical shape of literary studies than feminism. In making so bold a claim, I do not mean to minimize divergent or even opposing strains within feminism itself or to minimize the impact of other theoretical agendas. Rather, I want simply to state at the outset what should be obvious to anyone in my generation of academics: that we have all, whether deliberately or not, changed the ways we think about and teach our various literary figures and periods in the light of, and often under the intellectual, moral, or political pressure of, specific feminist arguments.

If this much can be granted without debate, I would make two further observations: first, the influence of feminism is more widespread among faculty members and graduate students than among undergraduates; and second, among those undergraduates who have been sensitized to feminist concerns there is a general lack of appreciation for the historical and theoretical complexities of those concerns. To the extent that these observations are accurate, they bear important consequences for our everyday teaching, consequences that I want to explore here by focusing on a particular issue that has shaped my own recent thinking about *The Faerie Queene*.

The issue I have in mind is the gaze, consistently analyzed in critical, psychoanalytic, and film theory as necessarily masculine and routinely shown in *The Faerie Queene* to objectify, dehumanize, commodify, and disempower Spenser's female characters.[1] Graduate and undergraduate students who have been exposed to feminist arguments are quick to seize on the poem's various scopic scenes. They accept without question the negative effects of the gaze, and they persistently assume that all gazes originate from a patriarchal position of domination and power. I suppose such assumptions are inevitable, especially among undergraduates: not only has feminist theory insistently repeated them, but the students themselves are probably too inexperienced to challenge them. Certainly my male students are too young to have felt the withdrawal of a specifically feminine gaze that convinces any man over age forty-five of its earlier presence. Similarly, in the absence of extended interpersonal relationships, undergraduates are hardly in a position to imagine the more constructive, supportive, or beneficial aspects of a gaze. One of the useful lessons, then, that our literary texts might offer such students is a warning about the too easy leap from the generalized models of theory to the varying particulars of experiential practice—a warning that can demonstrate the harsher social consequences of overly rigid gender characterizations or arbitrarily restrictive binary oppositions. This is a lesson that Spenser himself repeatedly offers, and thus one of the most useful pedagogical approaches to his text is an analysis of precisely these gender dynamics.

Spenser's treatment of the relations between the sexes has been the object of much recent criticism. Yet this work has tended to focus on a narrow set of characters—Britomart and Belphoebe, Amoret and Radigund—rather than on the structural device by which Spenser thematizes those relations. The gaze operates throughout the poem to transcribe a relatively nondramatic (and hence unempowered) act of looking into a highly charged set of consequences—responses to either seeing or being seen, responses that amaze or daze, grace or disgrace, allay or dismay.

The Spenserian gaze, in short, is a psychic scenario in which one gender confronts the radical alterity of its other and adopts certain postures of power to negotiate that difference. Those negotiations generally take place within the terms, both literary and courtly, of a Petrarchanism already problematized by what Reed Dasenbrock calls the inequalities of domination and desire, but I am here going to bracket Spenser's critique of Petrarchanism to situate the gaze at the imaginative center of his entire poetic project: in his desire to look upon and to be looked at by the queen, in his intention to offer her a series of mirrors in which she may see herself, and in his hope that amidst the various shadows of Elizabeth scattered throughout the poem a reader might glimpse the awesome figure of sovereignty itself.

Let me pause over this broadest of visual scenes. Spenser criticism routinely assumes that the intended reader of *The Faerie Queene* is Elizabeth herself; the poem is dedicated to her and she is consistently addressed in the six proems (Quilligan in *Milton's Spenser* is the major exception to this assumption). Yet Spenser tells us in the letter to Ralegh that his general end of all the work is to fashion a gentleman or noble person. The dedicatory sonnets would seem to corroborate this implied masculine audience insofar as they delineate and address the patriarchal authorities through whom sovereign power circulated within the realm: the lord high chancellor, the lord high treasurer, the lord high chamberlain, the right honorable earl of Northumberland, etc. (D. L. Miller, "Figuring"; Stillman, "Politics"). It is noteworthy that the queen herself is a conspicuously absent presence in this initial depiction of her court, although, as the final three sonnets suggest, other women are present. It might be argued, therefore—and despite the nod at a few selected court women—that the poem is specifically addressed to such men as are subject to the omnipresent gaze of the ever-absent queen and that the gentleman Spenser wishes to fashion is precisely one who understands the power of that gaze to constitute him as a subject.

At this level of political argument, the queen herself occupies an increasingly problematic position as both subject and object of the poem's, like the court's, various gazes. As subject of the royal gaze, Elizabeth may represent either an authoritative beneficence that literally "makes" men by "gracing" and rewarding them or a spying voyeurism that threatens to emasculate or unman her would-be courtiers by commodifying and consuming them. As regal object gazed on, Elizabeth may represent either an elevation of feminine authority by enforcing masculine subjection or an exhibitionism that threatens paradoxically to unmake that authority by subjecting it to masculine idolatry. We might play out these alternatives to show that they are not as neat or as clear-cut as I have posed them, but a more important point needs to be made—namely, that the would-be courtier to whom the poem may be addressed is also in a problematic position as both subject and object of sundry gazes. Indeed, it is precisely because the economy of the gaze can either empower or disempower both the queen and her subjects that it becomes thematized within Spenser's poem. *The Faerie Queene*, in consequence, should be conceived as under the scrutiny of competing doubled gazes: masculine courtiers watch a female sovereign watching the poem *at the same time* as feminine sovereignty watches male courtiers viewing that poem. The text itself is both constituted and made anxious by the continuous pressure of these contesting gazes. One of the broader tasks of reading Spenser is to reveal, on the level of the text, the effects of that pressure: where and how does Spenser try to protect his text from the potential "misdeemings" of these conflicting "readings" or "regards"?

To situate all of Spenser's gazes within this political context is to call attention to the gaze itself as a structuring of subtle negotiations: between masculine and feminine ego formations, between an eye that proffers judgment and the me made desperate or guilty by that judgment, between an individual subject and the conflicting forces of subjection and subjectification; between the object of one's sight and the self-objectifications enforced by the mere fact that one is also looked at; between the economics of appropriating power from and ceding power to the eye that gazes. If I now make the Spenserian gaze sound suspiciously like a Lacanian one, that is because I think Lacan provides a useful hermeneutic for disclosing the dynamics of Spenser's visual fields.

To cite one example that might follow from these suggestions, Lacan's mirror stage offers a provocative model for the poem's own "mirrors more than one." Just as Lacan's child first discovers and then assumes an ideal-ego presented to him by the image he sees held, sustained, and offered by his (m)other, so Spenser's "gentleman" or courtier receives an idealized image of himself only insofar as that reflection is authorized and sustained by feminine sovereignty. In both cases, the fantasy of "wholeness" or autonomous "power" of the masculine ego is dependent on the continual presence of the gaze of a female other (which, I repeat, itself depends on the absence of the real woman, mother or queen). And in this sense, for both Lacan's child and Spenser's implied reader, the misrecognition of the sustaining other is a salutary precondition of political ego identity. Elizabeth, that is, must appear in the poem not as such but as that powerful mirage known to the Renaissance as the body politic, "Unseene of any, yet of all beheld" (7.7.13), the paradoxical, problematic symbol that Lacan calls the Name-of-the-Father ("Subversion"; Bellamy, "The Vocative").

In what follows I do not intend to make extensive use of Lacan, even though my remarks depend obliquely on him; rather I wish only to resituate a single narrative moment of book 6 within Spenser's broader scopic field. The narrative I want to focus on is that of Serena, and my argument is that the gazes to which she is subjected in this book become meaningful only in relation to a host of other Spenserian women gazing or being gazed on. I am concentrating on Serena first because her character seems to confirm absolutely the general feminist model of the victimized female. Such an interpretation, however, needs to be qualified. Because Serena's subjection is the final "vision" of the second installment of *The Faerie Queene*, it assumes considerably more thematic importance than has yet been recognized. It needs to be viewed in the context of how Spenser repeatedly tries to demonstrate that his presumed "gentleman or noble person" is fashioned primarily by means of how he *or she* looks upon that other, synecdochically named woman *or man*, who is constantly looking at him *or her* looking.

It is necessary, then, to see that the narrative of Serena's humiliation before a sequence of masculine gazes is itself compelled by alternative and fearful images of a masculine subjection before a feminine gaze. In *Amoretti*, for example, Spenser tries over and over again to dramatize the act by which he looks upon his lover only to find her always already looking at him. Naming that act explicitly as a gaze, Spenser describes it as one "in which al powers conspire" and contest. In sonnet 5, it is precisely the lady's "lofty looks" that disarm and disempower his own "rash eyes" that have gazed on her so wildly and loosely as to threaten her with blame of "too portly pride" and "foule dishonor." In sonnet 35,

> My hungry eies, through greedy covetize,
> Still to behold the object of their paine
> With no contentment can themselves suffize
> But having pine, and having not complain.
> For lacking it, they cannot life sustain,
> And having it they gaze on it the more;
> In their amazement like Narcissus vain
> Whose eyes him starved; so plenty makes me poor.[2]

Here the gaze becomes both the source and the economy of desire, of a narcissism that must constantly empty itself so as to empower an appetite or demand for more, in a scenario that may remind us of Freud's *fort/da*—here played with the woman rather than the reel. And yet, as sonnet 37 shows, the very gaze that seeks to co-opt power from its object is immediately betrayed by a countergaze that not only "entraps" the lover's sight but censures and essentializes it as "mens frail eyes." In each of these sonnets the gaze becomes a field of contention, by turns empowering and disempowering masculine desire. In each instance, the real threat turns upon the moment of sur-prise, when the subject's own gaze is overtaken and mastered by the gaze of the female other. This latter gaze, as Lacan reminds us, is always one of censure or blame: it reinscribes the subject as guilty and imposes on him the condition of shame.

One obvious repetition of this contestatory visual field in *The Faerie Queene* is the Bower of Bliss, which is successively re-presented in book 2 in terms of selective gazes. In canto 5, one of the first of these repetitions, Spenser describes Cymochles wallowing "In daintie delices and lavish joys . . . amongst loose ladies" (28). These damsels—like the twins Guyon later encounters in the crystal fountain ("unheling" their amorous spoils to his greedy eyes [12.64]) or like Acrasia herself (whose "snowy brest was bare to ready spoil / Of hungry eyes" [12.78])—offer themselves specifically as objects of Cymochles's gaze. In turn,

> He like an adder lurking in the weeds
>> His wandering thought in deep desire does steep
>> And his frail eye with spoil of beauty feeds:
>> Sometimes he falsely fains himself to sleep
>> While through their lids his wanton eyes do peep
>> To steal a snatch of amorous conceit
>> Whereby close fire into his heart does creep
>> So he them deceives, deceived in his deceit.
>>   (5.34)

Cymochles's desire, initially incited and empowered by the simple fact that the damsels stare directly at him, is subsequently disempowered by the very gaze that produces it: as Atin rightly concludes, his vision is literally "entombed here in ladies lap" and he himself emasculated into "womanish" voluptuousness.

If Cymochles represents one dimension of the gaze's power to disempower —here analogous to the frustrated narcissism in *Amoretti*—Acrasia, in canto 12, represents another, more insidious threat. With Verdant lying in her lap, "her false eyes fast fixéd in his sight," Acrasia greedily depastures his delight and "through his humid eyes did suck his spright / Quite molten into lust and pleasure lewd" (st. 73). Whether we read this final image as symbolic or graphic, spirit or flesh, its dynamic is the same: feeding herself on the eyes that seek to feast on her, Acrasia both drains and devours all masculine "power" with her gaze.

We might be reminded at this point of another breast frequently bared to greedy spoil: Elizabeth herself, as Louis Montrose notes, occasionally appeared at court in a condition remarkably similar to that of the women in Acrasia's bower (Montrose, *"Midsummer"* 66–67). In 1597, the ambassador extraordinaire of Henri IV described one such appearance of the queen: "she kept the front of her dress open, and one could see the whole of her bosom, and passing low"; at a second audience, the queen again "had a petticoat open in front, as was also her chemise, in such a manner that she often opened this dress and one could see all her belly, and even to her navel." Montrose suggests that such displays signified Elizabeth's status as maiden and as bountiful mother to the realm; seen from the perspective of a courtly Petrarchanism, they may figure the conflicts inherent in the doubleness of the category of woman herself (cruel fair and *donna angelicata*). But seen from the perspective of Acrasia's bower, they may also figure a narcissistic exhibitionism that depends on eliciting, precisely to frustrate, the various desires that motivate a given subject's gaze. Such a scene of proffering her bosom to and withdrawing it from the courtly eyes that would gaze on it is not very different from the dynamics of Spenser's feminine tyranny in the bower. So powerful, in fact, are the images of such victimized males within the poem that Spenser may feel compelled, by book 6, to offer an inverted scenario.

Before I look specifically at book 6, however, it is necessary to clarify the argument thus far. The sketch I have made of the visual field that constitutes the scopic context for this book is admittedly skewed. But so too, I would posit, is the field offered by contemporary feminism. Victimization is not a horror visited upon one sex to the exclusion of the other. It is a consequence both suffer equally. Because the gaze operates destructively on either gender it assumes a central thematic role in Spenser's poem. My emphasis, therefore, on the victimizing of men rather than women is merely to offer a countertext to the one feminism has drawn concerning the gaze's effect. The narrative of Serena is situated exactly at the intersection of these divergent contexts.

In the proem to book 6, Spenser tries to recontextualize the analyses to follow by once again reminding the reader of his "sovereign Lady Queene" on whom "the eyes of all" have "fixéd been," whom so many "feeble eyes misdeem," and who is herself invited to gaze on this court of courtesy as "a mirror sheene" of her own "wisest sight." The visual reflexivities announced here are immediately echoed in the first incident of the book proper, in which Calidore meets Artegall: "Who whenas each of other had a sight, / They knew themselves, and both their persons read" (1.4). Each comes to know himself, in perfect Lacanian fashion, by seeing himself reflected in the gaze of the other. Recognizing themselves as beings-given-to-be-seen, both knights can then assume the identity of both self and other. The gaze that allows Calidore and Artegall such ego identification is what Eve Sedgwick has defined as a kind of homosocial insight that constitutes both as subjects as well as objects of the *unseen* gazes on and by the Faerie Queene. Such a moment, therefore, radically revises earlier masculine encounters in the poem, where the normative response is a militant struggle to promote the self as the sole object of the feminine gaze. This means, I think, that by book 6, Spenser has turned his attention more directly to ways in which that gaze draws men together as a social and political unit, not apart (and together, I would add, both negatively and positively). And to this extent, one would need to discriminate more carefully than I have time to do here between this homosocial gaze and the gazes of or at the other gender.

The next two incidents, involving Priscilla and Serena, return to Spenser's now inverted visual field as both women are stumbled on in compromising conditions. Each woman has naively assumed herself free from "gealous spies" and "too curious" or "envious eyes"; each is subsequently abashed by the sudden intrusion of an alien eye; each is subjected by that gaze to the threat of shame; and each seeks to withdraw herself from the gaze to escape its censure. At this point, Spenser orchestrates the narrative return of the Blatant Beast, which, under the combined forces of Envy and Detraction, pronounces aloud (babbles) the shame each woman feels. "Ne ever Lady of so honest name," the hermit tells us, "But he them spotted with reproach or secret shame" (6.12). Such shame is the principal threat Spenser sees to the courtesy he defines both as the book's social virtue and as the political grace that must motivate the reformed court. Book 6 might be seen, therefore, as an attempt to figure varieties of this shame, this "Regard of womanhead" (5.9.45), by emphasizing ways in which gazing on the queen at the center of that court perverts and distorts the very courtesy it ought to foster. If Elizabeth and her courtiers are both constituted by and empowered within the dynamics of gazing, both are subject to the tyrannies that gazing makes possible.

In this light, the significance of the poem's final vision—the threatened cannibalizing of Serena—needs to be read in terms of its correlative but opposite image. And that, I would suggest, is Mirabella, whose presumption that "her beauty had such sovereign might" (6.7.31) leads her to fashion herself deliberately as object of the masculine gaze. As Freud and Lacan remind us, this exhibitionism is the flip side of voyeurism, and as Spenser shows with Acrasia, the will to power through subjection of men's sight once again effects a loss of power altogether. Mirabella is thus "compelled by force" and fear: "loth to see, or to be seene at all," she becomes the image of sovereign beauty disgracing itself. Deceived in her own deceit, Mirabella is refigured as the gaze's effect: "Shame would be hid" (6.8.5).

If femininity can subjugate and disempower itself through an exhibitionist abuse of the masculine gaze, it can also be dominated by the voyeuristic force of that gaze. Serena and Pastorella demonstrate this destructive pole. The threat voyeurism represents can not only be specified but also shown to put both men and women at equal risk; after Lacan, we can argue that insofar as the gaze converts the other, either male or female, into an object to be consumed, the self loses the very grounds on which to constitute itself. If both the subject and its other are irretrievably caught in a want-to-be or lack of being, neither can satisfy the desire that lack occasions. I cannot be loved for what I am; I can be loved only as a signifier of what you lack. If, then, I am a metonymy of your desire, you are a metonymy of my want-to-be.

The trap of this Lacanian trope is that the inevitable failures of desire do not alter the fact that neither subject nor other can be constituted independently. Each arises, comes into existence, only as the structural signifier of or for the other. Loss of a (feminine) other, therefore, is the effective and concurrent loss of a (masculine) self. It is exactly this self-destructive loss of a necessary feminine other that the narratives of Pastorella and Serena try to describe. The threats against both women are the same: a kind of masculine idolatry that turns feminine beauty into bounty, flesh into food, and the female body into a commodity. The brigands who capture Pastorella are a "lawlesse people" who "feed on spoil and booty" and who convert neighbors, especially women, into objects to sell (6.10.39). In canto 11 Spenser describes the economy of such a sale: the brigands praise Pastorella's beauty "t'augment her price" (st. 11), thereby inciting the merchants to gaze on her bounty:

> These merchants fixéd eyes did so amaze
> That what through wonder, and what through delight
> A while on her they greedily did gaze
> And did her greatly like, and did her greatly praise.
> (st. 13)

The sequence Spenser dramatizes here charts the psychic and Petrarchan movement by which praise of the lady degenerates into the consumptive relations of prizing and pricing, commodifying and consuming.

The same terms govern the far grimmer narrative of Serena. Captured by the lawless cannibals, Serena is subjected to a grotesque parody of the conventional Elizabethan and Petrarchan praise of feminine beauty. Whetting their knives and lips, the cannibals gaze on the now naked woman:

> Her ivory necke, her alabaster breast,
>> Her paps, which like white silken pillows were,
>> For Love in soft delight thereon to rest;
>> Her tender sides, her belly white and clear,
>> Which like an altar did it self uprear,
>> To offer sacrifice divine thereon;
>> Her goodly thighs, whose glory did appear. . . .
>
> . . . .
> Those daintie parts, the darlings of delight . . .
> (6.8.42–43)

Here the typical blazon of female beauty is converted, through the gaze that records it, into "a common feast," into "the daintest of morsels" (st. 38, 39). Serena is literally despoiled, and while the remainder of the canto contrives her rescue, she herself remains subjected to inward shame and disgrace: she has lost the power not only to appear before her beloved but even to speak to him.

That Spenser intends Serena's humiliation to represent contemporary courtly dynamics might be suggested by our difficulties in accounting for her name. Hamilton thinks it is mere linguistic irony: Serena is anything but serene. We can politicize that irony, however, by noting that the merged narratives of Timias and Serena in book 6 encourage a direct historical allusion to Ralegh and his shamed wife, Elizabeth Throckmorton: Serena was Ralegh's pet name for his wife (s.v. "Walter Raleigh" and "Serena" in Hamilton et al.). A further historical reference might be possible: was Queen Elizabeth herself ever accorded the honorific epithet of "serene highness"? If someone could prove that—and I confess I cannot yet do so—we might argue that the Serena narrative allows *The Faerie Queene* to end precisely where the dedicatory sonnets do: in a question about how the political power relations between the queen and "all the gracious and beautiful Ladies of her Court" constitute the visual field of the various courtiers who, like Colin and Calidore on Mt. Acidale, gather to gaze on them. Linking two Elizabeths "both under one name," Spenser may be warning the queen that any court that uses women "To sharpe [the] sence with sundry beauties view" (dedicatory sonnet 17.7) subjects femininity as such to a kind of visual cannibalism.

If the court, then, as Spenser conceives and describes it, is the site of various masculine-feminine relations that produce and sustain transactions of power deriving from and returning to the queen, then the assorted gazes in *The Faerie Queene* attempt to reveal some of the likely products of those transactions. At the most dangerous poles, the gaze would chart scenarios of exhibitionism and voyeurism in which both Elizabeth and her surrounding courtiers might find themselves trapped. By exposing the paradoxical ways in which these gazes defeat rather than sustain the courtly flow of power, Spenser tries to suggest the visual field within which an appropriate recycling of that power might be generated. And this too could be analyzed by means of a registration in which subject and object are mutually dependent on a symbolic system of exchange conducted along the axes of a doubled gaze. Only a recognition of that doubleness, of the dialectic between seeing and being seen, or between demand and desire, can protect a gaze from the misdeemings and mirages that would ultimately disempower it. And here we might invoke two other Spenserian figures, for the psychic defenses the poet would put to work against the fearful threats of either exhibitionism or voyeurism may well be those two feminine others encountered in Alma's court—Praysdesire and Shamefastness. As the dialectic that both offers the self to and recognizes its dependence on the gaze of an other, these two map the productive limits of any and all ego identity, personal and political, of the queen or of those courtiers and court ladies who around her ring.

NOTES

[1]For theoretical arguments, see Lacan, *Four Fundamental Concepts* 67–122; Metz; and Mulvey. For Spenser studies, see "Gender," "Heroine," and "Sex" in Hamilton et al.; Cavanagh, " 'Beauties Chace' "; and Silberman, "Singing" and "The Hermaphrodite." For important exceptions to these generalizations see Snow; Krier, *Gazing*.

[2]All Spenser quotations are taken from Greenlaw et al.

"The Triall of True Curtesie": Teaching Book 6 as Pastoral Romance

Margaret P. Hannay

The current emphasis on diversity in the literary canon, while long overdue, can have the unanticipated side effect of limiting students' knowledge of other times, even while expanding their knowledge of other cultures. The English honors program at Siena College seeks to present works from the traditional canon in more saleable form, both presenting them on their own terms and "overreading" them with less traditional works. A course on the pastoral, for example, entitled Edenic Literature, emphasized Renaissance works such as *The Shepheardes Calendar* and *Paradise Lost*, but it also included more recent works such as Mary Shelley's *Frankenstein*, C. S. Lewis's children story *The Magician's Nephew*, and Sean O'Faolain's short story "The Man Who Invented Sin," as well as an excursion to the Albany Institute of History and Art to study the portrayal of our area as Edenic by the Hudson River painters.

My current honors seminar, on the pastoral romance, considers four related works: Philip Sidney's *Old Arcadia*; the *New Arcadia*, emphasizing book 3; Edmund Spenser's *The Faerie Queene*, emphasizing book 6; and Mary Sidney Wroth's 1621 *Urania*, emphasizing books 1 and 2. Students find that the addition of a work by a woman writer enriches their readings of Sidney and Spenser by sharpening our focus on issues of gender and class. Lady Wroth, the first English woman to write a prose romance, modeled her work on that of her uncle, Sir Philip Sidney. The first part of her romance was published in 1621 but had to be withdrawn because of complaints from Edward Denny, baron of Waltham, and the duke of Buckingham about topical references (Wroth, *Poems* 31–37, 236–41); the second part of *Urania* is extant in one manuscript only, owned by the Newberry Library. (A transcription of the 1621 *Urania* for classroom use is now available from the Women Writers Project, Brown University; Josephine Roberts's definitive edition of the entire work should be available soon.)

Because students in the honors program are not necessarily English majors and usually have not taken other courses in the English Renaissance, I begin with a film to orient them to the Elizabethan world. An effective introduction is "The Marriage Game" from the BBC *Elizabeth R* series, which dramatizes the use of Petrarchan and pastoral language as a political ploy and also presents the earl of Leicester as a major figure, thereby simplifying later explanations of Spenser's social position and of the Sidney family. Few of my students have traveled abroad and even fewer have an accurate mental image of the sixteenth century, so the film helps give them a sense of Elizabethan life—countryside, music, architecture, clothing, etiquette, gender roles, and the complexity of its political games. The film is followed by a lecture in which we put the pastoral romance into the wider Elizabethan context (Montrose, "Eliza" and "Of Gentlemen"; Norbrook; Sinfield, "Power"; Bernard) and into the history of the pastoral form (Ettin; Poggioli; Patterson, *Pastoral*).

Lest the sheer complexity of the romances discourage students, I include a handout of character identifications and thought questions for each work. For the relatively straightforward *Old Arcadia*, I suggest that students keep their eyes on the four royal teenagers: Musidorus, Pyrocles, Pamela, and Philoclea. Then we talk about the parents: Basilius, Gynecia, and Euarchus. Students have little difficulty with the added characters of Amphialus, Cecropia, Argalus, and Parthenia in the *New Arcadia*, although the entry of various disguised knights into the tournaments can confuse them. For *The Faerie Queene* 6, we concentrate on three major plot strands: Sir Calidore's quest to subdue the Blatant Beast and his pastoral retreat (cantos 1–3 and cantos 9–12); Serena's wounding by the Blatant Beast and her subsequent adventures (3.20–4.16; 5.1–6.16; 8.31–51); and Mirabella, the proud, disdainful mistress punished for her crimes against Cupid, god of love (6.16–17; 7.27–8.30). For their weekly short papers students are asked to consider such questions as the following: How do characters, episodes, and settings in *The Faerie Queene* 6 mirror, parody, or reverse those in the *Old* and/or *New Arcadia*? How does the pastoral retreat of Calidore compare and contrast with that of the princes in the *Arcadia*? How does the attitude toward social class or gender in *The Faerie Queene* 6 compare and contrast with that in the *Old* and/or *New Arcadia*?

Urania, with its enormous cast of characters, can quickly overwhelm students, so the handout focuses on the two royal families of cousins: the children of the king and queen of Naples—Amphilanthus, Leonius, and Urania —and the children of the king and queen of Morea—Pamphilia, Parselius, Rosindy, Philarchos, and Philistella. Because students are fascinated with biographical allusions, I let them indulge in enough speculation to help them find their way through the labyrinth of intersecting stories. Amphilanthus as William Herbert and Pamphilia as Wroth herself are well-established parallels; the queen of Naples clearly refers to Mary Sidney, countess of Pembroke, Wroth's aunt, godmother, and literary mentor (Hannay, "Your Vertuous"). The younger brothers and sisters in each royal family also have biographical references. For example, Leonius seems to figure Philip Herbert, named for the Pembroke lion; he loves Veralinda, probably a reference to Susan de Vere, Wroth's dear friend the countess of Montgomery, for whom the romance is named. The royal family of Morea includes Pamphilia's brother Rosindy, a transparent reference to young Robert Sidney; Pamphilia's other siblings include less obvious references to Wroth's many brothers and sisters. Students enjoy finding biographical clues in *Urania*, such as Amphilanthus's disguise as the "Knight of the Cipher" in the Pembroke crimson and blue, with his device a cipher (probably an anagram) that shows the "worth" of his mistress's name, thereby making the familiar Wroth-worth pun (sig. Oo2r–v). The danger is, of course, that students will read the work only as roman à clef, so once they have the plot straight, they are asked to consider other issues: How do characters, episodes, and settings in *Urania* mirror, parody, or reverse those in the *Arcadia* or *The Faerie Queene* 6? What notable images of vice or virtue are presented? What rules for conduct are thereby presented or assumed for each gender and class?

Our first reading is the *Old Arcadia*. It is the first chronologically and the most accessible to students, who can readily identify with the teenaged protagonists, find the language less opaque than that of the later works, and enjoy Sidney's humor. The comedy of Basilius and Gynecia in the cave, Mopsa's adventures in the wishing tree, and the revival of Pyrocles in Philoclea's bedroom assuage their fear of an unfamiliar genre and make possible the teaching by delight that Sidney advocated. The *Old Arcadia* also introduces standard romance motifs and conventions that students will encounter in *The Faerie Queene* and *Urania*, such as disguised princes, princesses raised as shepherdesses, singing shepherds, attacks by wild beasts, kidnapping, and the rescue of the princesses (Chang 114–51; Tonkin, *Spenser's Courteous* 285, 296).

For discussions of gender roles, we begin with the comic treatment of Pyrocles disguised as the Amazon Cleophila. Students laugh together at Cleophila's protestation that "for all my apparel, there is nothing I desire more than fully to prove myself a man in this enterprise" (21). Although pastoral fiction is usually presented from a male viewpoint, as Andrew Ettin demonstrates (146), Helen Hackett reminds us that Renaissance romance was perceived as having a mainly female readership and therefore was "denigrated" (40). Gender issues are highlighted by the authors' assumptions about audience. I have found Mary Ellen Lamb's study *Gender and Authorship in the Sidney Circle* particularly useful in introducing the idea of gendered reading. Rather than present Lamb's findings to students directly, I assign each of them one of Sidney's addresses to his audience as "fair ladies," giving them five minutes to analyze the significance of the reference, and then have them explain to the class what narrator assumes about the reader. They quickly discover for themselves the implication of the reader in the morally dubious actions of the characters and then in the condemnation of those actions by Euarchus; the students, however, give the romance the "compassionate readings" that Lamb believes Sidney desires (80). Later in the semester we discuss the audience implied by Spenser and by Wroth.

The power of the male gaze, implicit in the blazon, is also introduced in the *Old Arcadia* through Musidorus's blazon of Pamela before his attempted rape and through the song Pyrocles recalls as he lays Philoclea on her bed, "What tongue can her perfections tell." The blazon is transferred to the comic bathing scene in the *New Arcadia*. Students contrast Sidney's blazons with Spenser's story of Serena, subjected by the cannibals to a bizarre literalization of the blazon tradition: "Some with their eyes the daintest morsels chose; / Some praise her paps, some praise her lips and nose" as they "whet their kniues" and prepare for the feast (6.8.39).[1] We consider the implied power of the male gaze in the light of Theresa Krier's *Gazing on Secret Sights*; A. Leigh DeNeef's essay in the present collection should also prove helpful. Students note also the problematic use of poetic blazons in *Urania*, the "internalization by a female author" of a way of seeing that is "associated with masculine sexuality" (Hackett 58).

The *Old Arcadia* introduces students to the *querelle des femmes* in the early debate between Pyrocles and Musidorus, who summarize centuries of invective in a few comic pages, thereby providing the necessary background for a consideration of the influence of gender on identity formation (Jordan, *Renaissance* 225). We then consider models presented for female behavior: the saintly patience of Pamela and Philoclea, the gracious passivity of Pastorella, and the constancy of Pamphilia are set against the negative female figures, such as the lustful Gynecia, the ambitious Cecropia, the scornful Mirabella, and the aggressive Nereana, who serves as "Pamphilia's alter ego" (Beilin 224).

Students recognize that Renaissance strictures of chastity make the women particularly vulnerable to the Blatant Beast, or slander. In the essentially comic *Old Arcadia*, Gynecia is prevented from accomplishing her lustful desire, and her reputation is maintained, "fortune something supplying her want of virtue" (4). Because those who knew the truth "never bewrayed her," she is celebrated as "the perfect mirror of all wifely love" (360). Philoclea does consummate her love with Pyrocles, in a hilarious adaptation of the Pyramus and Thisbe tale, but her reputation is saved by their marriage. Students note that failures of chastity are so serious that in the *New Arcadia* the stories of the young princes and princesses are rewritten; all of these characters act virtuously, while lust is safely displaced onto Amphialus and his mother, Cecropia. *The Faerie Queene* presents a series of women who stray from chastity. Calidore's impact on such women in book 6 reveals the problematic nature of the virtue of courtesy. The misadventures of Serena are particularly instructive, for the courteous Calidore stumbles on a pastoral love scene in which a knight in the "couert shade . . . did safely rest," enjoying the love of his lady. Though "it was his fortune, not his fault," to blunder into this situation, Calidore does not tactfully withdraw; instead, he engages the knight, Calepine, in shoptalk, leaving Serena unprotected and vulnerable to the bite of the Blatant Beast (6.3.20–24). Her subsequent misadventures, including the attack of the cannibals, all result from this courteous knight's insensitivity to her reputation. Students are quick to notice that chastity is not given quite the same prominence in *Urania*, probably because Wroth, who had two illegitimate children by her cousin William Herbert, is far more sympathetic than Sidney or Spenser to the plight of a woman who loves one man but is forced to marry another.

My students understand problems caused by a system of arranged marriage, since some of them are children or grandchildren of immigrants who had such marriages. After mentioning more cheerful arranged marriages among their own relatives, students are eager to discuss Cecropia's attempts to coerce Pamela or Philoclea to marry Amphialus. They also remark that, in the story of Priscilla, Spenser seems rather oblivious to the suffering such coercion causes women. Calidore does restore Priscilla to her father and save her reputation, but he immediately goes on to his next adventure— leaving her to marry the "great pere" she had originally fled (3.7). Students observe that the theme of forced marriage recurs with increased intensity in the *Urania*, but no viable options are presented for avoiding such a fate. In the first half of book 1, for example, five women are forced to marry against their wills. Only one woman attempts resistance and flees her wedding, but her action brings about the death of both husband and lover, whereupon she enters a religious house—and then quickly dies of grief.

In addition to being interested in gender roles, students are particularly concerned about the presentation of social class. As a way of approaching the topic, we note that the quest for self-discovery is objectified by each of these pastoral romances in formulaic terms, as shepherds or shepherdesses are revealed to be of royal blood. Sidney includes the theme in the *Old Arcadia* and expands it in the *New Arcadia*. The princess Pamela is fully aware of her identity, disdaining her subjection under the "lout" Dametas, a shepherd imposed as her guardian. Although she has, "to show an obedience, taken on shepherdish apparel," she chooses to assert her true identity by wearing a diamond set in horn with the motto "Yet still myself" (*Countesse* 145–46).[2] Because Pamela is conscious of her superior status, Musidorus discovers that his disguise as shepherd bars him from her love. He may rescue her from a bear, but he "found that a shepherd's service was but considered of as from a shepherd" (221). To win his princess, the shepherd-knight Musidorus must teach Pamela to read his identity. I ask students to list his strategies for self-revelation: his metapastoral poem, "My sheep are thoughts," sung "to show what kind of shepherd I was" (232); his courtship of Mopsa, a dense reader, as a sign to the more astute Pamela; his narration of his story as that of another, with the standard device of slipping into the first person; the comic revelation of his birthmark, whose significance rests only on his own word; his demonstration of prowess on horseback and in armor. Attempting these strategies to establish that "I am no base body," Musidorus concludes that they have been futile: "all I do is but to beat a rock and get foam" (234). But Pamela, understanding the allegorical nature of his disguise, asks her sister, "did you ever see such a shepherd? . . . did you ever hear of such a prince?" (249). Students discover that Musidorus succeeds in revealing his true social rank under the veil of fiction to win Pamela.

We then consider Calidore's problems of social class, almost a mirror image of Musidorus's situation; to win the love of a shepherdess, he must veil his known aristocratic identity under a transparent pastoral fiction. Like Musidorus, Calidore deliberately adopts the garb of a shepherd to be near his beloved, a princess living as a shepherdess, but his position is rather more delicate than that of Musidorus, whose princess fully understands her own allegorical garb. Calidore first attempts to woo Pastorella in the courtly Petrarchan mode, entertaining her "with all kind courtesies, he could inuent" (9.34), but she does not understand "such queint vsage, fit for Queenes and Kings" and will not read "His layes, his loues, his lookes" as Calidore intends (35). Pastorella deems herself a shepherdess and is therefore not impressed with his courtly courtesies, for she "ne euer had such knightly seruice seene" and therefore "Did litle whit regard his courteous guize," preferring "Colins carolings" (35). Knowing Calidore to be a knight but believing herself to be a shepherdess, Pastorella "did them all despize," forcing him to adapt his strategies to her reading. Not until Calidore exchanges "his bright armes" for "shepheards weed" and his "steelhead speare" for "a shepheards hooke" (36) and deigns to excel in the shepherds' games does Pastorella begin to favor his suit. Like Pamela, Pastorella is kidnapped; like Musidorus, Calidore must abandon his shepherd's weeds and resume his knightly armour to rescue her and restore her to her royal rank.

After we have compared the treatment of the self-discovery motif in Sidney and Spenser, I ask students to consider Wroth's presentation of her shepherdess-princess Urania. They quickly discover that Urania does not rely on a knight to restore her to royal rank; instead, this resourceful woman undertakes her own "quest for identity" (Swift 329). The romance opens with the usual pastoral scene of a shepherdess bewailing her fate, but it is not unhappy love that troubles the fair Urania—it is the loss of her own identity. Challenging all the assumptions about love controlling the lives of women, she cries, "Can there be any neare the vnhappinesse of being ignorant, and that in the highest kind, not being certaine of mine owne estate or birth?" (sig. B1). Like Pamela and Pastorella, Urania eventually returns to her royal father and exchanges her shepherdess garments for the "rich robes fit for her birth" (sig. Cc1). Urania, however, is a far more active agent in her resumption of rank than is either Pastorella or Pamela. Instead of demonstrating the passivity natural to Pastorella or that forced on Pamela by imprisonment, Urania demonstrates courage, wisdom, and true friendship. For example, she is shown in the active role of standing watch on shipboard during a storm, "neuer shewing feare or trouble: incouraging all" (sig. F3v). Notable for her good sense, she offers excellent advice to the distraught Perissus, even though he at first scorns her words with the comment "I see you are a woman; and therefore not much to be marked" (sig. B2v). Like Britomart rebuking Scudamour, Urania eventually convinces Perissus that dying for love is pointless and ensures that he resumes his quest to right Limena. Similarly, she advises her cousin Pamphilia, who suffers from her love for the inconstant Amphilanthus, to reconsider the value of constancy as the primary virtue for women. Urania's friendship with Pamphilia becomes more important than her participation in the love games that form most of the plot of *Urania*; the role of female friendships in the development of female identity is thereby emphasized (N. Miller 124–25). Yet these friendships also confirm the former shepherdess in her royal rank.

Once we have established that each of these tales of self-discovery involves an ascent from shepherd status to the aristocracy, we discuss the unstated assumption that aristocratic status is a condition for love. Knowing her responsibility to her kingdom, Pamela must initially rebuff Dorus because of his apparent low social rank. Even believing herself to be a shepherdess, Pastorella disdains Coridon: "Though meane her lot, yet higher did her mind ascend" (9.10). For his part, Calidore is not interested in Pastorella until he decides that "her rare demeanure" is a mark of social class, setting her above the shepherds and making her worthy to be "a Princes Paragone esteemed" (9.11). Students observe that Wroth softens the emphasis on rank slightly, for Parselius hopes that Urania is a princess but decides to love her even if she is not. Wroth also incorporates a moving scene of farewell between Urania and her "good friends, and formerly supposed Parents," who would grieve if she disappeared (sig. D4). Nor is there a complete gulf between the princes and the shepherds, for "though poore, yet were they ciuill." When the foster parents kneel to kiss the hand of Parselius in reverence for his rank, he so much "respected them for their care of *Vrania*" that he raises them, embraces them, and gives them a detailed explanation of his reasons for believing her to be the lost princess, before a tearful goodbye. If their age had not prevented such a journey, we are told, the foster parents would have accompanied Urania to court.

Issues of social class trouble my students, many of whom are the first generation to attend college. Siena is a Franciscan college, originally founded to give the children of local Catholic immigrants the opportunity for an education that they could not otherwise afford. Although it has evolved from a commuter school to a residential college drawing students from throughout the Northeast, that early sense of mission continues. Many of the students must earn most of their tuition, even while carrying a full academic load. They question the aristocratic preconceptions in the comic portrayal of the cowardly Dametas and Coridon, who having never been trained in knightly skills, are ridiculous on horseback or in armor. When Musidorus addresses his suit to Pamela through his attentions and gifts to Mopsa, presented by the narrator as hilariously inappropriate, they feel considerable sympathy for Mopsa. Similarly, they resent the patronizing courtesy of Calidore to the shepherd Coridon, whose primary fault seems to be that of social class. Yes, he is cowardly, but students note that it is far easier to confront brigands when one holds a sword instead of a sheep hook, wears armour under shepherd's weed, and has training in combat. Students are troubled that Spenser defines courtesy in terms of decorous behavior within the social hierarchy: "to beare themselues aright / To all of each degree, as doth behoue" (6.2.1). The presentation of the "Saluage Man" raises even more disturbing questions for students, since his innate goodness is shown by his protection of the upper classes. An analogy to the Elizabethan ideal for the behavior of the Irish (and possibly of Native Americans) seems implicit in his servility (see Sheila Cavanagh's discussion of Irish stereotypes in this volume). He demonstrates his gentleness to Calepine by "creeping like a fawning hound, . . . Kissing his hands, and crouching to the ground." Like Shakespeare's Caliban, he is presented as lacking true language:

> For other language had he none nor speach,
> But a soft murmure, and confused sound
> Of senselesse words, which nature did him teach,
> T'expresse his passions, which his reason did empeach.
> (4.11)

Obviously, the "soft murmure, and confused sound / Of Senselesse words" could be a language unknown to Calepine, although the narrator does not grant that possibility. For my predominantly Irish American students, even more ominous is the presentation of the "saluage nation" of Celtic cannibals, who prepare for human sacrifice by playing "bagpypes" (8.46), a dark mirroring of the piping of shepherds before Pastorella (9.5) and of Colin Clout before the graces in canto 10.

The assumptions implicit in Spenser's treatment of the lower classes and those whom he sees as savage peoples leads into a discussion of conflicting views about the success of Calidore's courtesy, a courtesy that may be tainted by assumptions about gender or class. Is it true that Calidore "acts with the greatest courtesy man can display," although his courtesy often shades into policy (Shore 161)? Or is his "chivalry reduced to empty forms" (Helgerson, *Elizabethan* 333)? Does he lack "the spiritual faculty that would allow him to sense the mystery of courtesy" (Neuse, "Book VI" 352)? Does Calidore himself exemplify the limits of courtesy, a virtue inadequate to restore justice (Poggioli, ch. 10)? With his peculiar gift for blundering into idyllic pastoral situations and destroying them, he also chases away the graces from Mount Acidale, as Colin Clout sharply reminds him (10.20). In his devious courtship of Pastorella, he undermines the suit of the lower-class shepherd Coridon with an appearance of courtesy, thereby introducing the kind of envy and jealousy that produce the slander of the Blatant Beast. His presence may even, in some unspecified way, provoke the attack of the brigands who destroy the pastoral world. Calidore may slay the brigands, give Coridon back some of his sheep, and by chance restore Pastorella to her true place at court, but Meliboe and that whole pastoral world are obliterated. Each of these incidents is connected with *Arcadia*, for Sir Calidore combines qualities found in the shepherd-knight Musidorus and in

Amphialus, who mars everything he touches. Like seventeenth-century readers, students find the story of Argalus and Parthenia particularly moving; these lovers who avoid forced marriage only to be slain by Amphialus most fully reveal the inadequacies of "the courteous Amphialus."

At the end of the semester, we tie the course together through consideration of the political nature of the pastoral, demonstrating Sidney's contention that the pastoral "under the pretty tales of wolves and sheep" can be useful for social and political comment (*Defence* 95). Students draw parallels between Sidney's and Spenser's use of the political discourse implicit in this form that "sometimes under hidden forms [utter] such matters as otherwise they durst not deal with" (*Countesse* 84). They enjoy pursuing Richard McCoy's idea that Amphialus may represent Sidney's own position (*Sir Philip* x), as well as Annabel Patterson's discussion of Sidney's deliberate use of pastoral convention to "break through the political restraints and cultural assumptions" (*Pastoral* 43). Students are keenly interested in "strategies of indirection" used to criticize the state (Patterson, *Censorship*), noting particularly Spenser's final reference to "a mighty Peres displeasure" (6.12.41). They see the consequences of a peer's displeasure most clearly in *Urania*; Wroth may have continued to write, but her public voice was effectively silenced after she was forced to withdraw her 1621 *Urania* from publication.

Students begin the course with some curiosity but little knowledge about the pastoral romance. By the time we have discussed the ways both male and female writers use the pastoral to reflect and to challenge cultural assumptions about gender and class, students have come to see the Arcadian world as a microcosm for our own, a place for "the triall of true curtesie."

NOTES

[1]Quotations from *The Faerie Queene* are taken from the Hamilton edition.
[2]Quotations from the *New Arcadia* are from Wroth, *Countesse*.

CONTRIBUTORS AND SURVEY PARTICIPANTS

The editors gratefully acknowledge the help of the following contributors and the scholars and teachers who responded, often in considerable detail, to the survey conducted for this volume.

Judith H. Anderson, *Indiana University, Bloomington*
Robert P. ApRoberts, *California State University, Northridge*
Nancy Arnesen, *North Park College*
Wilson G. Baroody, *Arizona State University*
Tom Bulger, *Siena College*
Sheila T. Cavanagh, *Emory University*
Caroline Cherry, *Eastern College*
Edwin D. Craun, *Washington and Lee University*
A. Leigh DeNeef, *Duke University*
Donald Dickson, *Texas A&M University, College Station*
Richard Y. Duerden, *Brigham Young University, Utah*
Matthew A. Fike, *Augustana College, Illinois*
Raymond-Jean Frontain, *University of Central Arkansas*
Richard C. Frushell, *Penn State University, McKeesport*
Sayre N. Greenfield, *Denison University*
A. C. Hamilton, *Queen's University*
Margaret P. Hannay, *Siena College*
Diana E. Henderson, *Middlebury College*
M. Thomas Hester, *North Carolina State University*
A. Kent Hieatt, *University of Western Ontario*
Eugene D. Hill, *Mount Holyoke College*
Clark Hulse, *University of Illinois, Chicago*
Arthur F. Kinney, *University of Massachusetts, Amherst*
Theresa M. Krier, *University of Notre Dame*
Stuart M. Kurland, *Duquesne University*
Joseph F. Loewenstein, *Washington University*
Catherine Mars, *University of Virginia*
Anne Lake Prescott, *Barnard College*
Diana Akers Rhoads, *Hampden-Sydney College*
Barbara Roche Rico, *Loyola Marymount University*
Anne Shaver, *Denison University*
Wayne Shumaker, *University of California, Berkeley*
Dorothy Stephens, *University of Arkansas, Fayetteville*
Andrea Sununu, *DePauw University*
John Timpane, *Lafayette College*
Evelyn B. Tribble, *Temple University*
Julia M. Walker, *State University of New York, Geneseo*
John Webster, *University of Washington*
Faye P. Whitaker, *Iowa State University*

WORKS CITED

Abbreviations

C&L	Christianity and Literature
CLS	Comparative Literature Studies
CritI	Critical Inquiry
ELN	English Language Notes
ELR	English Literary Renaissance
HLQ	Huntington Library Quarterly
HSL	University of Hartford Studies in Literature
JDJ	John Donne Journal
JEGP	Journal of English and Germanic Philology
JMRS	Journal of Medieval and Renaissance Studies
L&P	Literature and Psychology
MLR	Modern Language Review
MLS	Modern Language Studies
MP	Modern Philology
NLH	New Literary History
N&Q	Notes and Queries
NOR	New Orleans Review
PLL	Papers on Language and Literature
PostS	Post Script: Essays in Film and the Humanities
PQ	Philological Quarterly
RenP	Renaissance Papers
RenQ	Renaissance Quarterly
RES	Review of English Studies
RQ	Riverside Quarterly
SAQ	South Atlantic Quarterly
SEL	Studies in English Literature, 1500–1900
SN	Studia Neophilologica
SP	Studies in Philology
SSt	Spenser Studies: A Renaissance Poetry Annual
TSLL	Texas Studies in Literature and Language
UTQ	University of Toronto Quarterly
WMQ	William and Mary Quarterly
YES	Yearbook of English Studies

Abrams, M. H., gen. ed., *The Norton Anthology of English Literature*. 5th ed. Vol. 1. New York: Norton, 1986.

Allen, Don Cameron. *Mysteriously Meant: The Rediscovery of Pagan Symbolism and Allegorical Interpretation in the Renaissance*. Baltimore: Johns Hopkins UP, 1970.

Alpers, Paul J. *Edmund Spenser: A Critical Anthology*. Harmondsworth, Eng.: Penguin, 1969.

———, ed. *Elizabethan Poetry: Modern Essays in Criticism*. New York: Oxford UP, 1967.

———. "Narration in *The Faerie Queene*." *ELH* 44 (1977): 19–39.

———. *The Poetry of* The Faerie Queene. Princeton: Princeton UP, 1967.

———. "Spenser's Late Pastorals." *ELH* 56 (1989): 797–816.

Anderson, Judith. "The Antiquities of Faeryland and Ireland." *JEGP* 86 (1987): 199–214.

———. "Arthur, Argante, and the Ideal Vision: An Exercise in Speculation and Parody." Baswell and Sharpe 193–206.

———. " 'A Gentle Knight Was Pricking on the Plaine': The Chaucerian Connection." *ELR* 15 (1985): 160–73.

———. *The Growth of a Personal Voice:* Piers Plowman *and* The Faerie Queene. New Haven: Yale UP, 1976.

———. " 'In Liuing Colours and Right Hew': The Queen of Spenser's Central Books." *Poetic Traditions of the English Renaissance*. Ed. Maynard Mack and George deForest Lord. New Haven: Yale UP, 1982. 47–66.

———. " 'Nor Man It Is': The Knight of Justice in Book V of Spenser's *Faerie Queene*." *PMLA* 85 (1970): 65–77.

Anderson, Ruth Leila. *Elizabethan Psychology and Shakespeare's Plays*. 1927. New York: Russell, 1966.

Aptekar, Jane. *Icons of Justice: Iconography and Thematic Imagery in Book V of* The Faerie Queene. New York: Columbia UP, 1969.

Aristotle. *Nichomachean Ethics*. Trans. Terence Irwin. Indianapolis: Hackett, 1985.

Baldwin, T. W. *William Shakspere's Small Latine and Lesse Greeke*. Urbana: U of Illinois P, 1944.

Bamborough, J. M. *The Little World of Man*. London: Longmans, 1952.

Barkan, Leonard. *The Gods Made Flesh: Metamorphosis and the Pursuit of Paganism*. New Haven: Yale UP, 1986.

———. *Nature's Work of Art: The Human Body as Image of the World*. New Haven: Yale UP, 1975.

Baswell, Christopher, and William Sharpe, eds. *The Passing of Arthur: New Essays in Arthurian Tradition*. New York: Garland, 1988.

Bayley, Peter, ed. The Faerie Queene: *A Casebook*. London: Macmillan, 1977.

———, ed. The Faerie Queene *I and II*. New York: Oxford UP, 1966.

Beacon, Richard. *Solon, His Follie*. Oxford, 1594.

Bednarz, James P. "Ralegh in Spenser's Historical Allegory." *SSt* 4 (1984): 49–70.

Beier, A. L. *Masterless Men: The Vagrancy Problem in England: 1560–1640.* London: Methuen, 1985.

Beilin, Elaine. *Redeeming Eve: Women Writers of the English Renaissance.* Princeton: Princeton UP, 1987.

Bellamy, Elizabeth J. "Androgyny and the Epic Quest: The Female Warrior in Ariosto and Spenser." *PostS* 2 (1985): 29–37.

———. "Colin and Orphic Interpretation: Reading Neoplatonically on Spenser's Acidale." *CLS* 27 (1990): 172–92.

———. "Reading Desire Backwards: Belatedness and Spenser's Arthur." *SAQ* 88 (1989): 789–810.

———. *Translations of Power: Narcissism and the Unconscious in Epic History.* Ithaca: Cornell UP, 1992.

———. "The Vocative and the Vocational: The Unreadability of Elizabeth in *The Faerie Queene.*" *ELH* 54 (1987): 1–30.

Belsey, Andrew, and Catherine Belsey. "Icons of Divinity: Portraits of Elizabeth I." *Renaissance Bodies: The Human Figure in English Culture c. 1540–1660.* Ed. Lucy Gent and Nigel Llewellyn. London: Reaktion, 1990. 11–35.

Belt, Debra. "Hostile Audiences and the Courteous Reader in *The Faerie Queene,* Book VI." *SSt* 9 (1991): 107–35.

Benjamin, Walter. "The Storyteller." *Illuminations.* Ed. Hannah Arendt. New York: Schocken, 1969. 83–109.

Benson, Pamela Joseph. "Florimell at Sea: The Action of Grace in *Faerie Queene,* Book III." *SSt* 6 (1986): 83–94.

———. "Rule, Virginia: Protestant Theories of Female Regiment in *The Faerie Queene.*" *ELR* 15 (1985): 277–92.

Berger, Harry, Jr. *The Allegorical Temper: Vision and Reality in Book II of Spenser's* Faerie Queene. New Haven: Yale UP, 1957.

———. "Narrative as Rhetoric in *The Faerie Queene.*" *ELR* 21 (1991): 3–48.

———. *Revisionary Play: Studies in the Spenserian Dynamics.* Berkeley: U of California P, 1988.

———, ed. *Spenser: A Collection of Critical Essays.* Englewood Cliffs: Prentice, 1968.

Bergeron, David. *English Civic Pageantry, 1558–1642.* Columbia: U of South Carolina P, 1971.

Bernard, John D. *Ceremonies of Innocence: Pastoralism in the Poetry of Edmund Spenser.* Cambridge: Cambridge UP, 1989.

Bieman, Elizabeth. *Plato Baptized: Towards the Interpretation of Spenser's Mimetic Fictions.* Toronto: U of Toronto P, 1988.

Bloom, Allan. *The Closing of the American Mind.* New York: Simon, 1987.

Bloom, Harold, ed. *Modern Critical Views: Edmund Spenser.* New York: Chelsea, 1986.

Boehrer, Bruce Thomas. " 'Careless Modestee': Chastity as Politics in Book 3 of *The Faerie Queene.*" *ELH* 55 (1988): 555–73.

Bono, Barbara J. *Literary Transvaluation: From Vergilian Epic to Shakespearean Tragicomedy.* Berkeley: U of California P, 1984.

Borris, Kenneth. " 'Diuelish Ceremonies': Allegorical Satire of Protestant Extremism in *The Faerie Queene* VI.viii.31–51." *SSt* 8 (1990): 175–209.

———. "Fortune, Occasion, and the Allegory of the Quest in Book Six of *The Faerie Queene*." *SSt* 7 (1987): 123–45.

Boswell, Jackson C. "Spenser Allusions: Addenda to Wells." *N&Q* 24 (1977): 519–20.

Bradner, Leicester. "Forerunners of the Spenserian Stanza." *RES* 4 (1928): 207–08.

Brady, Ciaran. "Spenser's Irish Crisis: Humanism and Experience in the 1590's." *Past and Present* 111 (1986): 17–49.

Brathwaite, Richard. *The English gentlewoman, drawne out to the full body: Espressing, what habilliments doe best attire her, what ornaments doe best adorne her, what complements doe best accomplish her.* London: B. Alsop and T. Fawcet for Michaell Sparke, 1631.

Broaddus, James W. "Renaissance Psychology and Britomart's Adventures in *Faerie Queene* III." *ELR* 17 (1987): 186–206.

Brooks-Davies, Douglas, ed. *Edmund Spenser:* The Faerie Queene: *Books I to III.* 1976. Rutland: Tuttle, 1991.

———. *Spenser's* Faerie Queene: *A Critical Commentary on Books I and II.* Manchester: Manchester UP, 1977.

Burchmore, David W. "Triamond, Agape, and the Fates: Neoplatonic Cosmology in Spenser's Legend of Friendship." *Sst* 5 (1985): 45–64.

Burke, Kenneth. *A Grammar of Motives and a Rhetoric of Motives.* New York: Meridian, 1962.

Burrow, Colin. "Original Fictions: Metamorphoses in *The Faerie Queene.*" *Ovid Renewed: Ovidian Influences on Literature and Art from the Middle Ages to the Twentieth Century.* Ed. Charles Martindale. Cambridge: Cambridge UP, 1988. 99–119.

Bush, Douglas. *Mythology and the Renaissance Tradition in English Poetry.* 1932. Rev. ed. New York: Norton, 1963.

———. *The Renaissance and English Humanism.* 1939. Toronto: U of Toronto P, 1968.

Cain, Thomas H. *Praise in* The Faerie Queene. Lincoln: U of Nebraska P, 1978.

Cambrensis, Giraldus. *Historical Works of Giraldus Cambrensis.* Ed. T. Wright. London, 1892.

Canny, Nicholas P. "The Ideology of English Colonization: From Ireland to America." *WMQ* 20 (1973): 575–99.

Cantor, Paul A. *Shakespeare:* Hamlet. Cambridge: Cambridge UP, 1989.

Carpenter, Frederic Ives. *A Reference Guide to Edmund Spenser.* 1923. New York: Kraus, 1969.

Carroll, Clare. "The Construction of Gender and the Cultural and Political Other in *The Faerie Queene* 5 and *A View of the Present State of Ireland*: The Critics, the Context, and the Case of Radigund." *Criticism* 32 (1990): 163–92.

Carscallen, James. "The Goodly Frame of Temperance: The Metaphor of Cosmos in *The Faerie Queene,* Book II." *UTQ* 37 (1968): 136–55.

Caspari, Fritz. *Humanism and the Social Order in Tudor England.* Chicago: U of Chicago P, 1954.

Cassirer, Ernst, Paul Oskar Kristeller, and John Herman Randall, Jr., eds. *The Renaissance Philosophy of Man.* Chicago: U of Chicago P, 1948.

Cavanagh, Sheila T. " 'Beauties Chace': Arthur and Women in *The Faerie Queene*." Baswell and Sharpe 207–18.

———. " 'Such Was Ireland's Countenance': Ireland in Spenser's Prose and Poetry." *TSLL* 28 (1986): 24–50.

Chang, H. C. *Allegory and Courtesy in Spenser*. Edinburgh: Edinburgh UP, 1955.

Charlton, Kenneth. *Education in Renaissance England*. London: Routledge, 1965.

Cheney, Donald. "Spenser's Fortieth Birthday and Related Fictions." *SSt* 4 (1984): 3–31.

———. "Spenser's Hermaphrodite and the 1590 *Faerie Queene*." *PMLA* 88 (1972): 192–200.

———. *Spenser's Image of Nature: Wild Man and Shepherd in* The Faerie Queene. New Haven: Yale UP, 1966.

Cheney, Patrick. " 'And Doubted Her to Deeme an Earthly Wight': Male Neoplatonic 'Magic' and the Problem of Female Identity in Spenser's Allegory of the Two Florimells." *SP* 86 (1989): 310–40.

———. " 'Secret Powre Unseene': Good Magic in Spenser's Legend of Britomart." *SP* 85 (1988): 1–28.

———. "Spenser's Completion of the Squire's Tale: Love, Magic, and Heroic Action in the Legend of Cambell and Triamond." *JMRS* 15 (1985): 135–55.

Cheney, Patrick, and P. J. Klemp. "Spenser's Dance of the Graces and the Ptolemaic Universe." *SN* 56 (1984): 27–33.

Coleridge, Samuel Taylor. *The Statesman's Manual. Lay Sermons*. Ed. R. J. White. Vol. 6 of *Collected Works*. Ed. Kathleen Coburn. London: Routledge, 1972. 3–114.

Collins, Arthur. *Letters and Memorials of State*. 1746. New York: AMS, 1973.

Collinson, Patrick. *The Elizabethan Puritan Movement*. Berkeley: U of California P, 1967.

Comito, Terry. *The Idea of the Garden in the Renaissance*. New Brunswick: Rutgers UP, 1978.

Coughlan, Patricia, ed. *Spenser and Ireland: An Interdisciplinary Perspective*. Cork: Cork UP, 1989.

Craig, Martha. "The Secret Wit of Spenser's Language." Alpers, *Elizabethan Poetry* 447–72.

Cropper, Elizabeth. "The Beauty of Women: Problems in the Rhetoric of Renaissance Portraiture." Ferguson, Quilligan, and Vickers 175–90.

Crosman, Robert. *Reading* Paradise Lost. Bloomington: Indiana UP, 1980.

Cullen, Patrick. *Infernal Triad: The Flesh, the World, and the Devil in Spenser and Milton*. Princeton: Princeton UP, 1974.

Cummings, Robert M., ed. *Spenser: The Critical Heritage*. New York: Barnes, 1971.

———. "Spenser's 'Twelve Private Morall Virtues.' " *SSt* 8 (1990): 35–59.

Curtius, Ernst Robert. *European Literature and the Latin Middle Ages*. Trans. Willard R. Trask. New York: Harper, 1963.

Dasenbrock, Reed Way. "Escaping the Squire's Double Bind in Books III and IV of *The Faerie Queene*." *SEL* 26 (1986): 25–45.

Davies, Stevie. *The Feminine Reclaimed: The Idea of Woman in Spenser, Shakespeare, and Milton.* Lexington: U of Kentucky P, 1985.

Dees, Jerome S. "The Narrator of *The Faerie Queene*: Patterns of Resonance." *TSLL* 18 (1977): 553–76.

DeNeef, A. Leigh. *Spenser and the Motives of Metaphor.* Durham: Duke UP, 1982.

Dickens, A. G. *The English Reformation.* 2nd ed. London: Batsford, 1989.

Dubrow, Heather. "The Arraignment of Paridell: Tudor Historiography in *The Faerie Queene* III.ix." *SP* 86 (1990): 312–27.

Dubrow, Heather, and Richard Strier, eds. *The Historical Renaissance: New Essays on Tudor and Stuart Literature and Culture.* Chicago: U of Chicago P, 1988.

Dundas, Judith. *The Spider and the Bee: The Artistry of Spenser's* Faerie Queene. Urbana: U of Illinois P, 1985.

Dunseath, T. K. *Spenser's Allegory of Justice in Book Five of* The Faerie Queene. Princeton: Princeton UP, 1968.

Elliott, John R., Jr., ed. *The Prince of Poets: Essays on Edmund Spenser.* New York: New York UP, 1968.

Ellrodt, Robert. *Neoplatonism in the Poetry of Spenser.* Geneva: Droz, 1960.

Emerson, Ralph Waldo. *The American Scholar. Selections from Ralph Waldo Emerson.* Ed. Stephen E. Whicher. Boston: Houghton, 1957. 63–80.

Emig, Janet. "Writing as a Mode of Learning." *The Web of Meaning.* Upper Montclair: Boynton/Cook, 1983. 123–31.

Empson, William. *Seven Types of Ambiguity.* London: Chatto, 1947.

Ettin, Andrew V. *Literature and the Pastoral.* New Haven: Yale UP, 1984.

Evans, Dorothy F. Atkinson. *Edmund Spenser: A Bibliographical Supplement.* 1937. New York: Haskell, 1967.

Evans, Maurice. *Spenser's Anatomy of Heroism: A Commentary on* The Faerie Queene. Cambridge: Cambridge UP, 1970.

Evett, David. *Literature and the Visual Arts in Tudor England.* Athens: U of Georgia P, 1990.

Falkiner, C. L. *Illustrations of Irish History and Topography.* London: Longman, 1904.

Falls, Mary R. "Spenser's Kirkrapine and the Elizabethans." *SP* 50 (1953): 457–75.

Fanon, Frantz. *The Wretched of the Earth.* New York: Grove, 1963.

Ferguson, Arthur B. *The Chivalric Tradition in Renaissance England.* Washington: Folger Shakespeare Library, 1986.

Ferguson, Margaret W., Maureen Quilligan, and Nancy J. Vickers, eds. *Rewriting the Renaissance: The Discourses of Sexual Difference in Early Modern Europe.* Chicago: U of Chicago P, 1986.

Fichter, Andrew. *Poets Historical: Dynastic Epic in the Renaissance.* New Haven: Yale UP, 1982.

Fineman, Joel. "The Structure of Allegorical Desire." *Allegory and Representation.* Ed. Stephen J. Greenblatt. Baltimore: Johns Hopkins UP, 1981. 26–60.

Fletcher, Angus. *Allegory: Theory of a Symbolic Mode.* Ithaca: Cornell UP, 1964.

————. *The Prophetic Moment: An Essay on Spenser.* Chicago: U of Chicago P, 1971.

Fletcher, Anthony, and John Stevenson, eds. *Order and Disorder in Early Modern England.* Cambridge: Cambridge UP, 1985.

Flower, Linda. "Introduction: Studying Cognition in Context." Flower et al. 3–32.

————. "Negotiating Academic Discourse." Flower et al. 221–52.

Flower, Linda, et al., eds. *Reading-to-Write: Exploring a Cognitive and Social Process.* New York: Oxford UP, 1990.

Fowler, Alastair. *Spenser and the Numbers of Time.* New York: Barnes, 1964.

Frantz, David O. "The Union of Florimell and Marinell: The Triumph of Hearing." *SSt* 6 (1985): 115–28.

Freeman, Rosemary. The Faerie Queene: *A Companion for Readers.* Berkeley: U of California P, 1970.

Frushell, Richard C. "Spenser and the Eighteenth-Century Schools." *SSt* 7 (1987): 175–98.

Frushell, Richard C., and Bernard J. Vondersmith, eds. *Contemporary Thought on Edmund Spenser.* Carbondale: Southern Illinois UP, 1975.

Fulwiler, Toby. *Teaching with Writing.* Portsmouth: Boynton/Cook, 1989.

Fumerton, Patricia. *Cultural Aesthetics: Renaissance Literature and the Practice of Social Ornament.* Chicago: U of Chicago P, 1991.

————. "Relative Means: Spenser's Style of *Discordia Concors.*" *PLL* 24 (1988): 3–22.

Genette, Gérard. *Narrative Discourse: An Essay in Method.* Ithaca: Cornell UP, 1980.

Gent, Lucy. *Picture and Poetry, 1560–1620: Relations between Literature and the Visual Arts in the English Renaissance.* Leamington Spa: Hall, 1981.

Giamatti, A. Bartlett. *Play of Double Senses: Spenser's* Faerie Queene. New York: Norton, 1975.

Gilligan, Carol, and Jane Attanuicci. "Two Moral Orientations." *Mapping the Moral Domain: A Contribution of Women's Thinking to Psychological Theory and Education.* Ed. Gilligan et al. Cambridge: Center for the Study of Gender, Education, and Human Development, 1988. 73–85.

Gilman, Ernest B. *Iconoclasm and Poetry in the English Reformation: Down Went Dagon.* Chicago: U of Chicago P, 1986.

Glasser, Marvin. "Spenser as Mannerist Poet: The 'Antique Image' in Book IV of *The Faerie Queene.*" *SEL* 31 (1991): 25–50.

Goldberg, Jonathan. *Endlesse Worke: Spenser and the Structures of Discourse.* Baltimore: Johns Hopkins UP, 1981.

————. "The Mothers in *The Faerie Queene* III." *TSLL* 17 (1976): 5–26.

Grafton, Anthony, and Lisa Jardine. *From Humanism to the Humanities: Education and the Liberal Arts in Fifteenth- and Sixteenth-Century Europe.* Cambridge: Harvard UP, 1986.

Graziani, René. "Elizabeth at Isis Church." *PMLA* 79 (1964): 376–89.

Greenberg, Jeff, S. L. Kirkland, and Tom Pyszcynski. "Some Theoretical Notions and Preliminary Research concerning Derogatory Ethnic Labels." Smitherman-Donaldson and van Dijk 74–93.

Greenblatt, Stephen. "Murdering Peasants: Status, Genre, and the Representation of Rebellion." *Representations* 1 (1983): 1–29.

———. *Renaissance Self-Fashioning: From More to Shakespeare*. Chicago: U of Chicago P, 1980.

Greene, Thomas. *The Descent from Heaven: A Study in Epic Continuity*. New Haven: Yale UP, 1963.

Greenfield, Sayre N. "Reading Love in the Geography of *The Faerie Queene*, Book Three." *PQ* 68 (1989): 425–42.

Greenlaw, Edwin, C. G. Osgood, F. M. Padelford, et al., eds. *Works of Edmund Spenser: A Variorum Edition*. 10 vols. Baltimore: Johns Hopkins UP, 1932–58.

Gross, Kenneth. *Spenserian Poetics: Idolatry, Iconoclasm, and Magic*. Ithaca: Cornell UP, 1985.

Grossman, Marshall. "Augustine, Spenser, Milton, and the Christian Epic." *NOR* 11 (1984): 9–17.

Guillory, John D. *Poetic Authority: Spenser, Milton, and Literary History*. New York: Columbia UP, 1983.

Guy, John. *Tudor England*. Oxford: Oxford UP, 1988.

Hackett, Helen. " 'Yet Tell Me Some Such Fiction': Lady Mary Wroth's *Urania* and the 'Femininity' of Romance." *Women, Texts, and Histories, 1575–1760*. Ed. Clare Brant and Diane Purkiss. London: Routledge, 1992. 39–68.

Halpern, Richard. *The Poetics of Primitive Accumulation: English Renaissance Culture and the Genealogy of Capital*. Ithaca: Cornell UP, 1991.

Hamilton, A. C., ed. *Edmund Spenser: The Faerie Queene*. New York: Longman, 1977.

———, ed. *Essential Articles for the Study of Edmund Spenser*. Hamden: Archon, 1972.

———. *The Structure of Allegory in The Faerie Queene*. Oxford: Clarendon–Oxford UP, 1961.

Hamilton, A. C., et al., eds. *The Spenser Encyclopedia*. Toronto: U of Toronto P, 1990.

Hankins, John Erskine. *Source and Meaning in Spenser's Allegory*. Oxford: Clarendon–Oxford UP, 1971.

Hannay, Margaret P. " 'My Sheep Are Thoughts': Self-Reflexive Pastoral in *The Faerie Queene*, Book VI, and the *New Arcadia*." *SSt* 9 (1991): 137–59.

———, ed. *Silent but for the Word: Tudor Women as Patrons, Translators, and Writers of Religious Works*. Kent: Kent State UP, 1985.

———. " 'Your Vertuous and Learned Aunt': The Countess of Pembroke as a Mentor to Lady Mary Wroth." *Reading Mary Wroth: Representing Alternatives in Early Modern England*. Ed. Naomi Miller and Gary Waller. Knoxville: U of Tennessee P, 1991. 15–34.

Harvey, E. Ruth. *The Inward Wits: Psychological Theory in the Middle Ages and the Renaissance*. London: Warburg Inst., 1975.

Hawkins, Sherman. "Mutability and the Cycle of the Months." *Form and Convention in the Poetry of Edmund Spenser: Selected Papers from the English Institute.* Ed. William Nelson. New York: Columbia UP, 1961. 76–102.

Heale, Elizabeth. The Faerie Queene: *A Reader's Guide.* Cambridge: Cambridge UP, 1987.

———. "Spenser's Malengin, Missionary Priests, and the Means of Justice." *RES* 41 (1990): 171–84.

Heberle, Mark. "Aristotle and Spenser's Justice." *SN* 63 (1991): 169–73.

———. "The Limitations of Friendship." *SSt* 8 (1990): 101–18.

Helgerson, Richard. "Barbarous Tongues: The Ideology of Poetic Form in Renaissance England." Dubrow and Strier 273–92.

———. *The Elizabethan Prodigals.* Berkeley: U of California P, 1976.

———. *Forms of Nationhood: The Elizabethan Writing of England.* Chicago: U of Chicago P, 1992.

———. *Self-Crowned Laureates: Spenser, Jonson, Milton, and the Literary System.* Berkeley: U of California P, 1983.

Henderson, Katherine Usher, and Barbara F. McManus, eds. *Half Humankind: Contexts and Texts of the Controversy about Women in England, 1540–1640.* Urbana: U of Illinois P, 1981.

Heninger, S. K., Jr. *The Cosmographical Glass: Renaissance Diagrams of the Universe.* San Marino: Huntington Library, 1977.

———. *A Handbook of Renaissance Meteorology, with Particular Reference to Elizabethan and Jacobean Literature.* Durham: Duke UP, 1960.

———. *Sidney and Spenser: The Poet as Maker.* University Park: Pennsylvania State UP, 1989.

———. *Touches of Sweet Harmony: Pythagorean Cosmology and Renaissance Poetics.* San Marino: Huntington Library, 1974.

Herendeen, Wyman H. *From Landscape to Literature: The River and the Myth of Geography.* Pittsburgh: Duquesne UP, 1986.

Hieatt, A. Kent. *Chaucer, Spenser, Milton: Mythopoeic Continuities and Transformations.* Montreal: McGill–Queen's UP, 1975.

———. "A Numerical Key for Spenser's *Amoretti* and Guyon in the House of Mammon." *YES* 3 (1973): 14–27.

———. "The Passing of Arthur in Malory, Spenser, and Shakespeare: The Avoidance of Closure." Baswell and Sharpe 173–92.

Hieatt, A. Kent, and Constance Hieatt, eds. *Spenser: Selected Poetry.* New York: Appleton, 1970.

Higgins, Anne. "Spenser Reading Chaucer: Another Look at the *Faerie Queene* Allusions." *JEGP* 89 (1990): 17–36.

Holahan, Michael. "*Iamque opus exegi*: Ovid's Changes and Spenser's Brief Epic of Mutability." *ELR* 6 (1976): 244–70.

Holinshed, Raphael. *Chronicles of England, Scotland, and Ireland.* London, 1577.

Hollander, John, and Frank Kermode, eds. "Edmund Spenser." *The Literature of Renaissance England.* New York: Oxford UP, 1973. 152–334.

Hough, Graham. *A Preface to* The Faerie Queene. New York: Norton, 1962.

"How to Tell Your Friends from the Japs." *Time* 22 Dec. 1941: 33.

Hulse, Clark. *The Rule of Art: Literature and Painting in the Renaissance*. Chicago: U of Chicago P, 1990.

Hume, Anthea. *Edmund Spenser: Protestant Poet*. Cambridge: Cambridge UP, 1984.

Hurtsfield, Joel, and Alan G. R. Smith, eds. *Elizabethan People: State and Society*. New York: St. Martin's, 1972.

Imbrie, Ann E. " 'Playing Legerdemaine with the Scripture': Parodic Sermons in *The Faerie Queene*." *ELR* 17 (1987): 142–55.

Inhelder, Bärbel, and Jean Piaget. *The Growth of Logical Thinking from Childhood to Adolescence*. New York: Basic, 1958.

Jardine, Lisa. *Still Harping on Daughters: Women and Drama in the Age of Shakespeare*. Totowa: Barnes, 1983.

Jennings, Francis. *The Invasion of America*. Chapel Hill: U of North Carolina P, 1975.

Johnson, Francis R. *Astronomical Thought in Renaissance England: A Study of the Scientific Writings from 1500 to 1645*. Baltimore: Johns Hopkins UP, 1937.

———. *Critical Bibliography of the Works of Edmund Spenser Printed before 1700*. Baltimore: Johns Hopkins UP, 1932.

Johnson, John, John Dowland, et al. *English Lute Duets*. Cassette. Jacob Lindberg and Paul O'Dette, lutanists. Ocean: Musical Heritage Soc., 1984.

Jones, Howard Mumford. *O Strange New World*. London: Chatto, 1975.

Jones, H. S. V. *A Spenser Handbook*. New York: Appleton, 1930.

Jordan, Constance. *Renaissance Feminism: Literary Texts and Political Models*. Ithaca: Cornell UP, 1990.

———. "Representing Political Androgyny: More on the Siena Portrait of Queen Elizabeth I." *The Renaissance Englishwoman in Print: Counterbalancing the Canon*. Ed. Anne M. Haselkorn and Betty S. Travitsky. Amherst: U of Massachusetts P, 1990. 157–76.

Judson, Alexander C. *Life of Edmund Spenser*. Baltimore: Johns Hopkins UP, 1945.

Jussawala, M. C., ed. The Faerie Queene *I*. New York: Apt, 1982.

Kane, Sean. "The Paradoxes of Idealism: Book Two of *The Faerie Queene*." *JDJ* 1 (1983): 81–109.

———. *Spenser's Moral Allegory*. Toronto: U of Toronto P, 1989.

Kaske, Carol V. "Augustinian Psychology in *The Faerie Queene*, Book II." *HSL* 15–16 (1983–84): 93–98.

———. "The Dragon's Spark and Sting and the Structure of Red Cross's Dragon-Fight: *The Faerie Queene*, I.xi–xii." *SP* 66 (1969): 609–38.

Kellogg, Robert, and Oliver Steele, eds. *Books I and II of* The Faerie Queene, *the Mutability Cantos, and Selections from the Minor Poetry*. Indianapolis: Odyssey, 1965.

Kelso, Ruth. *Doctrine for the Lady of the Renaissance*. Urbana: U of Illinois P, 1956.

Kennedy, Judith, and James A. Reither, eds. *A Theatre for Spenserians*. Toronto: U of Toronto P, 1973.

Kermode, Frank. "Milton's Hero." *RES* ns 4 (1953): 317–30.

King, John N. *English Reformation Literature: The Tudor Origins of the Protestant Tradition*. Princeton: Princeton UP, 1982.

———. "Queen Elizabeth I: Representations of the Virgin Queen." *RQ* 43 (1990): 30–74.

———. *Spenser's Poetry and the Reformation Tradition*. Princeton: Princeton UP, 1990.

———. *Tudor Royal Iconography: Literature and Art in an Age of Religious Crisis*. Princeton: Princeton UP, 1989.

King, Margaret L. *Women of the Renaissance*. Chicago: U of Chicago P, 1991.

Kinney, Arthur F., ed. *Elizabethan Backgrounds: Historical Documents of the Age of Elizabeth I*. Hamden: Archon, 1975.

———. *Studies in* The Faerie Queene. Spec. issue of *ELR* 17 (1987): 119–242.

Knapp, Jeffrey. "Error as a Means of Empire in *The Faerie Queene* I." *ELH* 54 (1987): 801–34.

Knight, W. Nicholas. "The Narrative Unity of Book V of *The Faerie Queene*: 'That Part of Justice Which Is Equity.'" *RES* ns 21 (1970): 267–94.

Knox, John. *The First Blast of the Trumpet against the Monstrous Regiment of Women*. Ed. Edward Arber. London: English Scholar's, 1880.

Krier, Theresa M. *Gazing on Secret Sights: Spenser, Classical Imitation, and the Decorums of Vision*. Ithaca: Cornell UP, 1990.

———. "The Mysteries of the Muses: Spenser's *Faerie Queene*, II.3, and the Epic Tradition of the Goddess Observed." *SSt* 7 (1987): 59–91.

Kucich, Greg. "The Duality of Romantic Spenserianism." *SSt* 8 (1990): 287–307.

Lacan, Jacques. *The Four Fundamental Concepts of Psycho-analysis*. Trans. Alan Sheridan. New York: Norton, 1981.

———. "The Subversion of the Subject and the Dialectic of Desire in the Freudian Unconscious." *Ecrits: A Selection*. London: Tavistock, 1977. 292–325.

Lamb, Mary Ellen. *Gender and Authorship in the Sidney Circle*. Madison: U of Wisconsin P, 1990.

Levin, Richard A. "The Legende of the Redcrosse Knight and Una; or, Of the Love of a Good Woman." *SEL* 31 (1991): 1–24.

Lewalski, Barbara K., and Hallett Smith, eds. "Edmund Spenser." Abrams 528–781.

Lewis, C. S. *The Allegory of Love: A Study in Medieval Tradition*. 1936. Rev. ed. London: Oxford UP, 1951.

———. *Spenser's Images of Life*. Ed. Alastair Fowler. Cambridge: Cambridge UP, 1967.

Lockerd, Benjamin G., Jr. *The Sacred Marriage: Psychic Integration in* The Faerie Queene. Lewisburg: Bucknell UP, 1987.

Logan, George M., and Gordon Teskey, eds. *Unfolded Tales: Essays on Renaissance Romance*. Ithaca: Cornell UP, 1989.

Lord, George deForest. *Trials of the Self: Heroic Ordeals in the Epic Tradition.* Hamden: Archon, 1983.

Lotspeich, Henry Gibbons. *Classical Mythology in the Poetry of Edmund Spenser.* Princeton: Princeton UP, 1932.

Lupton, Julia Reinhard. "Home-Making in Ireland: Virgil's Eclogue I and Book VI of *The Faerie Queene.*" *SSt* 8 (1990): 119–46.

Lytle, Guy Fitch, and Stephen Orgel, eds. *Patronage in the Renaissance.* Princeton: Princeton UP, 1981.

MacCaffrey, Isabel G. *Spenser's Allegory: The Anatomy of Imagination.* Princeton: Princeton UP, 1976.

MacColl, Alan. "The Temple of Venus, the Wedding of the Thames and the Medway, and the End of *The Faerie Queene,* Book IV." *RES* 40 (1989): 26–47.

Maclean, Hugh, and Anne Lake Prescott, eds. *Edmund Spenser's Poetry.* 3rd ed. New York: Norton, 1993.

Mallette, Richard. "The Protestant Art of Preaching in Book One of *The Faerie Queene.*" *SSt* 7 (1987): 3–25.

———. "The Protestant Ethics of Love in Book Two of *The Faerie Queene.*" *C&L* 38 (1989): 45–64.

———. *Spenser, Milton, and Renaissance Pastoral.* Lewisburg: Bucknell UP, 1981.

"The Marriage Game." *Elizabeth R.* Dir. Claude Whatham. Prod. Roderick Graham. With Glenda Jackson. BBC. 1976.

McCoy, Richard C. *The Rites of Knighthood: Literature and the Politics of Elizabethan Chivalry.* Berkeley: U of California P, 1989.

———. *Sir Philip Sidney: Rebellion in Arcadia.* New Brunswick: Rutgers UP, 1979.

McNeir, Waldo F., and Foster Provost. *Edmund Spenser: An Annotated Bibliography 1937–1972.* Pittsburgh: Duquesne UP, 1975.

Meiss, Millard, ed. *The Belles Heures of Jean, Duke of Berry.* New York: Braziller, 1974.

Merkel, Ingrid, and Allen G. Debus, eds. *Hermeticism and the Renaissance: Intellectual History and the Occult in Early Modern Europe.* Washington: Folger Shakespeare Library, 1988.

Metz, Christian. *The Imaginary Signifier.* Trans. Celia Britton. Bloomington: Indiana UP, 1982.

Meyer, Russell J. The Faerie Queene: *Educating the Reader.* Boston: Twayne, 1991.

———. " 'Fixt in Heauens Hight': Spenser, Astronomy, and the Date of the *Cantos of Mutabilitie.*" *SSt* 4 (1983): 115–29.

Miller, David Lee. "Abandoning the Quest." *ELH* 46 (1979): 173–92.

———. " 'Figuring Hierarchy': The Dedicatory Sonnets to *The Faerie Queene.*" *RenP* (1987): 49–59.

———*The Poem's Two Bodies: The Poetics of the 1590* Faerie Queene. Princeton: Princeton UP, 1988.

———. "Spenser's Vocation, Spenser's Career." *ELH* 50 (1983): 197–231.

Miller, Jacqueline T. "The Courtly Figure: Spenser's Anatomy of Allegory." *SEL* 31 (1991): 51–68.

————. *Poetic License: Authority and Authorship in Medieval and Renaissance Contexts.* New York: Oxford UP, 1986.

Miller, Naomi. " 'Not Much to Be Marked': Narrative of the Woman's Part in Lady Mary Wroth's *Urania.*" *SEL* 29 (1989): 121–37.

Millon, David. "Positivism in the Historiography of the Common Law." *Wisconsin Law Review* (1989): 669–714.

Mills, Jerry Leath. "Prudence, History, and the Prince in *The Faerie Queene,* Book II." *HLQ* 41 (1978): 83–101.

————. "Spenser and the Numbers of History: A Note on the British and Elfin Chronicles in *The Faerie Queene.*" *PQ* 55 (1976): 281–87.

————. "Spenser, Lodowick Bryskett, and the Mortalist Controversy: *The Faerie Queene* II.ix.22." *PQ* 52 (1973): 173–86.

————. "Spenser's Letter to Raleigh and the Averroistic *Poetics.*" *ELN* 14 (1977): 246–49.

————. "Symbolic Tapestry in *The Faerie Queene* II.ix.33." *PQ* 49 (1970): 568–69.

Montrose, Louis Adrian. "The Elizabethan Subject and the Spenserian Text." *Literary Theory/Renaissance Texts.* Ed. Patricia Parker and David Quint. Baltimore: Johns Hopkins UP, 1986. 303–40.

————. " 'Eliza Queen of Shepheardes' and the Pastoral of Power." *ELR* 10 (1980): 153–82.

————. "*A Midsummer Night's Dream* and the Shaping Fantasies of Elizabethan Culture: Gender, Power, Form." Ferguson, Quilligan, and Vickers 65–87.

————. "Of Gentlemen and Shepherds: The Politics of Elizabethan Pastoral Form." *ELH* 50 (1983): 415–59.

————. " 'Shaping Fantasies': Figurations of Gender and Power in Elizabethan Culture." *Representations* 1 (1983): 61–94. Rpt. in *Representing the English Renaissance.* Ed. Stephen Greenblatt. Berkeley: U of California P, 1988. 31–64.

More, Thomas. *The Dialogue concerning Tyndale.* London: Eyre, 1927.

Morgan, Gerald. "Holiness as the First of Spenser's Aristotelian Moral Virtues." *MLR* 81 (1986): 817–37.

————. "The Idea of Temperance in the Second Book of *The Faerie Queene.*" *RES* ns 37.145 (1986): 11–39.

Mueller, William Randolph, ed. *Spenser's Critics.* Syracuse: Syracuse UP, 1959.

Mulvey, Laura. "Visual Pleasure and Narrative Cinema." *Film Theory and Criticism.* Ed. Gerald Mast and Marshall Cohen. 3rd ed. New York: Oxford UP, 1985. 803–16.

Murrin, Michael. *The Allegorical Epic: Essays in Its Rise and Decline.* Chicago: U of Chicago P, 1980.

————. "The Rhetoric of Faeryland." *The Rhetoric of Renaissance Poetry from Wyatt to Milton.* Ed. Thomas O. Sloan and Raymond B. Waddington. Berkeley: U of California P, 1974. 73–95.

————. *The Veil of Allegory: Some Notes toward a Theory of Allegorical Rhetoric in the English Renaissance.* Chicago: U of Chicago P, 1969.

Myers, James P., Jr., ed. *Elizabethan Ireland: A Selection of Writings by Elizabethan Writers on Ireland.* Hamden: Archon, 1983.

Neale, J. E. *Elizabeth I and Her Parliaments, 1584–1601*. London: Cape, 1957.

Nelson, William. *The Poetry of Edmund Spenser: A Study*. New York: Columbia UP, 1963.

Neuse, Richard. "Book VI as Conclusion to *The Faerie Queene*." *ELH* 35 (1968): 329–53.

———. "Milton and Spenser: The Virgilian Triad Revisited." *ELH* 45 (1978): 606–39.

Newman, Karen. "Renaissance Family Politics and Shakespeare's *The Taming of the Shrew*." *ELR* 16 (1986): 86–100.

Nicoll, Allardyce, ed. *The Elizabethans*. Cambridge: Cambridge UP, 1957.

Nohrnberg, James. *The Analogy of* The Faerie Queene. Princeton: Princeton UP, 1976.

Norbrook, David. *Poetry and Politics in the English Renaissance*. London: Routledge, 1984.

Nyquist, Mary. "The Genesis of Gendered Subjectivity in the Divorce Tracts and in *Paradise Lost*." *Re-Membering Milton*. Ed. Nyquist and Margaret W. Ferguson. New York: Methuen, 1987. 99–127.

O'Connell, Michael. *Mirror and Veil: The Historical Dimension of Spenser's* Faerie Queene. Chapel Hill: U of North Carolina P, 1977.

Oram, William A. "Elizabethan Fact and Spenserian Fiction." *SSt* 4 (1984): 33–48.

———. "Spenser's Raleghs." *SP* 87 (1990): 341–62.

Oram, William A., et al., eds. *The Yale Edition of the Shorter Poems of Edmund Spenser*. New Haven: Yale UP, 1989.

Osgood, Charles Grosvenor. *Concordance to the Poems of Edmund Spenser*. Washington: Carnegie Inst., 1915.

Packer, Nancy Huddleston, and John Timpane. *Writing Worth Reading*. 2nd ed. New York: Bedford, 1989.

Paglia, Camille. "Spenser and Apollo: *The Faerie Queene*." *Sexual Personae: Art and Decadence from Nefertiti to Emily Dickinson*. New Haven: Yale UP, 1990. 170–93.

Palliser, D. M. *The Age of Elizabeth: England under the Later Tudors, 1547–1603*. London: Longman, 1983.

Parker, Patricia. *Inescapable Romance: Studies in the Poetics of a Mode*. Princeton: Princeton UP, 1979.

Patterson, Annabel. *Censorship and Interpretation: Conditions of Writing and Reading in Early Modern England*. Madison: U of Wisconsin P, 1984.

———. "Couples, Canons, and the Uncouth: Spenser and Milton in Educational Theory." *CritI* 16 (1990): 774–93.

———. *Pastoral and Ideology: Vergil to Valéry*. Berkeley: U of California P, 1987.

Percival, Rachel, and Allen Percival. *The Court of Elizabeth the First*. London: Stainer, 1976.

Phillips, James E. "Renaissance Concepts of Justice and the Structure of *The Faerie Queene*, Book V." *HLQ* 33 (1970): 103–20.

Pinciss, Gerald M., and Roger Lockyer. *Shakespeare's World: Background Readings in the English Renaissance*. New York: Continuum, 1989.

Poggioli, Renato. *The Oaten Flute: Essays on Pastoral Poetry and the Pastoral Ideal.* Cambridge: Harvard UP, 1975.

Pomeroy, Elizabeth W. *Reading the Portraits of Queen Elizabeth I.* Hamden: Archon, 1989.

Pope, Emma Field. "The Critical Background of the Spenserian Stanza." *MP* 24 (1926): 31–53.

Prescott, Anne Lake. *French Poets and the English Renaissance: Studies in Fame and Transformation.* New Haven: Yale UP, 1978.

———. "Spenser's Chivalric Restoration: From Bateman's *Travayled Pylgrime* to the Redcrosse Knight." *SP* 86 (1989): 166–97.

Quilligan, Maureen. *The Language of Allegory: Defining the Genre.* Ithaca: Cornell UP, 1979.

———. *Milton's Spenser: The Politics of Reading.* Ithaca: Cornell UP, 1983.

Quint, David. *Origin and Originality in Renaissance Literature: Versions of the Source.* New Haven: Yale UP, 1983.

Radcliffe, John G., ed. *John Upton: Notes on* The Faery Queen. New York: Garland, 1987.

Rambuss, Richard. *Spenser's Secret Career.* Cambridge: Cambridge UP, 1993.

Reid, Robert L. "Alma's Castle and the Symbolization of Reason in *The Faerie Queene.*" *JEGP* 80 (1981): 512–27.

———. "Man, Woman, Child, or Servant: Family Hierarchy as a Figure of Tripartite Psychology in *The Faerie Queene.*" *SP* 78 (1981): 370–90.

———. "Spenserian Psychology and the Structure of Allegory in Books 1 and 2 of *The Faerie Queene.*" *MP* 79 (1982): 359–75.

Renwick, W. L., ed. *Spenser: Selections with Essays by Hazlitt, Coleridge, and Leigh Hunt.* 1923. New York: AMS, 1977.

———, ed. *A View of the Present State of Ireland.* By Edmund Spenser. Oxford: Clarendon–Oxford UP, 1970.

Rich, Barnabe. *Favltes Favlts, and Nothing Else but Favltes.* 1606. Ed. Melvin H. Wolf. Gainesville: Scholars Facsimiles and Reprints, 1965.

Roche, Thomas P., Jr., ed. *Edmund Spenser:* The Faerie Queene. New York: Penguin, 1978.

———. *The Kindly Flame: A Study of the Third and Fourth Books of Spenser's* Faerie Queene. Princeton: Princeton UP, 1964.

———. "The Menace of Despair and Arthur's Vision, *Faerie Queene* I.9." *SSt* 4 (1984): 71–92.

Rodríguez-Salgado, M. J., et al. *Armada: 1588–1988.* London: Penguin, 1988.

Rollinson, Philip. "Arthur, Maleger, and the Interpretation of *The Faerie Queene.*" *SSt* 7 (1987): 103–21.

Rooks, John. "Art, Audience, and Performance in the Bowre of Bliss." *MLS* 18 (1988): 23–36.

Rose, Mark. *Spenser's Art: A Companion to Book One of* The Faerie Queene. Cambridge: Harvard UP, 1975.

Roston, Murray. *Renaissance Perspectives in Literature and the Visual Arts.* Princeton: Princeton UP, 1987.

Said, Edward W. *Orientalism*. New York: Vintage–Random, 1979.

Sale, Roger. *Reading Spenser: An Introduction to* The Faerie Queene. New York: Random, 1968.

Sartre, Jean-Paul. *Anti-Semite and Jew*. Trans. George Joseph Becker. New York: Schocken, 1965.

Scardamalia, Marlene, and Carl Bereiter. "Knowledge Telling and Knowledge Transforming in Written Composition." *Reading, Writing, and Language Learning*. Vol. 2 of *Advances in Applied Linguistics*. Ed. S. Rosenberg. Cambridge: Cambridge UP, 1987. 142–75.

Schmitt, Charles B., et al., eds. *The Cambridge History of Renaissance Philosophy*. Cambridge: Cambridge UP, 1988.

Scott, Shirley Clay. "From Polydorus to Fradubio: The History of a *Topos*." *SSt* 7 (1987): 27–57.

Sear, Frank B. *Perpendicular and Tudor* and *Elizabethan and Jacobean*. Slide sets 4 and 5 of *The Architecture of England*. Santa Barbara: Visual Education, 1975.

Sedgwick, Eve Kosofsky. *Between Men: English Literature and Male Homosocial Desire*. New York: Columbia UP, 1985.

Sessions, William A. "Spenser's *Georgics*." *ELR* 10 (1980): 202–38.

Seznec, Jean. *The Survival of the Pagan Gods: The Mythological Tradition and Its Place in Renaissance Humanism and Art*. Trans. Barbara F. Sessions. New York: Harper, 1953.

Shaheen, Naseeb. *Biblical References in* The Faerie Queene. Memphis: Memphis State UP, 1976.

Shaver, Anne. "Rereading Mirabella." *SSt* 9 (1991): 211–26.

Shepherd, Simon. *Spenser*. Atlantic Highlands: Humanities, 1989.

Shire, Helena. *A Preface to Spenser*. London: Longman, 1978.

Shore, David. *Spenser and the Poetics of Pastoral: A Study of the World of Colin Clout*. Montreal: McGill–Queen's UP, 1985.

Shumaker, Wayne. *The Occult Sciences in the Renaissance: A Study in Intellectual Patterns*. Berkeley: U of California P, 1972.

Sidney, Philip. *The Countess of Pembroke's Arcadia*. Ed. Maurice Evans. Harmondsworth, Eng.: Penguin, 1977.

———. *A Defence of Poetry*. *Miscellaneous Prose*. Ed. Katherine Duncan-Jones and Jan van Dorsten. Oxford: Clarendon–Oxford UP, 1973. 59–121.

———. *The Old Arcadia*. Ed. Katherine Duncan-Jones. Oxford: Oxford UP, 1985.

Silberman, Lauren. "*The Faerie Queene*, Book II, and the Limitations of Temperance." *MLS* 17 (1987): 9–22.

———. "The Hermaphrodite and the Metamorphosis of Spenserian Allegory." *ELR* 17 (1987): 207–23.

———. "Singing Unsung Heroines: Androgynous Discourse in Book 3 of *The Faerie Queene*." Ferguson, Quilligan, and Vickers 259–71.

———. "Spenser and Ariosto: Funny Peril and Comic Chaos." *CLS* 25 (1988): 23–34.

Simon, Joan. *Education and Society in Tudor England.* Cambridge: Cambridge UP, 1966.

Simpson, J. A., and E. S. C. Weiner, eds. *Oxford English Dictionary.* 2nd ed. New York: Oxford UP, 1989.

Sims, Dwight J. "The Syncretic Myth of Venus in Spenser's Legend of Chastity." *SP* 71 (1974): 427–50.

Sinfield, Alan. *Literature in Protestant England, 1560–1660.* London: Croom Helm, 1983.

———. "Power and Ideology: An Outline Theory and Sidney's *Arcadia.*" *ELH* 52 (1985): 259–77.

Smith, J. C., ed. *Spenser's* Faerie Queene. Oxford: Oxford UP, 1909.

Smith, J. C., and Ernest de Selincourt, eds. *Spenser: Poetical Works.* Oxford: Oxford UP, 1912.

Smitherman-Donaldson, Geneva, and Teun A. van Dijk, eds. *Discourse and Discrimination.* Detroit: Wayne State UP, 1988.

Snow, Edward. "Theorizing the Male Gaze: Some Problems." *Representations* 25 (1989): 30–41.

Stallybrass, Peter, and Allon White. *The Politics and Poetics of Transgression.* Ithaca: Cornell UP, 1986.

Staton, Shirley F. "Reading Spenser's *Faerie Queene*: In a Different Voice." *Ambiguous Realities: Women in the Middle Ages and Renaissance.* Ed. Carole Levin and Jeanie Wilson. Detroit: Wayne State UP, 1987. 145–64.

Steadman, John M. *Milton and the Paradoxes of Renaissance Heroism.* Baton Rouge: Louisiana State UP, 1987.

———. *Milton and the Renaissance Hero.* Oxford: Oxford UP, 1967.

———. *Milton's Epic Characters: Image and Idol.* Chapel Hill: U of North Carolina P, 1968.

Stewart, Stanley. "Spenser and the Judgement of Paris." *SSt* 9 (1991): 161–209.

Stillman, Carol. "Nobility and Justice in Book Five of *The Faerie Queene.*" *TSLL* 23 (1981): 535–54.

———. "Politics, Precedence, and the Order of the Dedicatory Sonnets in *The Faerie Queene.*" *SSt* 5 (1985): 143–48.

Stone, Lawrence. *The Crisis of the Aristocracy, 1558–1641.* Oxford: Clarendon–Oxford UP, 1965.

———. *The Family, Sex, and Marriage in England, 1500–1800.* New York: Harper, 1977.

Strong, Roy. *The Cult of Elizabeth: Elizabethan Portraiture and Pageantry.* London: Thames, 1977.

———. *The English Icon: Elizabethan and Jacobean Portraiture.* London: Mellon Foundation, 1969.

———. *Gloriana: The Portraits of Queen Elizabeth I.* New York: Thames, 1987.

———. *The Renaissance Garden in England.* London: Thames, 1979.

———. *Tudor and Jacobean Portraits.* 2 vols. London: Her Majesty's Stationery Office, 1969.

Stump, Donald V. "Isis versus Mercilla: The Allegorical Shrines in Spenser's Legend of Justice." *SSt* 3 (1982): 87–98.

———. "The Two Deaths of Mary Stuart: Historical Allegory in Spenser's Book of Justice." *SSt* 9 (1991): 81–105.

Suzuki, Mihoko. " 'Unfitly Yokt Together in One Teeme': Vergil and Ovid in *Faerie Queene* III.x." *ELR* 17 (1987): 172–85.

Swift, Carolyn Ruth. "Feminine Identity in Lady Mary Wroth's Romance *Urania*." *ELR* 14 (1984): 328–46.

Temple, William. *William Temple's Analysis of Sir Philip Sidney's* Apology. Ed. and trans. John Webster. Binghamton: Medieval and Renaissance Texts and Studies, 1984.

Teskey, Gordon. "From Allegory to Dialectic: Imagining Error in Spenser and Milton." *PMLA* 101 (1986): 9–23.

Thickstun, Margaret Olofson. "Spenser's Brides Errant." *Fictions of the Feminine: Puritan Doctrine and the Representation of Women*. Ithaca: Cornell UP, 1988. 37–59.

Thomas Aquinas. *On Law, Morality, and Politics*. Ed. William P. Baumgarth and Richard J. Regan. Indianapolis: Hackett, 1988.

———. *Summa Theologiae*. 60 vols. New York: Blackfriars with McGraw-Hill, 1964–75.

Todorov, Tzvetan. *The Conquest of America*. Trans. Richard Howard. New York: Harper, 1984.

Tonkin, Humphrey. *The Faerie Queene*. London: Unwin Hyman, 1989.

———. *Spenser's Courteous Pastoral: Book Six of* The Faerie Queene. Oxford: Clarendon–Oxford UP, 1972.

———"Spenser's Garden of Adonis and Britomart's Quest." *PMLA* 88 (1973): 408–17.

Toulmin, Stephen E., Richard Rieke, and Allan Janik. *An Introduction to Reasoning*. New York: Macmillan, 1979.

Tratner, Michael. " 'The Thing S. Paule Ment by . . . the Courteousness That He Spake Of': Religious Sources for Book VI of *The Faerie Queene*." *SSt* 8 (1990): 147–74.

Tung, Mason. "Spenser's 'Emblematic' Imagery: A Study of Emblematics." *SSt* 5 (1985): 185–207.

Tuve, Rosemond. *Allegorical Imagery: Some Medieval Books and Their Posterity*. Princeton: Princeton UP, 1966.

Tyndale, William. *The Obedience of a Christian Man*. 1527. Walker 127–344.

———. *The Pentateuch*. 1530. Ed. F. F. Bruce. Carbondale: Southern Illinois UP, 1967.

———. *Prologue to Romans*. 1526. Walker 483–510.

Ulreich, John C., Jr. "Making Dreams Truth, and Fables Histories: Spenser and Milton on the Nature of Fiction." *SP* 87 (1990): 363–77.

Underdown, David. "The Taming of the Scold: The Enforcement of Patriarchal Authority in Early Modern England." Fletcher and Stevenson 116–36.

Vickers, Brian, ed. *Occult and Scientific Mentalities in the Renaissance.* Cambridge: Cambridge UP, 1984.

Vickers, Nancy J. "Diana Described: Scattered Women and Scattered Rhyme." *CritI* 8 (1981): 265–79.

Vink, James. "Spenser's *Straftraum*: Guyon's Evil Descent." *L&P* 34 (1988): 52–63.

Vondersmith, Bernard J. "A Bibliography of Criticism of *The Faerie Queene* 1900–1970." Frushell and Vondersmith 150–213.

Walker, Henry, ed. *Doctrinal Treatises and Introductions to Different Portions of the Holy Scripture.* Cambridge: Cambridge UP, 1848.

Wall, John N. "Orion's Flaming Head: Spenser's *Faerie Queene* II.ii.46 and the Feast of the Twelve Days of Christmas." *SSt* 7 (1987): 93–101.

———. *Transformations of the Word: Spenser, Herbert, Vaughan.* Athens: U of Georgia P, 1988.

Waller, Gary. "Spenser and *The Faerie Queene.*" *English Poetry of the Sixteenth Century.* New York: Longman, 1986. 177–214.

Warnicke, Retha M. *Women of the English Renaissance and Reformation.* Westport: Greenwood, 1983.

Waswo, Richard. "The History That Literature Makes." *NLH* 19 (1988): 541–64.

Wayne, Valerie, ed. *The Matter of Difference: Materialist Feminist Criticism of Shakespeare.* Ithaca: Cornell UP, 1991.

Weatherby, Harold L. "The Old Theology: Spenser's Dame Nature and the Transfiguration." *SSt* 5 (1985): 113–42.

———. "The True Saint George." *ELR* 17 (1987): 119–41.

———. "Two Images of Mortalitie: Spenser and Original Sin." *SP* 85 (1988): 331–52.

———. "What Spenser Meant by Holinesse: Baptism in Book One of *The Faerie Queene.*" *SP* 84 (1987): 286–307.

Webster, John. " 'The Methode of a Poete': An Inquiry into Tudor Conceptions of Poetic Sequence." *ELR* 11 (1981): 22–43.

———. "Oral Form and Written Craft in Spenser's *Faerie Queene.*" *SEL* 16 (1976): 75–93.

Weiner, Seth. "Minims and Grace Notes: Spenser's Acidalian Vision and Sixteenth-Century Music." *SSt* 5 (1985): 91–112.

Wells, Robin Headlam. "Spenser and the Politics of Music." *HLQ* 52 (1989): 447–68.

Wells, William. "Spenser Allusions in the Sixteenth and Seventeenth Centuries, Part I: 1580–1625." *SP* 68 (1971): 1–172.

West, Michael. "Spenser and the Renaissance Ideal of Christian Heroism." *PMLA* 88 (1973): 1013–32.

———. "Spenser's Art of War: Chivalric Allegory, Military Technology, and the Elizabethan Mock-Heroic Sensibility." *RenQ* 41 (1988): 654–704.

Whitman, Charles Huntington. *A Subject Index to the Poems of Edmund Spenser.* New Haven: Yale UP, 1919.

Whitman, Jon. *Allegory: The Dynamics of an Ancient and Medieval Technique.* Cambridge: Harvard UP, 1987.

Wiggins, Peter DeSa. "Spenser's Anxiety." *MLN* 103 (1988): 75–86.

Williams, Kathleen. *Spenser's World of Glass: A Reading of* The Faerie Queene. Berkeley: U of California P, 1966.

Wind, Edgar. *Pagan Mysteries in the Renaissance*. New York: Norton, 1958.

Winny, James, ed. *The Frame of Order: An Outline of Elizabethan Belief Taken from Treatises of the Late Sixteenth Century*. London: Allen, 1957.

Wittreich, Joseph A. *Visionary Poetics: Milton's Tradition and His Legacy*. San Marino: Huntington Library, 1979.

Wofford, Susanne Lindgren. "Gendering Allegory: Spenser's Bold Reader and the Emergence of Character in *The Faerie Queene* III." *Criticism* 30 (1988): 1–22.

Woodbridge, Linda. *Women and the English Renaissance: Literature and the Nature of Womankind, 1540–1620*. Urbana: U of Illinois P, 1983.

Woodhouse, A. S. P. "Nature and Grace in *The Faerie Queene*." *ELH* 16 (1949): 194–228.

Woods, Suzanne. "Closure in *The Faerie Queene*." *JEGP* 76 (1977): 195–216.

———. *Natural Emphasis: English Versification from Chaucer to Dryden*. San Marino: Huntington Library, 1984.

Wright, Louis B. *Middle-Class Culture in Elizabethan England*. Chapel Hill: U of North Carolina P, 1935.

Wrightson, Keith. *English Society, 1580–1680*. New Brunswick: Rutgers UP, 1982.

Wroth, Mary. *The Countesse of Mountgomeries Urania Written by the right honorable the Lady Mary Wroath, Daughter to the right Noble Robert Earle of Leicester. And Neece to the ever famous, and renowned Sir Phillip Sidney Knight. And to the most excelent Lady Mary Countesse of Pembrooke late deceased*. London: Marriott, 1621.

———. *Poems of Lady Mary Wroth*. Ed. Josephine A. Roberts. Baton Rouge: U of Louisiana P, 1983.

Wurtsbaugh, Jewel. *Two Centuries of Spenser Scholarship*. Baltimore: Johns Hopkins UP, 1936.

Yates, Frances A. *Astraea: The Imperial Theme in the Sixteenth Century*. London: Routledge, 1975.

———. *The Occult Philosophy in the Elizabethan Age*. London: Routledge, 1979.

Youings, Joyce. *Sixteenth-Century England*. Harmondsworth, Eng.: Penguin, 1984.

Zitner, S. P., ed. *The Mutability Cantos*. By Edmund Spenser. London: Nelson, 1968.

INDEX